IN THE
SHADOWS
OF JUSTICE

IN THE SHADOWS OF JUSTICE

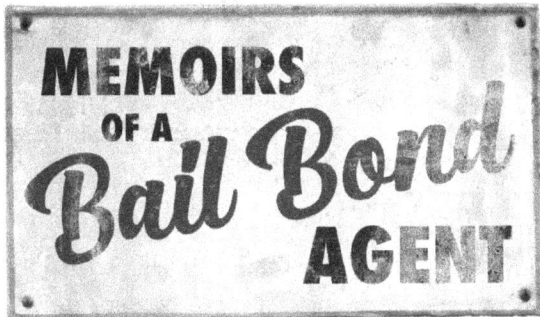

MEMOIRS OF A *Bail Bond* AGENT

JAMES A. GARSKE

To my wife, Patricia Garske, and daughter, Kristin Widing,
for their help as well as their patience with this project.

LETTER FROM THE AUTHOR

This book is a fictional account of incidents that took place during my fifty-plus years in the bail bond business. Names have been changed, characters have been merged, and situations have been altered. I did this in an effort to provide the reader with insights into the types of corruption that surrounded the criminal justice system and the bail industry in the state of Nevada and throughout many parts of the United States during the mid-1960s through the late 1980s.

CONTENTS

PROLOGUE

My name is Robert Wayne. My friends, family, and associates call me "Lefty," for obvious reasons. After spending nearly half a century dealing with hookers, slot cheats, drug dealers, biker gangs and white-collar criminals—without ever being tempted to join them—I now find myself in the San Diego County Jail facing more felony charges than an average criminal would face in a lifetime.

Not only am I trying to make sense of what the hell's going on here, I'm also questioning how a good Catholic boy like me, the apple of my grandmother's eye, could gravitate so easily, and so willingly, into a world rife with exploitation, corruption, and sleaze.

I guess the answer is simple. I wasn't a good Catholic boy. In fact, I was eliminated from the altar boy's roster for stealing wine from the sacristy when I was 11 years old. A year later, I was booked into the Reno City Jail for stealing candy from the corner drug store.

Being arrested, fingerprinted, and locked in the drunk tank of the Reno Police Department with a fresh bunch of drunken derelicts and weirdos was a sham, instigated by my old man to scare the shit out of me. He was a police lieutenant at the time and had planned to use this opportunity to teach me a lesson. He had the right idea; however, the lesson I learned wasn't the one he was hoping for.

In high school I kept stealing; this time it was beer from the Safeway store where I worked after school and weekends. I didn't like beer, so I sold most of it to my high school buddies. By the time I finished high school, I learned that crime paid better than any straight job—if you didn't get caught.

At one time or another during the past forty-five-plus years, I may have been guilty of almost all the charges rumored in this current indictment, but I've never before been arrested or convicted of anything. As a result, I always considered myself lucky, or maybe even immune from arrest, until now.

I'm currently waiting for one of the arresting officers to provide me with a copy of the grand jury indictment listing all the criminal charges being brought against me. The list is supposedly longer than my arm, and it most likely will include the amount of bail needed to get me out of this hellhole.

All I've heard from the booking officers is that the State of California, with a little help from the Feds, have indicted me and my business associate, Vance Parker, on charges of bribing judges, law enforcement officers, jailers and inmates, along with money laundering, fencing stolen property, and unlawful possession of firearms. Not to mention a long list of lesser, more ambiguous charges—the kind every prosecutor throws in for laughs, knowing they're only there in an effort to increase the amount of my bail, and will be tossed out during any meaningful plea bargaining.

Although I'm interested in learning all the charges against me, I'm more concerned about the chatter surrounding the actual amount of my bail. If the rumors are true, I could be forced to post a $2.5 million dollar bail bond; that would require paying a bail bondsman a minimum non-refundable premium of $250,000.

But right now, I'm not about to fork over that kind of cash just to get my sorry ass out of here anytime soon. That's because right now, the only thing I'm sure of is that whatever allowed law enforcement to snare me in this trap of theirs isn't going to be enough to convict me—because I'm innocent—this time!

Consequently, you'd be smart not to count me out just yet. At least not until you've heard the whole story about how I spent the past forty-five years working in the shadows of justice as a professional bail bondsman.

CHAPTER

#1

In May 1965, after spending a few years as a grunt in the Marine Corps learning how to kick ass and kill people, I received an honorable discharge and returned home to my old stomping grounds in Reno, Nevada. Since my older brother, Allan, moved to San Diego to attend law school, and my older sister, Diane, eloped with her high school sweetheart a month before I was discharged, Mom, who was in her late forties at the time, didn't like the idea of being alone. She insisted I move in with her, and since I needed some familiar surroundings to evaluate my options for the future, I took her up on her offer. Ever since I was a young kid, the only thing I'd wanted to do was hit it big. Back then, in my mind, a hundred grand a year or more made all the difference.

At Mom's suggestion, I took out a pad and pencil and began writing down my options. It took me less than ten minutes to figure out that high paying career opportunities were slim to none without a college degree. At the same time, I realized I was also lacking any specialized training to fall back on. The process of writing everything down left me with the realization that I didn't have the slightest idea what I wanted to do with the rest of my life.

With few options left, I decided to check out the local Help Wanted ads in hopes of getting a few new ideas, but almost all the listings came from local casinos looking for blackjack dealers, Keno writers, bartenders and maintenance workers, which, according to Mom, were all minimum wage jobs that relied more on tips than wages to make ends meet. What's more, most of the construction jobs I found were all temporary, dead-end opportunities.

Without looking any further, Mom and I agreed that my best option was to finish college. But as a temporary measure, I would take the highest paying, seasonal construction job I could find in order to avoid working during the school year.

After about a week of hitting all the new construction sites in the area, I found a local cement contractor in Sparks who was hiring laborers to help set forms and pour concrete curbs and cutters throughout a new housing development. He was paying twice the minimum wage plus double for overtime.

I began doing backbreaking work ten hours a day, six days a week. Although my schedule was grueling, repetitive, and boring, I was able to save a substantial amount of money; enough to sustain life without having to work until the following summer, or so I thought.

Shortly after the first semester started, I realized I was wrong. I was going to need a part-time job; one with flexible hours that paid more than minimum wage, if I was going to continue paying my way and helping Mom with the household bills.

As luck would have it, I found out that my old man was still working for the Reno Police Department. He and mom got divorced when I was a freshman in high school. They'd been together for almost twenty years before he decided to abandon her. He waited until Allan graduated from Catholic high school and joined the Navy. Being the first born and the first son, plus being one of those good Catholics who didn't believe in divorce and did believe in all that religious stuff, Allan had always been my dad's favorite. Diane was a senior when he left. After she graduated, and within a year after he pulled the plug, she got a job with the phone company and moved in with some girlfriends.

That left Mom and me living in an unfinished house together with all the bills that went with it, while Dad moved in with his new girlfriend and her two kids. Mom had to continue working from seven at night until three in the morning dealing blackjack in one of the local hotel/casinos. She'd worked six, and sometimes seven, nights a week so my sister and I could graduate from the private Catholic high school Mom insisted we attend.

Although I hadn't talked to Dad in more than five years, I was desperate enough to visit him and see if he had any employment ideas. As it turned out, he was still a lieutenant, and still going nowhere. His problems started when he was listed as a person of interest during the FBI's investigation of a burglary scandal that resulted in six other Reno police officers being sent to prison shortly after he dumped Mom.

When the dust settled, and a new police chief took over, he reassigned Dad to a desk job as the department's jail commander. I'm guessing after the chief reviewed the old man's personnel file, he determined Dad was a perfect candidate for overseeing the jail. He must have thought the old man was dirty and having an old crook like him watching over all the new recruits wasn't a bad idea.

When we met, I was still pissed at the way he'd treated Mom during their divorce, so I wasn't interested in renewing a father/son relationship—which in reality we'd never had. I just wanted to pick his brain in hopes of finding a job with flexible hours that wouldn't require busting my ass shoveling concrete.

Looking back, I can honestly say this was the only helpful tip he ever gave me. He said I should go next door (it was actually across the street from the jail) and meet a bail agent named Mickey Colter. He knew Mickey was looking for help, but he didn't know exactly what kind Mickey needed, or how much it paid. At the end of our little chat, I thanked Dad for the tip and told him I'd stop by Colter's office on my way home.

Mickey's office reminded me of a movie set, with Mickey as the main, gangster-type character. He was sitting behind an oversize wooden desk, sporting a small, stingy-brim straw hat and chewing on the stub of an old cigar, which, from its appearance, had never been smoked. He chewed on it regularly and spat into an old salon-style spittoon next to his desk. He had a potbelly the size of a basketball, which made him look a little pregnant sitting behind the desk. As I watched his actions and listened to him talk I was reminded of Edward G. Robinson, who starred in many of the gangster movies I'd watched on TV as a kid.

The two guys hanging around Mickey's office that day, Ernie and Leo Mullens, also reminded me of gangsters; guys like James Cagney, the tough guy in *Public Enemy*, and Bruce Gordon, aka Frank Nitti, who played the lead role in the television series *The Untouchables*. Although Ernie and Leo were brothers, you'd never know it. Ernie was six two and well built, while Leo, the older one, was maybe five eight and fat. After a few minutes of idle conversation with the three of them, I was ready to bet my entire summer savings I had stumbled onto the set of a *live* gangster movie being filmed in Mickey's office.

I spent the next few hours that afternoon learning everything I could about the bail bond business, how it worked, and what I would be doing if Mickey hired me. He and I hit it off from the beginning; he was the most interesting, charismatic person I'd ever met.

During that meeting, Mickey explained that to qualify for the job I had to pass a state insurance exam and obtain an insurance license from the State of Nevada. By the end of our meeting, my head was swimming with information, but Mickey assured me I'd have plenty of time to learn more about the bail business after I started working. In the meantime, he said, I should focus all my attention on passing the exam.

I walked away with two positive thoughts: First, Mickey agreed to hire me as soon as I passed the state exam and received my license. Second, after stepping into his world and experiencing what my future could be, I knew exactly how I wanted to earn my living for the rest of my life.

As I was leaving the office, I told him I'd start studying that very afternoon and assured him I would let him know just as soon as I felt ready to take the test.

I went straight to the Carson City office of the Nevada Department of Insurance to gather study material. Within minutes of asking my first question, I felt some of the air escape from the balloon of excitement surrounding my new career opportunity. I learned there was no specific test for surety bail bond agents. Instead, I had to take the entire insurance exam, which covered every line of insurance except life insurance.

I was overwhelmed, in a hurry, and pissed off. Not a good combination when someone wants to get on with his or her new lifelong career. But there was nothing I could do except study, and it took more studying than I ever anticipated, on subjects that were as dry as an old watering hole in the middle of the Sahara.

Despite my time and effort studying, I flunked the exam—not once, but twice. After the second time I went to Mickey's office. I said I was unable to pass the exam and didn't feel taking it again would help. I reluctantly suggested that he might want to think about looking for someone else, because I wouldn't be able to take him up on his job offer.

He laughed and said he hadn't thought I would pass but was surprised at how easily I gave up. He demanded that I take the exam again, at the earliest opportunity. He would hold the job open if I agreed to do this. As I was leaving, he insisted I call him as soon as I knew the exam's date and location. I agreed, and left the office thinking nothing would come of it. At least, nothing more than making a fool of myself for the third time.

After failing twice, my heart was in the toilet, and I was not in the mood to study. I knew that no matter how much time I spent studying, I couldn't retain enough knowledge about all the different lines of insurance, especially ones I didn't give a shit about, in order to pass a fucking exam that was absolutely, totally unrelated to my dream job. Especially knowing that taking the exam again only meant humiliating myself yet again.

By this time, I'd already told just about everyone in my life that I was going to be a bail agent. Failing a third and final time would be like pouring salt on an open wound. And having to admit failure to the world, especially to Mickey and my family, seemed even worse.

Knowing the inevitable outcome in advance, I didn't waste another minute studying. Instead, I went out drinking. The next morning, I checked with the Nevada Department of Insurance and learned that the next available date and location for the insurance exam was the following Monday in Carson City. I signed up, and as instructed, called Mickey to let him know. This time, he said it was urgent that I call him as soon as I finished the exam and received my results, which I agreed to do.

I was happy to tell him I would call, because having to tell him in person that I flunked again would have been too humiliating. Monday couldn't come soon enough. I just wanted it over, once and for all. It made me sick to my stomach to think I was going to lose the opportunity of a lifetime because of some stupid, unrelated exam.

In the '60s, all state insurance exams consisted of fifty multiple-choice questions and required a passing grade of 70 percent or better. This meant I needed a minimum of thirty-five correct answers. I was sure no one was lucky enough to guess 70 percent of the correct answers, especially, me. But guessing was my last and only hope, or so I thought.

Although the participants were given one hour to complete the exam, they could hand it in as soon as they were finished. When you're guessing all the answers like I was, who needs an hour? I was the first one finished. And since the exam administrator corrected each exam as soon as it was handed to him, everyone would know their test results before leaving the room.

He would place a correction sheet punched full of holes over your answer sheet, look up at you, and utter one of only two words. It didn't matter to him which of the two he chose: "passed" or "failed." He just uttered that one life-changing word with a *Who really gives a shit?* attitude. That's all it took. At least, that's what I thought at the time.

When I handed in my answer sheet, he placed his punched-out answer card over it and began counting the number of clear blocks. Clear boxes meant that I blacked out the wrong answer; the blacked-out boxes meant I picked the correct ones. I knew he'd find more than fifteen clear boxes on my exam, so I didn't stop to wait for his answer. I didn't want to hear "failed" a third time. There was no way this test would be my life-altering charm, especially given that I hadn't even studied this time. But I was wrong. When he was finished, he looked around, saw I was already walking out of the room, and yelled one word at me: "Passed."

I couldn't believe my ears. How in the hell did I pull that off? I felt like the luckiest guy in the world. So, with the biggest smile I'd had in my life, I ran, I danced, and I zigzagged directly to the nearest pay phone and called Mickey.

"Hey Mickey, I made it, I passed . . . I can't believe it; the third time actually turned out to be my charm!"

Mickey chuckled a little and said, "Congratulations, kid, I'm glad you passed. Now get your ass back to the office so we can talk about your new job."

I appreciated his comments, but he didn't seem surprised, considering I'd failed twice, and almost gave up on it. I thought maybe he had a customer in his office and couldn't talk, so I got in my car and headed back to Reno for a face-to-face celebration.

A week or so later I found out why I was so lucky, and that my ability at guessing correctly had nothing to do with it. Ernie Mullens, the younger of the two Mullens brothers I met the first day in Mickey's office, told me, "Lefty, my boy, luck had nothing to do with it. Mickey paid off one of his Scottish buddies from the Shriners Organization to put the fix in. His buddy happens to be a senior executive with the Department of Insurance. Mickey wanted to ensure that you passed. If luck had anything to do with it, I'd say you were just flat ass lucky to have crossed paths with him."

Since Mickey paid the exam administrator to ensure I received a passing grade, that meant the administrator really did give a shit—because he wouldn't have been paid if I failed. That's why Mickey was adamant about calling as soon as I knew when and where I'd be taking the test. He needed to let his buddy know, so he could arrange to be the one conducting the exam and correcting my paper that day. I always wondered how many questions I missed and how much my passing grade cost Mickey, but I never found out.

Shortly after I began working in the office, Mickey asked me to come in a little early one day. When I showed up, he handed me a small package wrapped in "congratulations" paper.

He said, "Kid, this is a little something you can use to level the playing field when manhandling some of the guys you'll be dealing with in this business."

When I opened the package, I was a little shocked, but not in a bad way. He'd given me brass knuckles and a pair of handcuffs—both of which I have to this day.

After I opened my gifts, he said, "I want you to carry these everywhere you go, but I don't ever want to see you packing a gun, under any circumstances. Somebody will end up taking it away from you and killing you with it. But to get these, they'll have to rip off your fingers. And no one would expect you to have them, so the element of surprise will always be on your side. Remember, when you hit someone, make sure you mean it, because it may be your only shot at knocking him down to size. But we can talk more about this, and chasing the bad guys, later.

"Oh yeah, knuckles are illegal as hell, so don't go showing them off to your girlfriends or taking them with you into the jail for an interview." Then, with a chuckle, he said, "If you do, you might find yourself calling me to bail you out."

This was my first exposure to carrying an illegal weapon and to the corruption and risks surrounding my new career. But I was sure it wouldn't be my last. As I found out later, paying off a state employee to fix someone's insurance exam was not that big a deal. Back in the late 1950s and early 1960s, anyone with the right amount of money and the right connections could get any state license, including a gaming license. Hell, as time went on, I even got a real estate license. And I never studied for that one, either.

There was an intense level of corruption within the Nevada criminal justice system, the type you might expect to find in small cow towns where everyone knows everyone. But I'm talking about Reno, "The Biggest Little City in the World," and Las Vegas, where the good guys controlled the hotels, while the East Coast mob controlled the casinos.

Being able to pay off judges, court clerks, cops, jailers, and even some prosecutors, was corruption at its best. For the right amount of money, certain attorneys, as well as a few well-connected bail agents like my mentor, Mickey, were able to have arrest records disappear, cases dropped, witnesses fail to appear, warrants issued, or warrants quashed when needed; especially those relating to out-of-state clients. You could also get felony charges reduced to misdemeanors, with negligible fines, which were usually paid from collateral deposits held by the bail agents who kept the excess for themselves as a bonus. You name it, it happened. And all of it made fixing my exam seem like child's play.

Over the next three years, Mickey taught me all he knew about the bail business, and most importantly, about "taking risks"—which meant doing things right most of the time but being ready to step into the shadows whenever needed. He constantly repeated himself, saying, "If you pay attention, follow my lead, never try to second-guess me or my way of doing things, you'll eventually be able to easily distinguish between the bonds you should write, and those you leave on the table for our competitors."

I learned how to take collateral like guns, jewelry, and cash from our shadier clients on a handshake, with no receipts or paper trails. I also learned the opposite: when to issue official receipts, and to make sure they were placed in the defendant's file. Or how to code files to reflect the type of collateral we were holding, and how to misappropriate it in the event we had to pay someone to make the case disappear. These coded transactions were always completed in cash.

Everything was fair game when a defendant failed to appear, regardless of whether we "sanctioned" it or not. When a defendant failed to appear and we were complicit in his flight to avoid prosecution, we usually paid off someone working in the system for their help. The famous expression "What happens in Vegas stays in Vegas," held true in Reno, too. People just didn't flaunt it as openly as they did in Vegas. We merely created the appropriate paperwork needed to fill the pockets of those who made these cases disappear. Then we would fill our pockets with whatever balance remained in the defendant's collateral account.

When it was necessary to hunt down a fugitive (always a kick in the ass), especially at the beginning of my career, we dummied up expense receipts totaling twice as much as we were holding in collateral so we could write off the unpaid balance as a loss. We were risking our lives, right? Well, that's not entirely true. As I got older and wiser, I stuck to apprehending the easy ones, and left the riskier ones, those with the propensity for violence, to professional bounty hunters. Usually, these so-called professionals were bikers looking for some excitement, or ex-cops who'd been kicked off the force for one illegal reason or another.

The only real professional I ever had the pleasure of meeting and hiring whenever I needed one (this happened in 1978), was Ralph "Papa" Thorson. He wrote a book in 1976 called *The Hunter*, which Hollywood made into a movie, starring Steve McQueen. I always wondered why Hollywood picked McQueen, since "Papa" was a huge burly guy with a beard, and McQueen was a clean-shaven peewee in comparison.

In the '60s and '70s, chasing bad guys was unlike the apprehensions you see on television today. There was no script. There was no guaranteed ending. And transporting them back to jail in the trunk of your car was a necessity. (Well, let's say it was safer.)

When I started in the business, I believed that corruption in the Reno Courts was the exception, not the rule. At least that's what I was led to believe—until I met Mickey. He was the first person to expose me to the corruption in our justice system, and the individuals that governed it, especially in Nevada. And he was the guy who taught me how easy it was to benefit financially from negotiating in the shadows that surrounded the justice system. He paid off judges, court clerks, prosecutors and cops, but only when he really needed their help. Most of the time, his attorney mitigated Mickey's losses using bribes in the privacy of a judge's chambers or behind closed doors in a clerk's office.

Corruption in Las Vegas was totally different. The mob not only infiltrated and corrupted the criminal justice system, but they also skimmed millions of dollars from the gaming casinos and controlled all the legal prostitution. They controlled not only the whore houses, but also the private escort services that catered to the companionship and sexual needs of the casinos' high rollers. Their involvement in everything was so blatantly transparent that the Feds regularly investigated corruption in Vegas.

As Mickey began to trust me, he taught me his personal system for handling certain "special" items of collateral. These questionable items were usually deposited by some of Mickey's regular customers, the ones who dealt in items that were *previously* lifted from some law-abiding citizen or business. They were always small, but usually quite expensive—the kind a burglar, booster, or thief could easily carry out of someone's home or retail store. They included jewelry, handguns, coin collections, stamp collections, etc. You get the idea. Mickey never touched drugs—not for his own use, or as collateral on a bond. Back then, he wasn't alone; even mob bosses were struggling with dealers and drug addicts popping up in their ranks.

Although Mickey showed me how to handle these "special" items, he made it clear that certain clients and their merchandise (all stolen, of course), were off-limits to me for the time being. In fact, many clients and/or co-signers who fell into this category would not even talk to me, let alone allow me to get within earshot of them during their business with Mickey.

As time went on, whenever I saw these individuals coming up the stairs, I'd excuse myself and retreat to another part of the office or the kitchen until they were gone. This put them at ease. Eventually, I was not only able to sit in, but could complete many of their business transactions when Mickey wasn't around. Some would take place in connection with their past or future bonds. Others were straight sales-type business transactions, where they needed immediate cash. Mickey and his wife, Elaine, liked to buy diamonds, jewelry, and coins, so Mickey always made sure they had first choice on everything these clients had to offer.

During my first few months of training, Mickey always let me handle the interviews with new clients, as well as their cosigners, friends, or family members willing to financially guarantee payment of the full amount of their bail in the event the defendant failed to appear. These were all the "straight" types, like moms, dads, brothers, sisters and wives; not his regular criminal type clients.

CHAPTER

#2

Early in my new career, Mickey started me out as a "runner." He told me a runner's only responsibility was to deliver a bond to a specific jail, wait for the release of the client, and return him or her to the office . . . period. His instructions were clear: "Don't take them anyplace other than the office; don't stop anyplace; don't let them out of your sight; and most importantly, don't accept money, or anything else from them."

After a few months of answering phones, taking messages, and delivering bonds and defendants, my job description changed from bail bond "runner" to commissioned bail agent. The upside of "just being a runner" is that you have no liability, and no worries about whether a defendant appeared in court or paid their premium. The downside was strictly financial. I received a flat fee for each bond I delivered, and an hourly pittance for being the office gopher and answering the phones. Neither of these paid enough to satisfy my need—or my greed.

The upside of being an actual bail agent was being able to share in a percentage of the premium collected on each bond you wrote. The more hours you were willing to work, or be on call, the more bonds you wrote, and the more commissions you received. But the downside was being on the hook for your portion of the loss if one of your clients failed to appear or skipped the country; it was also your job to find them. And if you were unable to find and return him or her to the custody of the court, you paid your share of the loss.

This also applied to your share of the expenses. If, somewhere down the line, you decided to hire a bounty hunter instead of going after the skip yourself, you personally paid for their services. And if you, or the bounty hunter, or the police were unable to find the fugitive in the time limit provided by the court, you, as a bail agent under contract with Mickey, would be forced to pay your contractual percentage of the whole loss, while Mickey paid the other part. You truly "shared in the liabilities" associated with the bonds you wrote.

I was chomping at the bit to start making more money. I was sure Mickey wanted me to start sharing in more of the financial responsibilities, as well as the riches. He said more than once, "Kid, I want you to start sharing in the wealth, but not without taking responsibility for your mistakes. Mistakes make you learn faster, but too many can cost you your job."

Mickey finally decided it was time to let me sink or swim, or as he put it, "It's time to put your ass in the wind and start flying by the seat of your pants." Then he sat back in his chair and said with a grin and a chuckle, "Let's just hope the wind is blowing in the right direction; I'd hate to see you crash and burn too soon."

He was right. It was time to either live well or die hungry, depending on how well I applied the things I learned from the Master, and how good I would be at making my own underwriting decisions.

He closed our little discussion by saying, "We'll see just how much you really like this business, especially when you start having second thoughts about some of your classier clients, like the druggies, pimps, hookers and bikers; or when you open the mail and find a forfeiture notice from the court on one of your $10,000 bonds. The days of my babysitting and holding your hand are over."

My contract, which his attorney drew up, didn't just guarantee my percentage of commission on all the bonds I wrote. It also stated that I would be holding Mickey harmless on an equal 50/50 percentage of any loss he sustained as a result of my making some stupid mistake or using poor underwriting judgment. It further explained that I would be held liable for an equal percentage of all the expenses incurred by him or the insurance company in connection with surrendering a fugitive back into the custody of law enforcement. It also mentioned some things I'd never thought about: the section covering all losses and legal fees incurred as a result of my actions, i.e., the wrongful death of a client, a co-signer, or an innocent bystander; the wrongful arrest of any person; wrongful breaking and entry into someone's home in pursuit of a fugitive; the list went on and on.

The contract seemed to have a never-ending list of financial responsibilities but failed to mention anything about my percentage of any misappropriated collateral, or any surplus revenue generated from the sale of a client's personal property or real estate. But it wouldn't be wise to insert language into any contract in an effort to cover criminal acts of fraud or corruption, especially when such a contract would be inadmissible in civil court. However, it could easily be used in a criminal action against you, as an admission of guilt by all parties concerned. In other words, it would be downright stupid. Any division of excess cash or other collateral would be done on a "trust basis." You know, the old "Honor Among Thieves" type of split. At this point, however, my only option was to trust Mickey's figures on how much cash he received from turning any of the questionable items, and what my split would be after he disposed of them.

Later in our relationship, Mickey told me, "Kid, everyone should take an active interest in what's going on around him or her—expecially when someone else is handling valuables or counting your money. This applies to everyone, even if the one you're trusting is your boss, or better yet, your mentor."

The attorney also provided a simple example of how our financial terms and conditions would work in connection with each bond: If I wrote a $5,000 bond, which required the collection of a 10 percent premium ($500), I would split that premium with Mickey on a 50/50 basis. However, if I elected to extend any form of credit to the defendant or his co-signer, I would still be responsible to pay Mickey his 50 percent at the time I reported the posting of the bond to him, regardless of whether the client paid me or not. This meant that all credit extended to my clients would come out of my pocket unless I collected at least 50 percent (Mickey's share) up front. And if I only collected 50 percent, he would get it all, and I would be the one chasing after the client to get the unpaid balance, which was my share. In addition, he flat refused to take anything other than cash as payment for his share. No drugs, no pussy, no hot jewelry, just cash.

While Mickey agreed to pay the insurance company's portion of each premium from his 50 percent, I would have to deposit 20 percent of my share of every premium into a personal savings account, which Mickey set up as a trust account in both our names. Mickey and/or Elaine were signatories on this account, which was only used to help cover my share of any actual bond losses, bounty hunter fees, court costs, motion fees, etc.—anything associated with obtaining the exoneration of any of my bonds. Mickey called this fund my "retirement account," because it was to be used only as a last resort.

Mickey was expecting me to pay any of my losses from my share of the earnings, not from my reserves. He also made it clear that I should not acknowledge the existence of this account until the balance reached a minimum of at least $10,000.

He pointed out that my reserve was my contract collateral, assuring that I lived up to all the terms and conditions of our contract, and he strongly suggested I start saving some of the money I was taking home.

He added a little caveat at the end of the financial discussions. "The only exception to this rule will be when I advance your 50 percent from time to time, based on the type, quality, and potential liquidity of the collateral you take in connection with any particular bond loss." He was saying if I used common sense and wrote only good, solid, secure bonds, or knew I could find anyone who failed to appear, I should never have to pay a loss. That's because he would always cover my action, then recover his advance from the collateral, unless it was short. Then he would be coming to me for any shortage.

That all sounds good on paper, but when you factor in the lack of financial quality and stability surrounding 80 percent of our customers, I would need to take some risks if I was ever going to make any money, especially the kind I was looking for.

Every time we'd talk about taking risks, he'd close our discussions with one of his famous zingers. "Remember, kid, if you're afraid to take a risk, you're in the wrong business. Maybe you should reconsider and become a plumber. They always get paid, no matter how much shit they have to deal with."

CHAPTER

#3

After we formalized our new arrangement by signing our contract, Mickey issued my first stack of blank surety bail bonds, while Elaine presented me with a brand-new leather briefcase. It was a gift from them both, but I knew it was Elaine's idea. Mickey interrupted her presentation. "Okay," he said, "the fun's over. It's time to discuss your work schedule."

I knew my schedule was going to change. Instead of hanging around the office all day, answering the phone, running bonds to the different courts, and collecting cash and signatures from defendants and co-signers, I would be covering a full working shift. But I was shocked to learn that Mickey's idea of a bondsman's shift included working in the office from 6:00 p.m. until 8:00 a.m., seven nights a week, then being on call the remaining ten hours of each day. In my case, he made exceptions for my college classes and permitted study time in the office—as long as answering the phone was my first priority.

In the '60s and '70s, answering services were the lifeline of every bail bond agency. Mickey made sure the one he chose was able to help him offer the best and fastest bail service in town.

He told me, "Kid, the last person you want to rely on is some ding-a-ling switchboard operator who can't keep her wig on straight long enough to page us. Or one who fails to provide us with all the information needed to follow up on the person that called for bail. You need to make sure that if, or when, you're picking an answering service you choose one that doesn't provide the same services to any of your competitors. You don't want some competitor paying the switchboard girls under the table to pass your calls and client information to them first."

Staying in contact with the office and the answering service was a lot different back then; we didn't have cell phones, email, or pagers. We had only pay phones, answering services, and landlines to rely on; you needed to keep change in your pocket for phone calls. And you had to be on the lookout for telephone booths and pay phones everywhere you went.

If I went to a friend's house, I had to leave his or her phone number with the answering service. Whenever I left home, I had to call in to the office and let them know where I was going, and when I expected to arrive. If I went to a movie, I had to check in by using a pay phone in the lobby every fifteen minutes or so, which made watching a movie almost impossible.

Mickey said, "Kid, bail is a 24-hour-a-day, seven-day-a-week business, and you'll spend half that time in the jail or in the office. Working anything less, like eight hours a day, five days a week, is considered part-time."

In addition, he made it clear that I was now a full-time independent agent/contractor, and the only way I'd get paid was by writing bonds and collecting premiums.

"You can answer the phone, interview clients, sleep on the office couch, study, read, play solitaire, review files, work on your skips, or mine. But no TV! And, under no circumstances can you miss a call, even if it means pissing your pants. And since you're on commission, you can hang around the office on your own time as much as you want, but you absolutely have to be here to cover your regularly scheduled shift. No excuses!"

Any time an agent, regardless of who he worked for, had to leave their office for any reason, including going to the jail, or court, he would call his answering service and have them take the calls. No one wants to remain in jail longer than necessary, so potential clients would call different agencies until they got a live person. No agent worth his salt could afford to miss a call either, especially me—not only because Mickey said so, but because I wanted to make money. And you never knew, until you answered the phone, whether the call was from some drunk needing a $25 drunk-in-public bond, or some gang member needing a $10,000 bond for assault, drug possession, or worse.

Every phone line in Mickey's office was linked to the answering service. I would call them every time I left the office, and then, as often as I could, to retrieve any messages. At the beginning, I seldom left the office, unless it was to interview a potential client in jail, write a bond, or go home to shower and clean up.

In most cases, I tried to interview a defendant in person. But if I had to meet a co-signer or someone dropping off cash for a bond, I'd have to interview clients over the phone, then follow up with a visit in jail as soon as I could. As a result, I spent a lot of time in phone booths retrieving messages, returning calls, interviewing clients in jail, or filling out applications with co-signers in a jail lobby.

Since my only time off was in the mornings to attend classes, I made the mistake of asking Mickey when I would get some actual days off. He laughed. "Kid, he said, "Tell you what, you can have a day off just as soon as one of these three things happen: The cops stop making arrests. All the jails are completely empty. Or you get fired for missing a bond call!"

After a long pause, he added, "You'll eventually be able to take real time off when you have enough experience writing bonds to provide me with some level of comfort when I leave you on your own. But even then, I'll expect you to check in with me or the answering service on a frequent basis. Especially when the cops make a big drug bust, or I need help covering any overflow of calls, jail interviews, or meetings with co-signers. And remember the unexpected times like holidays, or local events like rodeos or biker parties."

By this point, we had covered everything except posting actual bonds. He started this phase of my training by emphasizing that I could post any bail I felt comfortable writing, but only up to and including $5,000. Anything over that amount would require his verbal approval. This meant I had to call him, no matter what time of the day or night.

Although I could now write any bonds on credit, he had a much stiffer, and somewhat different, policy from the one he set when I was training.

His instructions went something like this: "Offering credit to any defendant, for any reason, rather than collecting the entire 10 percent premium up front is absolutely unacceptable. No Cash! No Bond!"

From day one, even when I was just a bond runner, Mickey repeatedly told me, "Kid, if I catch you getting some pussy instead of cash for a premium or taking drugs for collateral on one of my bonds, I'll fire you on the spot."

Mickey wasn't afraid to walk in the shadows of justice to make a buck, but he had his limits. He wouldn't take illegal drugs from addicts or pushers. Nor would he take pussy from hookers, or any other woman, as payment for their bonds. He never refused to post a bond for any of them regardless of their charges, as long as they qualified, meaning they had the premium money, collateral, or a track record with him.

He constantly reminded me, "In the American system of justice, everyone is considered innocent until proven guilty. It's not our job to judge the people we get out on bail, regardless of whether they're accused of dealing drugs, are just plain users, or peddling their ass for profit or a fix."

If I chose to extend credit to anyone, even with the best of intentions and the best of reasons, I'd still have to pay him his share. This meant it would most likely come out of my pocket. No exceptions! And he always enforced his "no pussy and no drugs" rules.

Although I could write bonds up to $5,000 without checking with him, I had to call him before I turned one down. He wanted to discuss my reasoning, even if he was dead asleep in the middle of the night. He didn't want to lose a good bond or a previous good customer as a result of my inexperience.

All the rules for posting bonds were clear, except one. He failed to mention anything about taking stolen property in lieu of the premium, or as collateral: things like jewelry, guns, simple electronics, coin collections, etc., which we both knew could easily be turned into quick cash from a local "fence" we used in the late '60s and early '70s.

I guess he thought I was smart enough to handle them correctly without calling; at least on bonds up to my $5,000 limit.

This meant we would always give all our clients, even the straight ones, a receipt, with a vaguely written description of their collateral and strict instructions for redeeming the item after their case was closed. When taking a separate type of collateral for any portion of an unpaid premium, the receipt was still the same; it just included a time limit for redemption.

The receipt for a women's gold Rolex watch was listed as "Woman's watch, gold in color." A diamond ring was listed as "Ring, gold in color, with a single (or multiple) clear white stones."

After they left, we'd switch the clients' or co-signers' items for some of the fake costume jewelry we kept in the office safe. We took the original jewelry and placed it under a section of the hardwood floor in the pantry, just off the office. Mickey took these precautions for two reasons: first, to prevent being arrested for receiving stolen property if the police raided our office immediately after the defendant left; second, to ensure against one of the defendant's friends coming in with gun in hand to retrieve everything. In either case, they would end up with the fake stuff.

Mickey was also concerned that sometime between the defendant's release and their first appearance in court, the police would knock on his door. They'd have a warrant allowing them to view—or confiscate—any of the collateral given in connection with posting the client's bond, and copies of any receipts given to the defendant, including those given for both premium and collateral. Or a subpoena requiring him to appear in court to testify under oath as to what was taken as collateral.

The police were not necessarily looking to hook Mickey for collaborating with the defendant to avoid his or her prosecution, but rather to assist in proving whether the cash or other items the defendants gave him were legit or ill-gotten gain.

Upon receipt of the bond exoneration from the court, which usually came at the close of a defendant's case, Mickey would return the costume jewelry to the defendant rather than the actual jewelry they'd deposited. That's because he had no way of knowing if the defendant had rolled over and turned state's evidence against Mickey for knowingly conspiring to get the defendant off with a lesser sentence.

In most cases involving his regular shady clients, giving back costume jewelry or other fake collateral was usually fine with them, because they expected to be re-arrested upon leaving Mickey's office on some new, bogus charge that would allow the cops to confiscate the jewelry Mickey had returned to them. If the cops found any of the original stolen items, they would add an additional charge for possession of stolen property and attempt to arrest Mickey, or me, for complicity in covering up their old crime.

Since the client's personal property was usually stolen in the first place, most of Mickey's friends and good clients would rather have him keep the jewelry, because having it in their possession would result in their returning to jail. They knew that if Mickey had it, he'd give them credit against any future bond premium. So we usually made out pretty well. I say "we," because as time went on, Mickey often shared some of the excess cash and/or the bounty after he disposed of it through his favorite local jeweler or fence.

At the beginning, Mickey required me to discuss taking collateral from my clients with him first. And if we discussed it over the phone, I was to use hypothetical terms. He then would discuss the stuff with a trusted third party before turning a bond away. That third-party "friend" was usually the same fence, or one of the same prominent jewelers he used many times over the years. These individuals would provide him with a value based upon what they would pay us for the stuff; not what they could get for it on the black market, or by selling it through their legitimate jewelry stores or pawn shops.

Jewelers were the worst to deal with. We knew they could separate the stones, melt down the settings, remake a new piece and sell it for more than its original value. The same went for pawn brokers. Then they'd come back with some bullshit attempt to pay us 10 cents on the dollar by expressing concerns that the stuff might be hot. Mickey usually settled for 25 cents on the dollar. When he was dealing with good client/friends, he'd give them the full value on anything he was holding by applying it toward their next bond. But most of the time we split any excess and forgot about it.

CHAPTER

#4

Although Mickey and I had discussed fugitive recovery earlier, I felt it was necessary to cover it again, since we were now entering into our new contract, and it outlined my responsibilities in greater detail. When I asked him about it, he gave me two options: I could do my own fugitive recovery, or we could hire one of his local skip chasers (another name for bounty hunters) and split the costs.

When I said I wanted to do my own skip chasing, the first words out of his mouth were: "Remember what I told you about carrying a gun. Someone will take it away and kill you with it. You'd better not get your young ass shot or killed on my watch, because Elaine will kill me if you do. By the way, where are the knuckles I gave you?"

Mickey recommended that I always notify the local police when I had information regarding a fugitive, especially if he or she had a history of violence. He said, "Try and make sure, as best you can, that the fugitive is actually there; and then, when they arrive, let them know you are prepared to make the arrest.

"Kid, it's important to be reasonably sure you're right when you make that final call to the cops. It will save you headaches later, because you don't want the police chasing their shadows all over hell and back for nothing. They may do it two or three times, but then you'll get a reputation for crying wolf, and they'll stop showing up; that's usually when you'll really need them. Remember, if you elect not to take backup with you on an arrest, you'll be giving the fugitives a 90 percent chance of getting away and giving yourself a 90 percent chance of getting seriously hurt—or even killed."

We completed a quick overview of the laws covering recovery, particularly the U.S. Supreme Court case of *Taylor v. Taintor*-83 US 366, which upheld the rights of a bail bond agent to arrest and surrender any person released into his or her custody on a bail bond. This case noted that a bail agent may cross state lines, enter any private home or business suspected of harboring one of his fugitives, and may do so without the need of a warrant or the owner's permission.

The Supreme Court also ruled that a bondsman could pass his "powers for the arrest of anyone out on his bond through to another person by simply providing them with a written and signed agreement giving them authority not only to apprehend, but also to transport that defendant back to the proper jurisdiction." This third person could be a properly licensed investigator, an off-duty police officer, or a local unlicensed and untrained bounty hunter, biker, or bum. At this point in my career, there were no federal, state, or local requirements governing the licensing or training of fugitive apprehension officers or bounty hunters anywhere in the United States.

Mickey said, "Kid, if you ever give someone your authority to apprehend a fugitive on one of our bonds, you better make damn sure it's in writing; I recommend you offer it to an off-duty police officer first, because he'll have the necessary experience and training for the job. That way, if an innocent bystander is injured or killed, you'll be able to prove that you made a reasonable and responsible decision regarding the apprehension and arrest of the fugitive. The downside in using them is the cost. They charge a hell of a lot more than a biker or a bum.

"If police officers or their equivalent aren't available, I suggest you do it yourself, or accompany whomever you hire. This way, you can claim that all the injuries to you, your team, or to the fugitive, were in self-defense. Especially if you smash his nose all over his face with those knuckles."

At the end of our meeting, he gave me another one of his famous "NO GUNS" lectures. He closed by reminding me that taking enough information before writing a bond is the best form of protection against future financial loss, but not necessarily the best way to make money in the business. And that at least half of all the future expenses and losses would be coming out of my pocket. This time however, all his comments hit home with a greater impact.

My Bail Bond 101 training classes were officially over. It was time to put all of Mickey's information and training to work. It was time to think about quitting school and starting to make some real money.

CHAPTER

#5

Writing bonds turned out to be much more difficult than learning the business. I began my newfound independence, as well as my opportunity to start making hundreds of dollars a week, on a sour note. I was taking way too much time on each individual bond: gathering too much information and asking for too many co-signers or trying to squeeze too much security out of my clients. As a result, I found myself losing too many good opportunities and good bonds to competitors. In fact, competitors were writing more business while I was making less in commissions than I'd made in salary as a runner.

My problems were Mickey's, too, because the business I was losing was his. He called me in for a little powwow, one which cured my underwriting issues. He reviewed my production, as well as the overall reduction in his business, and gave me two options.

"Kid, I've been thinking about hiring a couple of additional agents to pick up your slack. This means all your potential commissions will be split by two thirds, but it will guarantee that all my business will be handled. Or you could make all the commissions yourself by merely getting off your fat ass and working harder, smarter, and taking more risks. In my opinion, option two is your best choice since it would provide you with all the commissions, rather than continuing to lose two thirds of them to our competitors or the two new guys I'll be hiring. The choice is yours."

It didn't take a lot of thought to realize it was time to quit college and chose option two. I began reviewing Mickey's old files again to see how much information I needed to write many of the bonds I was losing. I started coming in earlier and staying later to watch the master at work; to see something—anything—I might have missed during my training.

With college out of the picture, my desire to make money took priority. I kept repeating some of Mickey's famous expressions: "Bail is a risk business. If you're afraid to take risks, become a plumber." Or, "Don't waste time taking a full application on someone who's lived here his whole life no matter what the charge, because he has nowhere to go, and if he does go, he'll leave an easy trail of tears, or collect phone calls to his mommy for you to follow."

One of his favorites was "Mommy, Daddy, or baby brother would rather visit him or her in a local jail cell on visiting day than continue receiving collect calls from him as a fugitive on the run. Especially if someone like you is willing to pay a handsome reward for information on his whereabouts."

I began taking greater risks with shorter applications. This resulted in writing more bonds. Now I began making the kind of money I'd imagined during my first interview with Mickey—the kind that would put me on track to join the millionaires' club before I turned thirty.

Spending as much time as I could around the office gave me more opportunities to casually pick Mickey's brain or have more open conversations. Like the time he told me his decision to hire me was based solely on greed. He'd hoped I'd receive special treatment from the jail personnel, since my old man was the jail commander, which he thought would lead to more client referrals.

But then, his thoughts turned to concerns. He wondered if I might be a direct conduit to the old man and would divulge any criminal activity I might stumble across. This resulted in reluctance to share valuable, yet questionable, underwriting information, associates, contacts or personal business with me. After all, he thought I was, and might always be, a cop's son first.

Once I explained how badly the old man treated Mom and me after my older brother joined the navy and left home, he realized the error in his thinking. Additionally, I told him I was willing to step onto the shadier side of justice to protect our relationship and my new career.

Once he put the pieces together, he began trusting me more and introducing me to more of his close friends and special clients. He also made it a point to include me in his special meetings whenever he could, and he let me work with many of the local old timers, as well as his favorite burglars, thieves, and boosters.

Many of these individuals worked throughout Nevada, not just in the Reno-Sparks area. We'd often find several of them in the bail office just about any time, day or night. They'd drink the coffee, shoot the shit about their latest scores, or make new bail arrangements with us for their next job "just in case."

As a result of Mickey's new openness around me, they were no longer afraid to include me in their conversations, especially when they could make me the butt of their jokes, like guys do with friends you could trust.

Of Mickey's friends and clients, burglars were the shadiest, and usually the only ones who crossed state lines to conduct their illegal business. As a result of their interstate business activities, they were also the only ones with FBI rap sheets, many of which were a mile long. But they also had fewer actual convictions. As time went on, I found out that Mickey fenced a lot of the jewelry, coin collections, gold, guns and other small valuables that his favorite burglars lifted from mansions, summer homes, and beach houses of the rich and famous throughout Nevada, Arizona, and California. In other words, he discretely sold them to many of his law abiding, legitimate friends behind closed doors.

Mickey always managed to keep some of the best items for himself or Elaine, but he always gave the thieves full-dollar value for each piece he kept when it was time to settle up on what they owed him, or if they wanted the money applied to any future bonds they might need. The rest of the items, those he didn't fence off or keep, he used as payoffs, bribes, or to fix any outstanding forfeitures.

Burglars caused Mickey most of his ongoing issues with the law. The most significant of those problems ended up in his FBI dossier—the one that contained extensive information on him and everyone with whom he'd ever associated. Not surprisingly, I also landed on his "known associates" list, which I learned from Mickey's insider at the local FBI office. This was the first time my name ever appeared in an FBI file, but you could bet it wouldn't be the last.

Although these burglars created problems with the police, they were the least of Mickey's problems with the courts. As I mentioned, if a burglar decided to run, he or she would first come in and either pay, or arrange to pay, whatever Mickey estimated would be enough to satisfy the courts or bribe the necessary officials. These arrangements allowed Mickey's lawyer to drag out the final payment of the burglar's bond forfeiture by filing motions to extend the trial dates or arrange to pay one of the court clerks to misplace a file for a while or lose it altogether.

Things got a little more complicated when a case received elevated publicity. At that point, the attorney might have to arrange with the judge to erroneously dismiss the case for lack of evidence after months of granting bogus continuances or, at the very least, provide adequate time for any interest in the case to die down.

On cases with little or no notoriety, Mickey would arrange for one of the evidence clerks or a deputy sheriff to assist the judge by losing the evidence, which would miraculously show up in Mickey's security locker in the basement of his country home. It was disguised as a wood worker's bench, with sawdust and all. He pretty much ended up with everything except illegal drugs.

Drugs, as well as the violence surrounding them, were becoming a big issue in some of the larger cities across the country, and Mickey wanted nothing to do with them, either personally or professionally. In his eyes, they weren't worth the risk.

The bondsmen taking drugs for payment of premium or collateral were having their homes and offices ransacked, their cars stolen, and in some cases, being killed by dealers or their associates in an attempt to recover drugs given as collateral or payment on their bail bond.

Occasionally, when a judge was uncomfortable dismissing a case in which he'd ordered Mickey's bond forfeited, he'd ask Mickey, through his attorney, to file a motion requesting a reduction in the amount of the bond obligation based on a bogus accounting of the money and resources Mickey allegedly spent attempting to locate the defendant. If the prosecuting attorney was playing hardball and pressing to have the judge order payment of the forfeiture, we always left some bucks on the table to satisfy him as well.

Mickey always arranged the payments. He paid the bribes, paid those responsible for losing files, paid the cops to lose the evidence, and even created most of the bogus accountings provided to the judges. These payoffs were illegal, no matter who delivered them, whether it was Mickey or his attorney. They'd been doing it long before I arrived on the scene.

The issue I had with Mickey regarding payoffs wasn't that he was doing it, or even that they were illegal. It was his level of overconfidence and self-righteous smugness. The longer you do stuff like this, I thought, the greater the chance of getting caught. His lackadaisical attitude reminded me too much of my own back in grade school, when I got caught stealing candy and promised myself I would never get overconfident again, and, more importantly, I would never get caught again. These so-called payoffs could send him, and everyone around him, to jail for much longer than I spent that afternoon when I was ten years old.

I promised myself I'd find the right time to discuss my concerns with him. In the meantime, I was going to write as many bonds as I could, always keeping in mind Mickey's ability to pay our way out of certain forfeiture problems and always remembering I was the student. My job was to learn all I could from the master, not to challenge his ways. I decided to learn as much as I could about the system without getting caught up in the actual payoffs—or anything else that might jeopardize my license.

CHAPTER

#6

Except for burglars and thieves, almost all the other characters Mickey did business with worked their trade throughout Nevada. Some were arrested so often that Mickey had to hire runners to drop off bonds at many of the jails in the smaller cities and townships between Reno and Las Vegas.

During my days as one of those runners, I became good friends with the two brothers I met the day I went to Mickey's office looking for a job. Ernie was twenty-five, just a few years older than me. Leo was in his late thirties. While Ernie was more relaxed, with an air of innocence about him, Leo was more of a gangster type. Both grew up around their father's slot machine repair shop, which enabled them to become world-class "slot cheats."

When we got to know each other better, Ernie brought me to the shop and showed me how slot cheating was done. He knew everything about the old-style machines, from their wooden cabinets and three spinning wheels to the hinged metal-door fronts on the cabinets that held the coin bags. These were nothing like today's computerized machines; the ones that post the number of coins you have left to play, then print a ticket listing your total winnings when you're ready to cash out. Although big winners still hear all the bells and whistles going off, the only way they receive payment in today's casinos is to redeem the winning ticket at the cashier's window.

Although both brothers were into rigging slot machines, being a "slot cheat" was Ernie's favorite thing. He loved the challenge of rigging the machines with the largest jackpots, then walking away and leaving his girlfriend to collect their winnings. In the '60s and '70s, cheating the clubs by rigging their machines was a fast, easy, yet dangerous way to make big bucks. It was significantly more dangerous in the clubs controlled by the mob.

Growing up, Ernie, being so much younger than Leo, spent much more time with his dad. As a result, he not only learned how the machines worked, he learned to make replacement parts for many of the ones being used throughout Nevada. And since his dad had a complete machine shop, he also learned how to manufacture special tools from scratch whenever his dad needed one to fix a machine.

As he grew up, he made his choice between right and wrong, and began using his newly acquired talents to manufacture all the special tools needed to easily break into or unlock slot machines, then rig them to pay jackpots. Over the years, Ernie had hundreds of slot machines of every type, size, and shape on which to practice his talents. His tool of choice became a pocket-size, battery operated drill he made to fit into the palm of one hand. He used it to drill an unnoticeable pin-sized hole into the side of a wooden slot-machine case, usually the machine with the highest jackpot. He practiced his technique of drilling the hole and subtly placing a small, stiff wire through it while his brother or his girlfriend was playing the machine.

His experience in the shop taught him just how far to insert the wire so his team could continue to play the machines while locking each wheel in place, one by one, as the bars appeared in the pay window. When all three wheels were locked, with a bar showing in each window, the jackpot whistle would automatically sound.

That's when Ernie or Leo would pull the wire out of the machine, place it up their sleeve, and walk away, leaving their "turn"—usually one of their partners or girlfriends—jumping with joy and screaming "Jackpot! Jackpot!" This drew attention away from the brothers as they left the club. They would all meet up later at a nearby watering hole to divide their winnings.

A "turn" is the name given to those who help slot cheats collect their jackpots. But "turns" also work with card muckers and craps players to set up their score by distracting change girls, security guards, casino floor managers, dealers, or pit bosses away from their team working the table.

They distracted employees by asking simple questions like "Where can I get change?" or "Where can I find a restroom?" The questions were designed to make an employee turn away from the team to point or direct them. Sometimes team members attracted the attention of dealers and pit bosses by spilling their drinks at the opposite end of a gaming table while their teammates palmed (switched) cards or stacked additional chips on their winning hand at a blackjack table. They also helped distract everyone at a craps table while their partner switched dice. This took the most talent, and it required special matching dice available through black market manufacturers in Chicago. Neither Leo nor Ernie used "turns" for anything other than slots, although they knew a lot of the drifters, and a lot about the different ways to cheat the casinos.

Leo often would ride along for a little excitement, but his favorite fiddle, or swindle, was to scam wealthy old ladies out of their money by pretending to be a bank security officer attempting to catch local bank employees suspected of stealing money from customer accounts. After gaining an old woman's confidence, he'd ask her to go to the bank, cash a check, and bring the money directly to him at a prearranged public place. Then he'd tell her the plan: He would mark the money in front of her, then give it to one of his female operatives. She, in turn, would pose as the little old lady's niece, and redeposit the money back into her account. Leo would assure the old lady that bank investigators would follow the marked money to catch the thieves. However, the female operative never redeposited the money, and there were no investigators. Instead, the operative met Leo at a nearby café, where they divided the money and skipped town.

Leo did a lot of sleazy things to pick up some quick cash on the side, like collecting $500 each time he drove some innocent young girl to Battle Mountain for an illegal abortion. But he was proud that he never pulled off one of his scams in his own hometown. He said he was afraid he'd get caught and embarrass his wife and kids, so Reno was off limits.

But one day, he got sloppy, overconfident, or just needed some fast money. He attempted one of his scams in Reno and was caught, arrested, and booked. He called Mickey's office during my shift, and asked me to post his bail, which I did. Later that day, he committed suicide. He left a typewritten note, which was unusual for a guy who never typed a word in his life. It told his wife and two daughters how sorry he was for embarrassing them.

Mickey, Ernie, and I wondered if he'd actually killed himself, or if he'd gotten a little help from the mob—since he didn't own a typewriter. The mob was known to dislike any criminal publicity, especially from petty crooks like Leo. They probably hit him due to his swindling the elderly out of their life savings. They knew this type of publicity would bring out all the goody-two-shoes in town, blaming legalized gambling for drawing Leo and his type of sleazy mobsters to town. The righteous were running around telling all the newspapers, TV, and radio stations about how these bad guys bilk little old ladies out of their money, while the casino owners were busy bilking everyone else. These virtuous advocates felt that gambling continually contributed to the high crime rate in the Reno-Sparks area and wanted all the crooks and gamblers run out of town.

As a result of the adverse publicity stirred up by Leo's suicide, I was hounded by the local news media. They wanted to interview the guy who bailed out Leo Mullens the day of his suicide. And they wanted to know if I felt there was any truth to the accusations brought by these pious complainers.

I later found my picture plastered across the front pages of the Reno Evening Gazette and the Nevada State Journal. The caption read: "Bail agent has no comment regarding ties between legalized gambling and the city's crime rate."

CHAPTER

#7

This unwanted publicity brought all kinds of people out of the woodwork. Some were friends I hadn't seen in a while. Others were assholes looking to blame me for helping criminals like Leo get out of jail. One of the friendlier ones was my brother's ex-girlfriend, Shirley. She called one afternoon and started the conversation with: "Hi, Lefty. I've wanted to talk to you since your brother and I broke up, but I wasn't sure how to get in touch with you until I saw your picture in the newspaper yesterday. I was hoping we could have a drink or something sometime."

Because I'd dropped out of school and spent almost every waking hour working on my new career, I had dated only a couple of old girlfriends. I'm sure it wasn't fun being on a date with someone who keeps excusing himself from the table to call the answering service or leaves them sitting alone in a restaurant while he goes to write a bail bond. I tried to be more sensitive, but the business was just too demanding. Sometimes I had to put them in a cab when I went to the office or the jail. Not the best arrangement for developing a lasting relationship. It was either work on a relationship or work on making money, and making money always won.

This time, something felt different. As we talked on the phone, I remembered the day my brother introduced me to her. She was younger than him and a few years older than me, and WOW! What a knockout! She was very nice, very pretty, and very sexy. With that vision in mind, I couldn't say no.

"I'm still working at Harrah's," she said, "and still writing Keno tickets in the main casino. Maybe you could stop by and chat during one of my breaks so we could get reacquainted and discuss going for that drink. What do you say?"

Without hesitation, I answered, "Sounds great, I'll stop by tomorrow." No sense letting moss grow under this invitation.

The next afternoon, I entered Harrah's Hotel and Casino and walked directly to the Keno counter where Shirley was working. I wrote a Keno ticket for the next game and handed it to her. I tried to act like any other normal customer in an effort not to draw attention to either of us. Her eyes were down as we exchanged pleasantries.

"Hello."

She responded, "Hello."

"Are you feeling lucky today?"

She looked up, realized who it was, and replied, "I am now." Then she added, almost in a whisper, "I get a twenty-minute break at the end of this game, so I'll meet you in the coffee shop, okay?"

I nodded and walked toward the restaurant. That's when it hit me. The only problem I'd ever noticed about her was her voice. It was nasally, squeaky, and hard to get past, because it sounded like she'd been sucking helium out of a party balloon.

We met in the coffee shop about fifteen minutes later, exchanged hugs, and some small talk about how long it had been since we'd last seen each other. Then she started to speak in a low, soft tone that subdued the squeak I remembered. Her voice had become almost as sexy as she was.

Since we had nothing else in common, she started off with a barrage of questions about Allan. "Did you ever speak to your brother about me? Did he ever tell you that we never had sex the entire time we dated?" Without waiting for a reply, she asked me to help her understand why.

"Lefty, do you think I wasn't attractive enough for him?"

That was a no-brainer. She was a knockout, and she knew it. She must have sensed my attraction to her when Allan introduced us, but now she needed to hear me say it. Why else would she call? I tried to explain how Allan, being raised Catholic, was one of those guys who believed in saving himself for marriage, which to this day, I'm sure was pure bullshit. I added that he and I were not only different ages, but our feelings about sex were different as well, so I wasn't sure I could help in defining his behavior.

She confided that she had been married before. This took me by surprise, since I didn't think Allan would consider dating a divorcée.

She said, "When I tied Allan's behavior toward me to the emotional letdown I was having from a failed marriage, it turned me off toward dating and sex. Your brother left me feeling less attractive as a woman, and heartbroken as well. Then, when he said he was leaving for law school without me, I realized our relationship was going nowhere. That's when I ended it."

She stood up and said, "I have to get back to work. Can we continue this tonight? Let's meet in the bar at the El Dorado Lounge on South Virginia Street at about eight o'clock, if that's okay?"

"Sure," I said. "I'll leave a message with the bartender in case I'm writing a bond and can't make it exactly at eight. But I'll definitely be there as close to it as possible."

After she left, I felt a little confused. I was looking forward to expanding our conversation on to something other than Allan, but then, a twenty-minute break didn't leave much time. Just then, my pager sounded. I decided to save my thoughts for later and walked toward the exit.

As I was about to leave, the chief of security came up, introduced himself, and asked if we could talk for a few minutes.

"Sure, what can I do for you?"

"I learned from reading the newspaper, that you obviously knew Leo Mullens. Did you also know his brother Ernie?"

"Yes. Why do you ask?"

His response came as a shock. "Leo and Ernie have been banned from setting foot in many of the casinos in Reno, including Harrah's, for quite awhile. And because of their friendship with the Mullens, we've banned a number of their friends and associates."

"What does this have to do with me?"

He said, "Please accept what I'm about to say as a friendly request. In the future, don't patronize any of Harrah's properties, clubs, hotels, or other holdings. As of now, you are no longer welcome, and our entire security staff has been notified."

I left the casino without saying another word—out loud, at least. I went directly to Mickey's office, and angrily explained what had happened.

He said, "I thought Ernie would have told you. He and Leo are listed in the casinos' infamous Black Book. They're banned from many casinos in Nevada for life on suspicion of slot cheating. And now, thanks to bailing Leo out, it looks like you may be as well."

"That's bullshit. I never cheated any casinos, and I've never been caught at anything, so how can they get away with this?"

"No one ever caught Ernie or Leo in the act either. And they were never arrested locally, that is, until Leo's last job. But minor incidents like getting caught cheating or being arrested don't matter when you're dealing with the mob and their casinos. They bar anybody they want from their clubs, regardless of whether it's justified or not. They also have the muscle to enforce it. You, at least, learned of your expulsion the easy way."

"Well, I'm too pissed off to work. I'm liable to punch a client or jailer just for the hell of it, so I'm leaving!"

I wasn't sure if I was really that pissed, or if I was looking for a good excuse to ensure I could spend a quiet, uninterrupted evening with Shirley. Either way, I needed the night off.

Mickey said, "Kid, go home and shake it off. Trust me, this won't be the only time you're treated disrespectfully while you're in this business."

As a result, I was able to show up a little early at the El Dorado bar and grab the only booth directly in front of the fireplace. It was the coziest, most intimate private space there; perfect for renewing, and hopefully expanding, our friendship.

Shirley had changed out of her Keno attire. She wore a short skirt with a silky clinging blouse, open just enough, with one extra button undone, to make it interesting. I stood up as she approached. We hugged, said hello, and gave each other a small kiss on the cheek. As we sat down, she started the conversation where we had left off. I interrupted her. "Your entry was unbelievable," I said. "You caught the eye of every guy in the place. You are absolutely gorgeous, which confirms the fact that my brother must have been nuts to let you get away!"

She thanked me for the compliments, gave me a flirtatious smile, and said, "I think we're in for a fun evening, unless you have a girlfriend, or someone else to go home to."

I laughed. "No one I know would put up with me being on call for work 24/7. I'm afraid I'm married to my career."

"Well," she said, "you know me, and I happen to think you're much better looking than your brother. And as for being married to the business, I'm sure we could find some time for fun."

One story led to another. Before I knew it, she took my hand, placed it under the table, and then up her skirt. She had on no panties. She sighed when I began to touch her and melted into quiet carnal ecstasy when the soft touch of my fingers penetrated her pussy. The next thing I knew, we were at the front desk of the hotel, renting a room.

Once there, we began ripping at each other's clothes, trying to get them off without missing a touch, a kiss, or a caress. I gently pushed her backward, onto the bed. I pulled her legs close and placed her feet up by my neck, while she softly placed me inside her. I began to thrust in and out very, very slowly. Because she was so horny she reached a climax before I did.

At the height of sexual exhaustion, we were undeniably weak, but neither of us wanted to stop, so we began to erotically caress, touch, explore and stimulate every part of each other's body. When we were too weary to continue, we rested. After a short while, she stood up, posed in some alluring and very erotic positions, and motioned me to join her in the shower, which I did.

Afterward, we returned to the bed, dripping wet, and continued for what seemed to be hours before we both fell asleep.

We both knew that having good, passionate, mutually satisfying sex required time and effort. And that's what this relationship was all about: raw sex.

We continued our relationship for months, meeting three, and sometimes four, times a week. Since she was sharing her apartment with a girlfriend from work, the El Dorado Hotel & Lounge became a comfortable, private spot away from prying eyes. Over time, the bartender and I became friends, so I always arranged to have a nice bottle of champagne and flowers waiting in our room, depending on how long it had been since our last little get together. We repeated that first night many, many times over the six months that we spent together.

As time went on, I could see a change in her. At the beginning, after one bad marriage and a poor rebound attempt with my brother, who didn't want sex with her for reasons only God and my brother knew, she was not only sexually unsatisfied, but also feeling unfeminine and unwanted. Now, at the height of our relationship, she was feeling very sexy, very feminine, and very satisfied—so much so that she felt it was time to begin looking for that certain sugar daddy who would carry her off into the sunset.

Since we knew from the beginning that person wasn't going to be me, she was open about her goals. Consequently, we began seeing less of each other as she began her hunt for Mister Perfect.

CHAPTER

#8

While Shirley went looking for her sugar daddy, I threw myself back into the bail bond business on more than a full-time basis. I found myself hanging around Mickey and the office, even when I didn't need to be there. I rented a one-bedroom apartment on High Street, just down the street from Mickey's office, and kitty-corner from the Reno police station. An elderly couple with no children owned the apartment complex. At the time, I had no idea just how much of an impact this couple would have on my future.

I left most of my things at Mom's house so she wouldn't worry about being left alone again. Although Sis lived in the area, her marriage, job, and the possibility of adopting a child gave her little extra time, so I wanted to make sure Mom knew I was going to be around.

I told her I'd stay at the apartment as needed, and at home as often as I could, depending on how busy it was at the office. Either way, I would still see her, or call her every day to make sure she was okay, and I would make sure she had everything she needed, especially money.

Since I was spending so much additional time at the office, Mickey decided it was time I gained some hands-on experience in bounty hunting. He set me up with a couple of his most experienced hunters. The three of us worked on Mickey's skips and on mine too. He felt the experience I'd gain from working with his "pros" would be well worth my time. I did everything Mickey's guys did, except carry a gun. However, I always had my personal set of brass knuckles close at hand, so I seldom felt the need to break Mickey's rule and carry my gun, the one I purchased upon my return home from the military, or one of the hunters spares.

My initial experience and training chasing bad guys started with watching these guys bust their way through doors, and literally kick the shit out of anyone who got in their way. This usually included the fugitive, or fugitives, they were hunting. Then they'd ask me to help drag one of the fugitives out and put him in the trunk of their car.

I was always the designated driver, which gave them a chance to sit in the back seat and clean themselves up. After all, kicking the shit out of uncooperative fugitives can get messy.

When we'd arrive at the appropriate jail, the booking officers would take one look at the fugitive and ask, "What the hell happened to this guy?" The hunters would smile and attempt to explain away the fugitive's injuries by saying how he'd fallen while attempting to run away; jumped out of a second-story window and landed on a pile of rocks; or simply tripped and fell down a flight of stairs.

All their comments were included in the jailer's booking reports, which were signed, under oath, by both bounty hunters and witnessed by me whenever necessary.

These "attempted escape" stories were always protested by the fugitives. But it came down to our word against theirs.

Since they were the fugitives and we were purportedly the good guys, no one gave a rat's ass about what they said, not even the judges.

In addition to having me ride with his two major hunters, Mickey suggested I pal around with Ernie, now that his brother was gone. He said Ernie needed a friend, and I could use someone to watch my back. Because Ernie and I got along so well, MIckey thought it would be good for the both of us. As usual, he was right.

No one could ever take Leo's place, but a good friend could keep Ernie's mind off his loss. And as Ernie was a lot bigger than me, he could intimidate a lot more people into surrendering without hesitation. This kept my bruises at a minimum when we looked for my skips. It was a good match, and we had a lot of good times, especially since the skips we hunted weren't using or dealing drugs.

Three years later, in late 1968, I was still writing bonds and helping chase skips in Reno full-time when Mickey called me into the office. He started our conversation by "making me an offer I couldn't refuse."

"Kid," he said, "there's more to the bail business than writing bonds and chasing skips. It's time you learned how to manage people and problems and to make decisions. With the influx of teamster money pouring into Las Vegas, the city is expanding, and I want to get my piece of the pie. I have a plan for two new offices down there, and I want you to manage them."

He said I'd be a minority partner and share in everything we did in Vegas. As the manager, I could still spend part of my time writing bail in the Reno office.

Mickey suggested that before I gave him my answer, I should check out potential office sites in Vegas, along with the competition we'd be facing. Rather than fly, I decided to drive, and asked Ernie to join me. He agreed and brought along his girlfriend, Kristy.

On the way down, Ernie and I discussed some of what we knew or had heard about Las Vegas. We knew that all the casinos, large and small, used the old-style, three-wheel slot machines, the ones Ernie was familiar with. In addition, the clubs all used a single deck of cards at their blackjack tables. We also knew that their "rent a cop" security guards were mainly used for controlling large gatherings of guests, like those near the showrooms and the high-roller tables. They also attended to guests with medical issues like heart attacks or seizures, but they never stuck their nose in the casino's business.

That's because the mob ran all the casino operations from behind the scenes, while the legitimate guys, the ones fronting for them, were responsible for hotel, restaurant, and floor-show operations. The mob bosses not only established casino security, they provided enforcement (muscle) when needed. They were careful never to allow outsiders to cheat any of the casinos that were indebted to, or about to be indebted to, the Teamsters Fund. Everything they did was done to protect their own skimming operations, which provided millions of dollars in compensation to the mob bosses. They, in turn, assisted the hotel owners and developers in obtaining Teamster expansion loans, among other things.

These mob thugs, acting as pit bosses and casino shift managers, were responsible for protecting the House from outside thieves and card cheats, as well as internal employees, especially dealers, who would palm chips right off their gaming tables and place them in false pockets sewed inside their aprons, pants, or skirts. At the end of their shifts, these dealers would take the stolen chips to neighboring casinos and exchange them for cash. At the time, casino chips were the same as cash in Vegas, and could be exchanged for cash in any casino.

These same thugs were also responsible for watching their own skimming operators, the guys sent from New York, New Jersey, and Chicago to skim cash from the drop-boxes retrieved from each of the gaming tables before they reached the counting room. That was before the Feds started investigating the casinos in the late 1960s. The mob bosses didn't like anybody, insiders or outsiders, stealing from them, and would have their thugs whack anyone, be it a skimmer, a pit boss, a dealer, an outside card mucker, or slot cheat. Money was the only thing that mattered to them and they protected it by setting examples.

One of the old casino advertising slogans went something like "We Send Out Winners to Get Players." Well, the thugs had their own jingle: "We Send Out Dead Guys to Stop Cheats."

Even though Ernie and I talked about the mob, and how much they hated cheats, the entire way to Vegas, it didn't faze him one bit. Upon arriving on the famous Las Vegas Strip, the first thing he wanted to do was hit the slots for some walking-around money. I barely had time to stop the car before he and Kristy jumped out and ran into a casino, leaving me to do my research.

Rather than staying in one of the strip hotels, we chose a small motel within walking distance of the downtown casinos—as well as the jail and the courthouse.

I suggested that we meet up each day for lunch and dinner so we could plan our return trip when I finished my research, and to make sure Ernie was staying out of trouble. During our first lunch meeting, Ernie started bragging about how easy it was to hit the clubs because they had machines everywhere, except in the restrooms (the shitters as he called them) and they'd already hit quite a few.

About four days later, on the day we planned to return to Reno, Ernie went for one more run at the machines. It turned out to be one run too many. The thugs must have been on the lookout for whoever was hitting their machines, because they caught him red handed, drill in hand. Fortunately, he wasn't far enough along with the drilling to involve Kristy. She watched as the thugs took Ernie away. The mob had little patience with outsiders like Ernie trying to take them, even if it was for peanuts compared with their skimming operation.

After taking him on a little trip to the desert and beating the living shit out of him, they dumped Ernie on the side of the road. At least, that's what we thought happened. We found out later the only reason they let him live was the money, their money. And they wanted it all back. Killing him left little opportunity to accomplish their goal. That was the only reason we found him stumbling along one of the main desert roads just outside of town.

After cleaning him up as best we could, we laid him in the back seat and headed for Reno. Kristy and I drove all night, switching drivers every few hours, watching to see if we were being followed. Until we reached Earnie's place, we didn't stop for anything except gas and takeout food. He was feeling pretty bad, but he didn't want us to take him to the hospital or a doctor, so Kristy stayed with him for the next few days.

A week or so later, he came down to Mickey's office and told us the whole story. Ernie had ripped off some of the big Vegas casinos for more than he'd previously admitted. He said even though it meant stepping on a few too many of the wrong toes, cheating their machines was so easy, and so profitable, he couldn't stop himself.

The beating they gave him was their way of sending a message to all his friends and associates. "Stop fucking with our machines. The only reason you're still alive is because we want our money back, every last fucking dollar of it."

Ernie knew he was a marked man; he knew they'd be coming back to finish the job, regardless of whether he gave them their money or not. It wasn't just about the money; they wanted to send a message. Although they left him alive on the outskirts of Vegas, this wasn't their long-term plan.

He told all of us, including Kristy, that he was going home to pack a few things, and would hide out for a while. He figured it was safer to spend their money on a hideout than giving it back to them. He said he'd call Mickey's office and let us know where he was staying.

That night, on his way home from Kristy's place, his car mysteriously ran off the road at high speed and careened through his neighbor's white-picket fence, smashing into a huge two-hundred-year-old oak tree in their front yard. No one was sure if the impact killed him, but by the time the police and the paramedics arrived, Ernie was dead.

Later, Kristy told Mickey that Ernie had all the money from Vegas with him when he came by her place. He left her house with all of it, except her share. When she went to the coroner's to learn the official cause of death, she was informed that Ernie died of a massive heart attack. The coroner said that Ernie's body was also severely bruised, which he attributed to the accident, but noted that he died instantly, when his heart exploded. And although it was unusual for someone his age, with no history of heart problems, to experience this type of trauma, he was unable to find any other cause of death.

"Unwilling" was probably a more accurate description.

Kristy went from there to the police department to retrieve Ernie's belongings. That's when she found out that all the money, including the hundred-dollar emergency fund he always had stashed in his wallet, was gone.

At his wake, we all knew in our heart of hearts that the thugs from Vegas finished him off and retrieved their money. That's where the bruising had come from. We also knew that an exploding heart may have been the official cause of death, but it wasn't the result of an accident.

According to the coroner, there was no evidence of Ernie being drugged or that he was even driving the car. It didn't take much to read between the lines of the report. If we pushed too hard, we might all end up like Ernie. So we said our goodbyes and moved on with our lives.

I lost a good friend, and I felt a little bit responsible, since I'd invited him along. But I also learned two valuable lessons. The first was not to mess with the mob casinos and not to hang out with anyone stupid enough to try to cheat them. I stopped hanging with any of the cheats taking money from a mob casino, no matter if it was in Reno, Tahoe, or Vegas. But I didn't stop bailing them out whenever or wherever they needed me. The second lesson was learning the depth of corruption in Vegas during that era—from the elected officials to the police. It seemed like everyone had their hand out and their eyes closed. Anyone could get anything they wanted, as long as they were prepared to pay the right person the right price.

CHAPTER

#9

Over the course of the next few months Mickey and I reviewed my proposal for the Vegas offices. It included items like our initial competition, the volume of arrests made by all law enforcement agencies within Las Vegas, North Las Vegas, and Boulder City, as well as the number of new casinos planned for the Strip and the number of casino expansions and renovation programs. Obviously, all this construction would add strong potential growth to the area, and, in turn, to the crime rate and the need for bail bonds.

If we were going to proceed, we also needed to discuss the rumors surrounding the use of the Teamsters' pension funds—because everyone knew the Teamsters' loans were being supplied via the mob for many of these projects. If the FBI and local law enforcement became engaged in numerous investigations, they could literally close down many of these projects, which would then have a negative impact on growth, which could leave us holding the bag on two Vegas offices we didn't need.

Everything pointed toward moving forward, especially since our meager investment in the two new bail offices was nothing compared with what the Teamsters and the mob stood to lose. And compared to the Reno-Lake Tahoe area, Las Vegas was definitely the place to be.

During our review, I also noted that there were only a small handful of bail agencies throughout the area, and only one or two of them would be able to muster the financial resources needed to compete against us. We decided to push ahead with our new plan. As Mickey put it, "It was time to get our slice of the pie."

This new opportunity was not only exciting and challenging, it was going to pay me thousands per week instead of the hundreds I was making. Under our new partnership agreement, I not only received my regular 50 percent commission on all the bonds I wrote in Reno whenever I was there, but I would also receive a 20 percent commission on every bond written by any of the agents working through the new offices, regardless of whether I was there, as well as my normal 50 percent on the bonds I wrote while I was in Vegas. The only drawback to receiving all this additional compensation was all the new responsibilities I had, and the amount of travel involved.

My new position meant frequent trips to Las Vegas, which left little time for a personal life. I always flew rather than drove so I could spend as much time writing or reviewing bonds as possible. In addition, I was on call 24/7 to either write or approve bonds no matter where I was, Reno or Vegas.

In retrospect, I can see three good reasons for Mickey's decision to expand his business, make me a partner, and send me to Vegas. Two of those decisions were strictly business. Reason #1: It gave him an opportunity to hire two of his burglar friends, who were tapped out mentally, physically, and financially after twenty years of literally living in the shadows while burglarizing expensive homes and financial businesses.

All Duke and Corey really wanted to do was retire into a "legit business," as they put it. I guess you could say the bail business was as close to "legit" as they could get, based on their previous career choices and their criminal records. If things didn't work out with them, Mickey believed our worst-case scenario would still mean bucks-up for us, because we had a chance to establish a strong working relationship with many of the criminals Duke and Corey had met and dealt with over the past two decades. In addition, many of them had relocated to Vegas or were interested in doing so soon.

Duke and Corey were not the brightest bulbs in the box, but their lack of business savvy didn't matter to Mickey, because he had me to watch over them. Mickey made sure they were able to pass the insurance exam the way I had, thanks to his friend in the DOI. Only this time, based on their past, I'm sure Mickey had to pull a few more strings, which amounted to paying out more money. From reading Mickey's file on each of them, I gathered that their history was more than a little tainted by several criminal arrests and minor convictions. There were also a few notes referring to some bribes and pay-offs Mickey made on their behalf along the way, which I guess didn't count.

All this taken together, including Mickey's financial influence over the DOI, meant he was only able to get each of them a restricted license. This meant they were obligated to work for a properly licensed bail bond agency and be supervised by the owner and/or a fully licensed bail agent employed as the managing agent by the owner.

Giving them a restricted license was enough for Mickey. He could still use them to post bail and he had me supervising them. As he put it, he had his scapegoat in place if anything went wrong. I had a significant number of reservations. If they fucked up, I could kiss my license goodbye while Mickey would skirt with a slap on the wrist. I could see him blaming everything on the lack of supervision provided by me, his sacrificial lamb, then paying a large bribe to keep his own license.

Yet I had a lot to gain and little to lose. My rationale went something like this: This whole business is so high risk, why should this be any different? What the hell. In for a dime, in for a dollar. Count me in, boss!

It turned out Mickey was right on target with Reason #1. With all their friends and contacts from years of dealing on the shady side, these guys were naturals. As I learned from dealing with them daily, not only did they write bonds on their past associates, on their time off they joined them in a few high-end home burglaries in Arizona, California, and elsewhere—but never in Nevada, under any circumstances. I guessed that, having done it for twenty-plus years, they couldn't pass up the excitement.

Duke had been a numbers runner back in Chicago, one of the guys who covered bets at the races for Anthony—"Tony the Ant"—Spilotro. That was before Duke became a burglar. When Antonio moved to Las Vegas, Duke pedaled all his stolen jewelry through Carmella's Pawn Shop or his almost-legit jeweler friends. They would would remove the valuable stones, restyle new settings, and melt down the old ones, making them impossible to trace.

Corey was also involved with sports books in Chicago, and knew the mobster Frankie Rosenthal from their early days in Chicago, and later from the Stardust Hotel Casino in Vegas. While Rosenthal became the mob's number-one gangster in Vegas, Spilotro became their number-one ballbuster. Rosenthal was credited with bringing sports book betting to Vegas while skimming millions from the casinos for the mob and himself.

Spilotro was running several Teamster casinos on the Strip from behind the scenes.

Mickey was also right on with *Reason #2*. Moving into Las Vegas was a no brainer, because he now had someone he could trust to watch his back; someone young, ambitious, trustworthy, and savvy when it came to his bail operations. He had someone who could underwrite bonds and secure collateral (regardless of where it came from) while never pocketing or misappropriating any of it. And he had someone who would never take, use, or even touch illegal drugs of any sort. He had me.

Reason #3 was the sticky one; it was personal. His wife, Elaine, had a daughter from a previous marriage. Crystal was in her early twenties, divorced, with no kids. She lived alone in an apartment near Mickey's Reno bail office. Although I had overheard a lot of conversations about her during the first couple of years I worked in the office, neither Mickey nor Elaine ever mentioned her directly—because I'm sure Mickey didn't want anyone in or around his office getting involved with her. By this point in our working relationship, Mickey especially meant me.

In Mickey's mind, business and personal lives were two different animals, and he didn't want anything fucking up his business or his marriage—especially a romantic falling-out between his stepdaughter and his prize employee. He knew that if (or when) we ended a relationship, regardless of how amicably it transpired, it would undoubtedly spill over into every facet of his life.

One day, Elaine, knowing full well that I'd be at the office, decided to play Cupid. She suggested that Crystal stop by and say hi. That afternoon was the first time I laid eyes on her, because rumor had it she'd been involved with a boyfriend the entire time I'd been working for Mickey.

Crystal was attractive, with long straight brown hair, a few freckles, and a nice body—as far as I could tell. She was also bright and personable. After a short and friendly introduction, Crystal left the office and, I suspected, went directly home. Within the hour, she called to ask if I'd like to come over for dinner "sometime." I said, "I'd love to, but it might be best if I discuss your offer with Mickey first, since I'm not sure if he would be amenable to mixing business with . . . pleasu . . . umm . . . personal dating." She laughed at my stuttering over a simple word like "pleasure," suggested I call her when I grew a set of balls, and hung up.

She called her mother and relayed our conversation. Elaine came into the office and asked to talk in private. She suggested that I accept her daughter's invitation and leave Mickey to her. She said Crystal and I should see how well we got along and if we'd want to have a relationship. If we did, we could all approach Mickey. If not, nothing would be lost. I said it sounded reasonable and I'd call Crystal as soon as I could. The trap was set, and I didn't see it coming!

Without informing Mickey, Crystal and I set a date for dinner at her place for the following week. As always, I brought fresh flowers and a bottle of quality champagne. After small talk over drinks, we had a wonderful dinner, then moved into the living room for champagne, quiet music, and some pleasant conversation.

After about an hour, the answering service called, and I had to leave. Crystal escorted me to the front door, kissed me on the cheek, and said, "I hope we can do this again soon," while politely nudging me out as she closed the door.

A few days later, Mickey and I met to discuss my progress with opening the new Las Vegas office. Not one word was mentioned about my dinner with Crystal, so I was comfortable with our little secret. Mickey and I talked about my departure date and a schedule for traveling and working between the two cities. We also discussed my accommodations while away from Reno.

It appeared I was going to spend more than half my time in Vegas, at least at first. Mickey suggested I look for a furnished apartment to rent month-to-month. He said it should be somewhere near downtown, and located between the city and county jail sites, while still being close to the courthouse. Staying in hotels, especially on the Strip, would be "too expensive," at least for him, since expenses would be coming out of his pocket, not mine.

As soon as I arrived in Las Vegas, I found exactly what Mickey had recommended: a new one-bedroom furnished apartment, payable on a month-to-month basis, and less than three blocks from the downtown casinos, as well as the Las Vegas City Jail and the new courthouse. I began to feel that this project was going to be easier than I'd originally thought.

After unpacking and settling in, I checked in with our new answering service, the one I picked using Mickey's formula. First, I made sure it was able to help us offer the best and fastest bail service in town, and it didn't represent any competitors. I also wanted one that would page our agent, provide him with factual information on the caller, and track his response time from the time she called until he responded. I needed to ensure that the agent didn't finish watching his favorite TV show or rolled over and went back to sleep after the call.

At our first agent meeting, Corey, Duke, and I went over the work schedules and created a plan to begin introducing ourselves to the local jail commanders, court clerks, and some of the local Vegas gang of thieves we'd been servicing long distance from Reno over the past few years.

After we finished scheduling shifts, shaking hands, and learning the proper procedures for posting bonds day and night in the different jails and courts, I added a little twist of my own. I told the agents I wanted them to call the answering service as soon as they arrived at a jail. That way, the service would not only know where they were and how long it took them to respond, she could give a future caller an idea of how soon they'd be available to meet or call them back.

We parted company for the day, giving me an opportunity to work on a backup plan I'd been quietly working on since the day Mickey put me in charge.

Since the only agents I had working for us were down-and-out ex-burglars, I didn't feel comfortable relying on them for what could become a large part of my livelihood. Even though Mickey was satisfied with these guys, I couldn't get my mind around the thought of leaving them alone. I began looking for licensed insurance agents who were hungry enough to quit their jobs selling insurance and start a new career writing bail bonds. I wanted a few straight guys working in the office while I waited to see if our over-the-hill burglars were reliable enough to service our calls twenty-four hours a day, seven day a week.

I placed an ad in the Help Wanted section of the local newspapers: "Wanted: Nevada insurance agents looking for a new and exciting career." Soon, I'd found three hungry insurance agents who were sick of cold calling prospective clients and ready to let some excitement into their boring lives.

These new prospects were already licensed through the Department of Insurance and wouldn't need to take additional exams. This meant I had no worries about asking Mickey to bribe anyone at the DOI. In addition, they were experienced with completing applications and documenting paperwork.

It didn't take long to train them on that portion of our business either.

On the flip side, although my two former thieves left a lot to be desired when it came to office procedures and paperwork, they were good at dealing with career criminals. While the insurance pros wanted to take three times as much collateral to secure their bonds, my two old-time thieves had enough street smarts to talk the talk and walk the walk when it came to pushing the rules of thumb for taking collateral on one of their own.

Within a few weeks, this odd group of misfits was not only willing to learn from each other, but also assist each other as needed. This meant quicker response times, better quality bonds, and more business for both offices. This also meant more money in everyone's pocket, including mine and Mickey's.

At the beginning, I limited their ability to post bonds at $1,000 per client, without their need to check with me before releasing anyone from jail. But they began working together so well, I increased this amount to $5,000. This gave me a little more freedom to check out our competitors, the court clerk's offices, and even the casinos, which made me feel a little like a tourist.

CHAPTER

#10

Nevada legislators legalized many things other states found to be disgusting, repulsive, or repugnant. Things like gambling, prostitution, and quickie divorces went hand-in-hand with corruption, and anyone with half a brain knew it. Money ruled the day, and payoffs tipped the scales of justice in favor of those willing to deal in the shadows.

All these legalized vices provided lawyers and bail bond agents with many opportunities to pad the pockets of city and county employees, judges, court clerks and local jailers with easy cash. These bribes, or "monetary tokens of appreciation" as we called them, were made behind closed doors. Individuals were paid either to participate—or to look the other way. Criminal cases, especially those on tourists, were being reduced to misdemeanors, erroneously dismissed without due process, or entire files were mysteriously lost. That's how the catchphrase "What happens in Vegas, stays in Vegas" originated.

After a few months of doing business in and around the greater Las Vegas area, I began to realize what was going on, and just how corrupt the criminal justice system really was. Although we were writing many bonds, my agents noticed that many of the bonds we were passing up, mostly those on out-of-state defendants, were being bailed by agents from one or more of the old established bail agencies: the guys that had been doing business in Vegas long before we arrived.

Although the execution of these bonds and the release of these defendants might have seemed coincidental to anyone else, I knew full well there was no such thing as coincidence when it comes to writing bail bonds. I decided to track some of these cases to their conclusion, noting things like the agencies and agents that posted the bonds, the deputies on duty at the time of release, the court to which the cases were assigned, the clerk processing all the paperwork on these cases, and the attorneys of record for the defendants.

I soon learned the names of the individuals who provided services to the old-time bail agents in exchange for bribes. The question was, how should I approach someone in order to get in on the action?

Somehow, walking up to a jailer, a court clerk, a judge or an attorney and asking if they'd be interested in accepting a bribe for letting me in on the scam they had going seemed like the wrong approach. Nor did the thought of asking the owner of a competitive bail agency, even a friendly one, if he would be interested in introducing me to all the participants in the bribery scam he had going between the courts and his out-of-state clients. Even the thought of discussing these options bordered on insanity.

In Reno, with the exception of a few winos I'd befriended along the way, I never found it necessary to pay anyone for referrals or favors. I felt it was Mickey's job to make sure his phones rang off the hook with business. And when it came time to pay off a loss to the court because I was unable to locate a skip, Mickey always turned them over to his attorney or handled them himself. Now, having to witness and deal with bribery on a much larger scale than I was used to, I decided to discuss the issue with my partner and mentor.

I explained the situation to Mickey, including my research project. He said, "Look, kid. First, talking to competitors is the kiss of death, if not for our business, then you for sure, because I'll fire your ass in a heartbeat if you're that stupid. Second, we want in on the action. If they're running this scam on all the out-of-town clients, there's big money in this, and we need to get our share.

"I don't want to discuss this over the phone. I want you to fly back to Reno tonight. I've nicknamed this new program 'The Collateral Scam.' I'll show you how it works when I see you. In the meantime, make an appointment with the attorney you noted most in your investigation. Tell him who you are, who you represent, and that we're looking to hire him to represent us on all our future court-related business in Vegas. Don't tell him anything else: no names, no numbers, no details, until you and I have a chance to talk face-to-face. Got it?"

"Don't worry. See you this afternoon."

I called Mickey as soon as my plane landed. It was almost 1:00 p.m. and I was starving, so I asked if we could meet someplace for lunch. He said he'd rather discuss our business in the office; he'd have food delivered. Considering the topic of our anticipated conversation, this was a wise choice.

By the time my cab arrived, Mickey and the food were waiting. After our hellos and a little small talk with Elaine, Mickey and I excused ourselves and went to the kitchen for lunch. Mickey said, "Kid, you eat, and I'll talk. Don't interrupt me with comments or questions until I'm finished. But write them all down so we're sure you grasp the concept before you head back."

Mickey detailed the collateral scam. He said it would work like this: "You get a call from a client who's been arrested for aggravated assault on a customer or security guard. Let's say it took place in a casino, or in their parking lot. You receive the call, do a short phone interview with him. You find out he's from out of town, and more importantly, he knows no one in Vegas. You learn he's here for, let's say, the Beer Convention. He owns his home back in Milwaukee, Wisconsin. He's the V.P. of sales for his company, has plenty of money in the bank, and is concerned that his arrest may cost him his job.

"You tell him you'll have your assistant make a few calls to our friends in Milwaukee to verify the bullshit he's feeding us. You know, some bounty hunters, or a few retired cops we've used in the past; discreetly of course, because we wouldn't want his company, his boss, or his family, especially his wife, to hear anything. Now he can relax, because we know everything he told us was the truth. Then you tell him you're on your way to the jail and will post his bail shortly. Upon his release you bring him back to the office, complete the interview, and make arrangements for him to have the $500 premium wired via Western Union.

"Then you discuss the charges against him and tell him he's looking at a year in the county jail if he's convicted. And since he is from out of state, he shouldn't expect any sympathy from the local judges. You say that without the right help, he will be found guilty.

"Now comes the good part. You tell him he can return home and go about his normal life as though nothing ever happened. After all, what happens in Vegas stays in Vegas!"

Mickey chuckled and added, "Depending on how much help he can afford."

He went on: "We tell him that first, he must wire the entire amount, $5,000, to us as collateral on the bond. That way we'll be able to use some of the money to hire the attorney—not just any attorney, but the one we trust and have confidence in. Someone we know can get the charges reduced to a misdemeanor, or dropped completely, which will prevent anything from going on his record . . . if he pays the fine, if any. And we will allow the fine to be paid from the collateral as well, because this way, our bond will be exonerated, and his case will be closed for sure.

"If he says he thinks he can go it alone, without our help, we tell him he still has to have the full amount wired to us as collateral on his bond before we can let him return home. Either way, we get the money, and he gets to go home. Ninety percent of these guys are so concerned about losing their jobs, or about their wives finding out, they beg us to handle everything. 'Just make it all go away, please!' is what you can expect to hear every time.

"If he refuses to let us handle his case, we tell him that if he thinks he can just go home and forget about it because he's thousands of miles away, we will use every penny of his $5,000 in collateral to hire bounty hunters who will pick up his stupid ass and return him to Vegas for trial. And the ride in the trunk of their car will make for a memory he'll never forget.

"After we get the original five grand and are assured that our attorney will be able to work his monetary miracles by greasing the palms of either the judge or the court clerk to have his case disappear, we set him up for some extra cash. We let him know that the $5,000 may not be enough to cover everything, depending on whether there was any property damage or personal injury involved, which may require some additional financial soothing; we'll know more after the attorney has a chance to review all the arrest reports and meets with the prosecuting attorney. The squeeze is now set."

Mickey said the extra money we'd get from squeezing the guy would always be enough to cover all the attorney's fees, including all the monetary tokens of appreciation and the payment of our client's fine, in the event he was unable to get the charges dropped completely. That would leave us with the original $5,000 collateral deposit to split between us.

He continued, "We let the client know that to ensure that this information stays in Vegas, we can only provide verbal receipts for all the expenses, but we can provide a copy of the 'case closed' documents, which reflect the actual amount of the fine paid to the court, if he really wants them. But if he wants them, we would no longer be able to guarantee that copies of his case file would not fall into the wrong hands back home. That eliminates having to provide receipts."

Mickey emphasized that this scam could only be used with out-of-state clients. Residents of Vegas could take care of themselves, unless they were new to the area. If we did this right, he said, and I kept him in the loop, we could each make a good $10,000 a month.

Because I knew exactly what we were doing and had no questions, I said I wanted to use the time before my flight to visit Mom. As I was leaving the office, I stopped and quietly asked Elaine if she knew whether Crystal was at home. She said, "Yes, I just talked to her."

My question about Crystal made Elaine happy, because it showed her we were still interested in seeing each other, and it showed me that Mickey had no idea what Elaine, Crystal, and I were up to behind his back.

The first thing I did when I got back to Vegas was meet with the attorney, a guy named Mike Rosano. I felt he would be our best bet for establishing our new program. Mike was open and amenable to working with us, especially after having us sign a contract to hire him. From that point on, everything we discussed was covered by attorney-client privilege. The things he did, and that we did to make these cases go away, were borderline legal . . . well, maybe somewhat over the line—depending on who was drawing the line.

Mike said, "Look, Lefty, the defendants or bail-clients you're referring to always want to get back home and forget this bad dream ever happened. So it's important that you have them sign an agreement allowing your agency to do whatever you can to assist in making their case *just go away*. That includes, but isn't limited to, using their cash collateral to hire our law firm, pay a fine, or to pay bounty hunters to arrest and return them to Vegas if they fail to cooperate."

The attorney fees for his service would be based on how much he had to do and who he'd have to bribe to close the case. Paying a clerk to lose the file cost less than paying a judge to dismiss a case or, as Mike put it, working with the court clerk, or with the judge, to settle the case would determine the total amount of his fees. But he assured me that the fees would never amount to more than half of the face amount of their bail bond; usually it would be less.

Within days, we initiated our first case. Although it went smoothly, I remember it being a little nerve racking. The attorney did his job, and his bill came to $2,000. Because we didn't want to squeeze our first mark, Mickey and I split the remaining $3,000. But we knew it worked, and it would get better from there.

I still remember the first time we got a real sucker on the hook, and I put the squeeze on him for an extra two grand. It went something like this: "Hey Charlie, it's me, your favorite bail bondsman from Vegas. Listen, we need a little more cash to bury your case. It appears the judge is playing hardball with the attorney and is looking for more cash."

Charlie replied, "No way, you got the full five thousand bucks, and I'm not giving you, or any crooked judge, another nickel."

My response was clear. "Look, asshole, I could give a shit whether you pay up the extra two grand to close your case. Either you send the money, or I'll send my bounty hunters after your stupid ass. Better yet, I'll come there myself and give you a free ride to Vegas in the trunk of my car. That way, you can be a badass and call the judge a crook to his face. When I tell the judge how you feel about him, it will go a long way toward influencing the length of your prison sentence.

"Whichever way you decide to go, you'll still be out your five grand. The difference is, you'll be in jail and unemployed rather than at home. So wire the additional money by the close of business today, or start looking over your shoulder tomorrow, because sooner or later, you'll be seeing my smiling face, or some of my bounty hunters, real soon.

The two grand showed up within two hours of my call, and Mickey and I split the five-grand collateral. This was the first of many.

Finally, between all the things I had going, especially the collateral scam, I started making ten grand a week.

CHAPTER

#11

I continued traveling between Reno and Las Vegas for a little over two years, making money hand over fist. I was raking in my share of the profits from the new Las Vegas offices, as well as my share of the commissions from Reno and Vegas. I was also receiving my share of the cash from the Vegas collateral scam in addition to my share of all the excess collateral from all the Reno bonds I wrote.

Since I was working 24/7 every week, either in Vegas or Reno, I had little or no time to spend it, or anyone to spend it on. I was able to stash more than a $150,000 in my savings in less than two years, not counting the 20 percent reserve deposits Mickey was holding as security against any actual losses in the event I screwed up.

Between surrendering most of our skips and paying off the judges and clerks on the ones we didn't catch, we seldom, if ever, paid an actual loss. And when we did, we usually had enough collateral to cover the loss without reaching into our own pockets. This business was a money machine made in heaven. But since we were no angels, we had to work a lot harder from within the shadows to make our money.

Being as smart and as careful as I was about all aspects of the bail business (both legal and illegal), I was surprised at how stupid I was when it came to personal relationships.

I spent a lot of the time in Vegas the first few months after I met Christal. This helped me make sure we took things nice and slow. That way, If we broke off our relationship before having sex, I foolishly thought I'd be able to convince Elaine that her daughter and I were just friends, and I wasn't an asshole just trying to get into her panties.

Or, if either of them was to tell Mickey, I could explain how I never touched her, and we were only going out occasionally as friends, to see if we enjoyed dating. What a dreamer I was on all counts.

Going slow may have worked for me, but Crystal had other ideas. Every time we got together, she began kissing me while trying to rip off my clothes. She'd unzip my pants and fondle me with one hand while using her other hand to unbutton her blouse and put my hands all over her breasts.

This heavy petting went on until the day she called me in Vegas and asked me to stop by her place when I returned to Reno. She met me at the door stark naked. She began by kissing me while placing one of my hands between her legs, and the other on her butt. Then she began to unbuckle my pants and massage me. So much for my attempts at going slow. They ended right there.

The next thing I knew, we were in her bedroom, on her bed, sharing some of the hottest foreplay I'd ever enjoyed. But when I attempted to penetrate her, she froze up like an ice cube and stopped cold! She took a deep breath and asked me to start over. Then, it happened again.

Although we were great at foreplay and spent hours working at it, we couldn't get her past freezing up whenever we tried intercourse. And although entry or even the attempt was always very emotional for her, it wasn't easy or fun for either of us. But she wanted to keep trying.

After a few more trips from Vegas, I felt as though Crystal had never cared about having a long-lasting relationship. All she wanted was my help getting over her physical and emotional problems with sex. I guess she felt I was more experienced than some of the guys she'd dated, and therefore I could be the catalyst she needed to get over being frigid.

At some point during our months-long ordeal, I told her we should stop seeing each other on an intimate basis while we were still friends and, hopefully, before Mickey found out, which would make a real mess out of all our lives. Somewhat reluctantly, she agreed. At least, that's what she said. We tried hanging out as friends, with no physical contact other than a simple kiss good night.

One day, Crystal decided to tell Elaine that we'd broken up, up, but she failed to tell her mom that it was mutual. In fact, she blamed it all on me. I would have appreciated some honesty, something like, "We both decided it was best to just stay friends." But no, she left me hanging out there like a molester.

I'm sure she felt it was okay to blame me, and ruin my relationship with her mother and Mickey, never mind mentioning that she was using me to get over what I thought might be her hopelessly inept sex life. Then I began to wonder if she might have been assaulted by her ex-husband. Had she told her mother, Mickey might have gone to jail for cutting the guy's nuts off. So I sucked it up and shouldered the blame.

Although Elaine never said anything to my face, I was certain she thought the worst of me for dumping her daughter.

That's when she decided to let Mickey know that he couldn't count on me to watch his back anymore, and that she wanted Mickey's and my relationship to change. Not end, mind you, just change. I'm sure she felt ending it could be financially devastating for everyone involved, as Mickey was now spending most of his time working on his new bail bond general agency, as well as his latest interest in possibly purchasing his own insurance company.

It wasn't long after, while I was in Las Vegas making my regularly scheduled rounds between offices, that I received a message from Mickey: "Get your ass back home. Now!"

CHAPTER

#12

I met Mickey in time for lunch at a little Italian bar and restaurant called the Halfway Club. At the time, there was a three-mile stretch of open land and sparse housing between Reno and Sparks. The owners were a great, hardworking Italian couple. Steamboat ran the bar while his wife, Ines, worked the kitchen. I never knew their last names, but they made the best pizza ever. Anyway, Mickey and I talked for at least three hours about everything except Elaine and Crystal. But after we caught up on all the business-related stuff, we got down to the real reason for our meeting.

"Kid," he said, "you went behind my back, and against my wishes in getting involved with my stepdaughter. You know I've grown to trust you with anything and everything in my life, and still believe I can. However, because this one infraction involves my family, and not just me, I have to make some hard decisions about how we deal with our future together."

He repeated over and over how much he wanted to leave things as they were, how we made a good team, and how he was grooming me to take over his entire operation, including his newly formed bail bond general agency. He wanted to retire with Elaine and travel the USA, and then Mexico, where they hoped to build their new retirement home. And how he still hoped that somehow there might still be a chance to work things out for us.

But in the meantime, he said, we had to give Elaine time to get over her disappointment about the breakup, because she'd truly wanted me as their son-in-law.

"Kid, I don't believe you were stupid enough to break off your relationship with Crystal without letting her do it first, even though you were stupid enough to get involved in the first place. I know you're a stand-up guy and would never do anything to hurt Elaine or me. I believe time will eventually heal this problem, so I've come up with a solution."

He said he'd been thinking long and hard about what to do to appease Elaine and continue working with me, or at least keep us in close touch. He offered to sponsor a bail bond office of my own. He said I could take my choice, either open it in Reno or Vegas, and he would provide me with all the bonds and financial backing I would need to ensure my success. Of course, if we were to do this, I would be obligated to write all my business through his newly formed managing general agency.

He had already started putting his friends into business throughout Northern California and Nevada. Even though I'd be in direct competition with one of his offices in whichever city I chose, he knew my office would fast become the leading example for his new stable of agents.

I could see it in his eyes and feel it in his voice; he wasn't ready to let me go. We were as close as any real father and son could ever be. Over the past few years, I'd helped build his business and expand it into new areas like Las Vegas. He knew I could build mine just as fast and just as large as we had built his. Plus, becoming a cornerstone in his new general agency business would not only keep me around to discuss and monitor any new issues that might arise in his business, but he could gain financially from every move I made.

The shrewd old bastard figured out a way he could make money from my screwup, save his family, and keep me around to watch for any new problems. He also knew the business was in my blood, and I was going to stay in the business regardless of his decision. He knew I was clever enough and smart enough to keep working, if not for him, then someone else. After all, I'd learned from the best.

And so, with his blessing and his financial support, I slowly began withdrawing from his retail bail operation and began looking for a new location to branch out on my own, as my own boss, in a business I knew was perfect for me.

I made it a point to stay away from Mickey's office in Reno whenever I knew Elaine was there. She loved me, but she loved her daughter more. I knew she was mad at me, but I felt she may have been a little mad at herself as well. Regardless, the question now was how long would it take for our relationship to heal, if ever? Unfortunately, only time would tell.

CHAPTER

#13

I picked Reno over Las Vegas for good reasons. First, Reno had been my home for almost twenty-five years. Second, Mom, bless her heart, had always been there to support me, and I felt I owed it to her to stick around.

The most convincing reason, however, was the fact that Las Vegas was too openly corrupt. Not just the casinos, the wild nightlife, and the mob influence; it was also the bail business, the jailers, court clerks and judges. Everyone involved was becoming too loose and too lax, especially when it came to bribes, payoffs, pocketing collateral, and literally burying problems in the desert.

And everything we were doing could eventually become big issues for all of us in the future; issues I could do without, especially if I was going to invest long hours and tens of thousands of dollars in a new business.

So Reno, the biggest little city in the world, it was. Mickey drew up our contract listing me as an independent bail agent/owner with him as my exclusive general agent.

A general agent in the bail bond business is an individual that personally reinsures all the bail bonds written by smaller local agents within a limited, but exclusive territory, one provided to the general agent by the surety insurance company he represents. The general agent's reinsurance is provided to protect the insurance company—not the bail agent. In other words, when a bail agent fails to return his client to court and is unable to pay the court the full amount of his client's bail, his general agent must pay every penny. In exchange for the general agent's reinsurance, the bail agent pays him a percentage of every premium charged on every bond written.

Although the agent's financial responsibility has been met by his general agent, the bail agent must reimburse his G.A. through the liquidation of any collateral he is holding or out of his own pocket. Failure to arrange a satisfactory reimbursement to the general agent can result in the bail agent's immediate suspension from writing future bonds.

"Timing and lighting are everything" and "Location, location, location," have become forever maxims for every business. Believe it or not, it's no different in the bail business. Getting into the business at the right time, and in the right location, could mean the difference between great success and dismal failure.

I knew the timing was right, especially in Reno, because the city was growing at an unbelievable pace while competition in the bail bond business was still limited to the same old, complacent companies, all of which were operating under old, traditional ideas.

In fact, they'd become so content about their business, none felt the need to advertise or promote their businesses. They just listed their trade names in the local telephone directory and had the jailers place their flyers on information boards posted near the pay phones in all the local jails. One of them, Mimi Collins, operated her business from home after her husband died. She and her husband were the first ones in Reno with a bail bond business. This was long before Mickey came along. Another was my mentor, Mickey himself, with his office right across from the jail. Since he had the best location at the time, he didn't feel the need to waste money on advertising. In his eyes, having the prime location was enough, especially when an older woman without an office was his primary competition. Plus, his business interests now lay elsewhere. In attempting to build his new general agency, he had lost interest in expanding his retail bail office.

I'd been working off and on between Reno and Vegas for more than three years, watching how things were being done, so I knew exactly what I could expect from all my soon-to-be competitors. I also noted that another answering service was opening, and their advanced systems included providing personal pagers to all their clients. This meant I could develop new contacts and promote my new business without having to call in every few minutes to get messages or to stay in an office for hours on end waiting for the phone to ring. This new paging system allowed the operators to take messages when necessary, page me with bail calls when necessary, and patch me through to the caller so I could talk directly to potential clients or their potential cosigner.

I was sure neither of my two old-time competitors would change answering services just to get some new-fangled piece of equipment like a pager, especially if I was already doing business with them. And, because I was their first customer, the new answering service would give me priority care.

My first major decision involved how I would conduct business. Should I operate my new business from the small apartment I'd been renting for the past few years, which was down the street but still visible from the police station? Or did

I operate from a separate new office location? This is where timing came into play. It happened that the older couple, David and Martha Russo, from whom I rented my apartment, also owned the small dry-cleaning shop directly across the street from the front entrance of the Reno Justice complex that housed the police department, the city jail, the municipal courts, and the municipal court clerk's office.

They also owned the property adjacent to their cleaners, which included an old gas station building that had been closed for longer than I could remember.

Over the years, David, Martha, and I got to know each other well, and became good friends. As part of that friendship, Martha would often stop by my apartment or Mickey's office with a dessert she'd baked, and I'd occasionally help them with small chores around the properties they owned throughout the neighborhood. Little did I know, these gestures of friendship would change all our lives in a positive way.

It didn't take long to make my decision. I wanted to put my new business in an office, not my apartment. I knew exactly where I wanted that office to be. I walked over to the cleaners and told David I was interested in renting the old gas station. He was almost as excited about the idea as I was, mainly because the city had recently contacted him about cleaning up what they described as the "eyesore on the corner."

He said I could have the place for $1 per month, if I agreed to clean up the lot at my own expense, and paint and repair the building as needed to appease the city. This also meant the building had to meet all the necessary building codes, licensing conditions, and health standards to obtain the business occupancy certificate I'd need to open my business. I agreed, and after about six weeks of hard work, I not only got the certificate of occupancy, I also registered my two new trade names: Lefty's Bail Bonds and Freedom Bail Bonds, and I was chomping at the bit to open them.

I decided to open both businesses in Reno as a means of discouraging any other newcomers from even thinking about it. In addition, listing the two names in the jails and the directories gave me twice the opportunity to reach potential customers or family members who were looking for a bail bond agency.

I fixed up the old gas station building, cleaned up the entire lot, and replaced the old gas pump locations with flower boxes. The single greatest idea came when I sealed up the two huge garage doors in front of the mechanic's area and hired a sign company to paint billboard-style signs across the front to advertise my two new agencies. No one entering or leaving the police station, the municipal court, or just driving by on either Second Street or High Street could miss them.

This cost me a few bucks, much more than I intended to spend. So I decided to hit Mickey for a withdrawal from the trust account he was holding in my name as collateral for my contract. I'd never needed to use it since I started writing bonds, and the balance had grown in excess of $250,000.

With an advance from my reserves, and his blessing, I also purchased a 1930 Buick four-door sedan, the kind with running boards on both sides of the car. This was the kind of car that instantly reminded people of the Elliott Ness gangster series on television at the time. I had the entire car painted black, put real 14-karat gold lettering on the sides, and had the interior reupholstered in original mohair.

Part of my idea in purchasing the car was to enter it into all the parades throughout the year, hiring a half-dozen guys dressed in black-and-white striped prison suits to walk in front of the car, which was featured just behind the sheriff's mounted posse. These "jailbirds" were paid to walk between the car and the sheriff's posse, scooping up horse shit from in front of the car whenever necessary. In addition, I'd drive my little gangster car around town, especially when I needed to visit the different jails or the clerk's office to post a bond.

While I was working on the old gas station's restoration and conversion project, David and I became even closer. I found out that he and Martha were in their mid-70s and had no children or extended family. They had worked all their lives and had been able to purchase a significant number of properties throughout the immediate neighborhood. This included the two-story building that housed my apartment, as well as a second apartment on the upper floor, and a third apartment in a small separate building directly behind it.

They also owned two other identical properties adjacent to it, as well as the Jet Motel. The motel had fifteen kitchenette units and was located in the middle of the block, directly across the street from their third two-story apartment building. They had a motel manager for the Jet, but he was about as old as they were, and in no shape to do maintenance. He attempted to rent as many of the motel kitchenette units as he could, but many of them went empty due to their need for attention.

Counting the three two-story apartments, the three small houses directly behind them, and the motel, they had a total of twenty-four units they were attempting to rent, and not having much success. Each month, the properties lost potential revenue.

During the many, many conversations we had while I prepared my new office location, David told me that Martha was ill and unable to keep up with the work at the cleaners, so they were going close it. In addition, they wanted to sell all the apartments and the motel, but not the corner property housing the cleaners and the gas station. If I was interested, they'd make the terms very affordable, because the property they owned was mortgage-free.

I told Mickey about my opportunity to buy some rental properties, which I could manage while operating the bail bond businesses. But since I was improving my new office location, buying and rebuilding the gangster car, and preparing an ad campaign to promote my agencies, even with the money Mickey had advanced me, I'd need at least another $100,000 from my savings to make the down payments. If he'd allow me to use a hundred grand from my security deposits, I would provide him with second mortgages on all the real properties I purchased until I replenished my reserve through the future 20 percent deposits I'd continue to make from the future bail bonds I would be writing.

After getting Mickey to agree with my second withdrawal request, I told David that I'd raised only $50,000 to acquire all twenty-four units, but I'd give him an additional percentage of the rental profits, over and above the agreed upon monthly mortgage payment, until the additional $50,000 for the down payment was met.

Even though David and Martha owned all the properties free and clear of all liens, and could borrow money to meet their needs, my program appealed to them more. They wouldn't have to make payments to a bank, and would receive a significant monthly income from me, between the mortgage payments, the bail office rental, and the extra percentage of the profits I was offering them. Plus, they would no longer have to worry about managing these buildings.

I'd be building equity in all the properties, securing a significant cash flow to help meet all the expenses involved, and have a fantastic location for my new bail businesses—all of which would happen almost instantly.

David and Martha agreed. In fact, they felt so secure in my ability to provide them with a steady income flow that they elected to close the cleaners and begin spending some of their well-deserved time off enjoying life. They were pleased to provide a young, ambitious, trustworthy person like me with such a great opportunity, especially since they had no one else in their lives.

In a matter of months, and at the age of twenty-seven, I became the managing owner of twenty-three rental units within walking distance of the downtown casinos and the strip clubs; two new bail bond businesses with the best office location in town; and had my own apartment as the twenty-fourth unit, which was now rent-free. I was able to meld my new rental business and my two bail bond businesses into one large profit center, and still have time to enjoy working, thanks to my new answering service and its new pager system.

CHAPTER

#14

After closing the deal with David and Martha and giving Mickey a second deed on all the properties, one that didn't require a monthly payment or reimbursement, I began spending the last $50,000 of the advance from my trust account on remodeling as many units as I could. One by one, I began working on each of them in between answering bail bond calls, doing much of the work myself in order to keep the costs down.

The jailers always laughed when I came strolling into the jail to interview a client wearing my carpenter-style coveralls. They would make comments like, "Gee, if the bail business is that bad, maybe you should apply for a jailer's job." Or, "Are you here to fix our overflowing shitters? You'll need a plunger, not a briefcase." My response was always the same: "Remember, those who laugh last, laugh best."

I was determined not to use all my personal savings to complete the projects. Instead, my plan was to do what I could with the money from Mickey and any surplus cash flow from the newly finished units and the bail business. I needed to hold my savings in reserve to ensure that I met all my personal and business obligations while continuing to help Mom. I also needed to keep some cash on hand to pay my bail losses, should I ever have any.

As I completed the cleaning, painting, and refurnishing of each unit, I began looking for tenants to fill them. But instead of using traditional advertising methods, I looked for people in need of an immediate place to live; people willing to pay higher-than-normal rent, and who didn't mind foregoing long-term rental or lease agreements. And I wouldn't require references. That way, if I needed to kick someone out, I could do it on the spot, rather than spending time and money evicting them—especially if they caused any trouble. In addition, if they owed me money, I was sure I could find them and collect it, one way or another.

At the same time, I looked for new bail clients in places like the strip clubs, brothels, biker hangouts, babe bars, and men's clubs. My thought was that most of the people working in these places were single, unattached girls—with a few pimps and boyfriends in the mix.

I also put out the word to all the divorce lawyers, because their clients were mostly potential divorcees from out-of-state who needed a clean, comfortable, safe place to hide out on a short-term basis. Many of these out-of-state women needed to establish residence for a minimum of six weeks to qualify for one of Nevada's quickie divorces. I could provide them with this in the form of weekly rent receipts. I gave these receipts to their attorneys, regardless of whether they stayed in the units or not. If they chose not to stay in a unit, I'd give them the receipts and rent that unit to someone else. This provided me with double—or even triple—expense-free rental income.

Most of these potential clients usually had access to more money than the average working woman. In addition, most, except for those staying only six weeks for a divorce, had zero credit and didn't hold jobs that would make most landlords happy or secure. None of these issues bothered me; after all, some smart old guy once told me: "If you're afraid to take a risk, you should become a plumber."

I began renting my units to topless dancers, ladies of the night, bartenders (females preferably), potential divorcees, and any other hustler I could find. I charged them double the rent previously collected by David and Martha. I always required payment in cash, in advance. They could pay weekly or monthly. Rent included utilities, mandatory weekly cleaning services, and damage deposits in differing amounts depending on if, or how well, I knew them or their attorneys. The attorneys soon started using my bail services for clients other than the divorcees.

The girls appreciated the safety and tranquility surrounding the apartments, and that when their boyfriends or pimps got drunk and out of hand, I was always around to quiet them down, kick their ass out, or have them arrested. Those things didn't happen often, because I made sure the guys, as well as the girls, understood all the rules. I made sure the guys understood that the girls were my tenants, and the boys were welcome only as their guests.

In exchange, the girls provided referrals, both for my rentals and my bail businesses. It was like having twenty-three sales agents and their friends soliciting new customers for me, and rather than having to pay them, they paid me in the form of higher rent, higher fees, and free advertising.

Once I got all the units remodeled and rented, I focused my time and energy on the bail business. I hadn't been out on a date or gotten involved with anyone in months, especially any of my bail clients or my new tenants. I always considered myself a quick study, and I'd learned the pitfalls of mixing business and pleasure.

Between more free time on my hands and writing more bonds, I started to see an increase in clients failing to appear in court. Many of them were working girls; ones who had a tough time balancing their court appearances on Monday mornings after working the streets or the strip clubs all weekend. To curb the number of no-shows, I initiated the use of what I called a "cop-out sheet" for court. These were written authorizations, signed by each of my clients, giving me authority to appear in municipal court to enter a plea of guilty on their behalf. Of course, I always collected the bond premium, a fee for my appearance in court, and a few hundred bucks for their fine. Since these individuals were all my clients and out on my bonds, most judges had no objection to my appearing on their behalf and paying their fines. Although collecting money for my court appearances could have been construed as practicing law without a license (a felony), no one really cared, especially on Mondays, when arraignment court was a zoo.

My "cop-out" program gave the judges an opportunity to collect a fine rather than forfeiting bail. This saved the court clerk's office a lot of work, kept the court calendar open for more important cases, and provided a sizable increase in revenue from fine payments.

Helping the girls took up a lot of my time, but it allowed them to stay on the streets turning tricks. I always collected the entire premium as well as the extra fees for my time. And I stuck to Mickey's rule: no credit, no pussy, no drugs.

Bail on street whores and hookers was usually $1,000 per arrest, and street walkers were arrested more often than girls working out of the casinos or the local downtown bars. That meant I would collect a hundred dollar premium for each bond posted every time they were arrested and an additional two hundred dollars each time I had to appear on their behalf or to hire an attorney, if necessary. Fines never exceeded fifty dollars per charge. When I did use attorneys, I used deadbeats and paid them only fifty dollars. The girls loved doing business with me because they didn't have to appear in court.

Some worked at the Mustang Ranch Whore House, which was minutes outside of town by car, or at the Monterey Tavern, another house of ill repute, located in Lovelock, about thirty miles east of Reno. These girls lived and worked in these houses three weeks a month, with one week off. You can guess why they needed a week off. Some of their pimps or boyfriends stayed in one of my units while the girls were literally working their asses off to pay the rent. These guys hung out and partied with the women when they were home for their week off.

Some of the pimps had more than one girl, and they hung out with whichever one was off on any given week. Some of the girls that shared a pimp also shared an apartment together and split the rent, because they stayed there only part of the time.

If any girl got in trouble and was arrested while she was at home, I'd bail her out, take care of her court appearance, and collect my fees, plus the extra two hundred. I made an exception for the girls who worked at the Ranch. I would go to Mustang on Sunday mornings, have breakfast with the owners, and settle each girl's individual bill, which always included court appearance fees, fines, and, of course, their bail premiums for the previous week.

This was a necessary courtesy I extended because most of the girls ran out of money before their week off was up, or their boyfriends or pimps would lose it gambling and drinking. The owners, in turn, paid what the girls owed, and arranged for the girls to reimburse them over the next three work weeks at the Ranch.

If their boyfriends or pimps got in trouble, especially while they were at home waiting for the girls, they were on their own. I seldom bailed these jerks, even if the girls begged me to, because I felt that any guy who was pimping his girlfriend or wife and living off their hard work was a scumbag, and scumbags were "bad risks," period.

Whenever these assholes got out of line around one of my units, I'd kick their asses out and notify the girls that they were still welcome as long as they came back alone or with a new beau.

Even with all the guidelines, experience, and cop-out sheets at my disposal, I had my share of forfeiture problems, which led to looking for a "friend" in the clerk's office; someone I could pay to help clear some of the more complicated forfeiture cases without having to pay the courts. In other words, someone willing to accept some "monetary tokens of appreciation."

It didn't take long to find the right "someone" who might be interested. She was young, cute, divorced from a Sparks police officer, had a young son, and was clearly in need of some financial assistance, because her ex was a complete jerk-off who failed to pay child support. In the '60s and '70s, those in a position to do something about deadbeat dads didn't give a shit.

Her situation reminded me of my mom and my deadbeat old man. The only difference between her ex-husband and my old man was that this guy was a runt, in both mind and body, whereas my old man was a big guy with a pea-brain.

It made me wonder what someone as attractive as she was could see in a deadbeat like him—why would she marry him? It boggled my mind. Maybe she was desperate to get away from her parents, because since he was a cop, you could bet your ass she didn't marry him for his money.

CHAPTER

#15

Her name was Misty Clover. Since I hadn't seen her around the courthouse or the clerk's office prior to opening my own bail bond agencies, I assumed she was either a permanent new addition to the staff or temporary help.

When I started posting my own bonds and taking care of all the related paperwork, I found myself spending more time in and around the courthouse. This also meant spending more time in the municipal court clerk's office filing paperwork, delivering bail bonds, paying fines, or settling forfeitures. These were all the things that Elaine usually handled, while Mickey and I wrote bonds or worked on skips. But since I was now on my own, I had to do all the paperwork as well.

Misty and I hit it off immediately. I found myself spending more time on paperwork; especially the paperwork dealing with misdemeanor cases that Misty was conveniently able to assist with, and things that gave me a reason to talk with her every chance I got.

I'd spent the past few months literally working day and night on the units and the bail business. This had made dating impossible, at least until now, and hopefully with Misty. One day, after a few weeks of friendly business-related conversations, I decided to ask her to dinner. I thought it was a bad idea to ask her in front of her co-workers, so I told her a little white lie. I said my sister needed to find a good daycare center for my niece and was wondering which one Misty was using for her son and if she would recommend it. The next day I waited until her shift ended and she left to pick up her little boy from the center. When she came out with her son, she was surprised to see me standing by her car, but she relaxed when I explained that I wasn't stalking her. I admitted to the white lie and explained the real reason I was there. She thanked me for not asking her at work, and then, with a cute little smile, graciously accepted my invitation.

I made reservations at Trader Dick's, which was just across the street from the Dick Graves Nugget Casino in Sparks. It was one of the nicest dinner restaurants in the Reno–Sparks area at the time, and I wanted to make a good first impression. I brought her a beautiful bouquet of red roses, and when we were seated at one of the restaurant's more intimate corner tables, ordered a fine wine. The cozy atmosphere coupled with the excellent Polynesian cuisine made for a wonderful dinner. In fact, everything made for a fantastic evening.

It was as if we'd known each other all our lives. We laughed, joked, danced, and held each other's hand. It was a special night, and I didn't want to spoil it by trying to get her into bed. After dessert, I took her home, kissed her on the cheek, thanked her for a wonderful evening, and asked her to marry me. . . .

The thought was on my mind, but the words never reached my lips. She was an exceptional woman, and I really wanted to see her again. I asked her if and when. She responded with an offer for dinner at her place the following evening, which I eagerly accepted.

She was all I could think about the rest of the night and the entire next day. I kept reviewing how I should behave. Should I bring more flowers? Some candy? Just more wine? I think this was the first time in my dating life I was at a loss and scrambling for the right thing to do. All I knew for sure was I didn't want to screw this up. I settled on a nice bottle of champagne with a little card that read, "To celebrate our new friendship," and a small stuffed animal to win over the kid.

She met me at the door with a kiss—a nice, "I like you a lot" kind of kiss—and introduced me to her little boy, Ricky. I told him how lucky he was having such an attractive mom, and how thankful I was that he took after her in the looks department instead of his daddy. He was too young to understand what I meant, but she knew that I knew her ex-husband—just in passing—so she laughed and thanked me for the nice compliment.

Not only was she attractive, smart, and funny, she turned out to be a pretty good cook. After we ate dinner, did the dishes, and got Ricky ready for bed, we sat down on the couch, turned on some music, and opened the champagne. After about an hour, she said it was time to put her son to bed, so I said goodnight to him as he wandered into his bedroom carting his new stuffed animal.

I asked Misty if I should leave, since tomorrow was a workday for her.

She replied, "Absolutely not. You sit down and wait. I'll be right back."

It took her only a few minutes to put Ricky to bed, change into something more comfortable, and refill our champagne glasses. She sat down, snuggled up against me, put my arm around her shoulder, and started listening to the music again. Since I didn't want to screw this up, I decided to let her take the lead on how our relationship should develop. Music it was.

After about twenty minutes of easy listening romantic music, my damn pager let out one of those loud screeching beeps, the kind that makes everyone within earshot jump out of their shoes.

It turned out to be an exceptionally large bond from a very good attorney, whose very important client wanted out of jail, NOW! He instructed the answering service to have me meet him at the sheriff's office ASAP.

I did my best to explain how important this call was to my business, making sure she knew I'd rather be with her, and I wanted to see her again. She told me she understood on all counts, kissed me goodnight, and said she was looking forward to picking up where we left off sometime soon.

I responded with, "How about tomorrow, and every tomorrow after that!"

She giggled and said, "It's a date. Same time, same place," and kissed me goodnight again.

When I saw her the next day in the clerk's office, I apologized again for leaving, and said I'd bring either Italian or Chinese, depending on which one she liked best. Her answer was simply, "I like you the best, just bring either."

That night I brought Chinese. In the days and weeks that followed, we hardly missed a chance to see each other, and after we started having sex (which happened the very next night, about halfway through the Chinese food) it was hard for either of us to focus on anything other than each other.

In between having some of the best sex I'd ever enjoyed in my young life, we'd roll over and talk about lots of different things; but our conversations always ended up focused on my business.

We talked about everything from how I chased bad guys when they failed to appear, to how easily I could get hurt if my fugitives were a little on the crazy side. She asked if I should be carrying a gun, and before I could answer, she said, "When do you find time to sleep, since you're on call 24/7, in court every day, and with me most of the night?"

She was full of questions, but for the most part, they reverted to questions concerning the hookers and professional prostitutes I dealt with. She asked how many of the girls worked at Mustang Ranch, and if I ever went out there. I said a few did, while the others worked the streets or out of the clubs, and yes, I went to the ranch almost every Sunday for breakfast with Joe and Sally, the owners. She thought that was cool and asked if she could go along sometime. I said, absolutely not!

My relationship with Joe and Sally was strictly business; we needed to settle up on whatever bonds I wrote for their girls, all of which revolved around how many of them got arrested during their week off from the Ranch each month. I told her their girls never got arrested for trying to turn a trick on the streets, because there was a strong policy against working outside the house. They usually got arrested for things like disturbing the peace, fighting in public, drunk and disorderly, or misdemeanor assault.

The real reason for not taking Misty along was that Joe wouldn't talk business in front of anyone, let alone someone working in the municipal court clerk's office.

Every answer I gave her led to another question, and another, until I started to kiss her; but sometimes, even that wasn't enough. It was obvious she was fascinated with my business, but she was especially fascinated by the "ladies of the night."

She once asked about the volume of business I was doing with the local hookers and professional prostitutes, other than those working in the whore houses. She was not only amazed at the numbers, but also by the vast number of smart, attractive, well-educated women willing to spread their legs at the drop of a hat when asked by complete strangers willing to pay big bucks for the pleasure of screwing them.

Then she began talking about the court and how a few things were happening with regard to the way some cases were being handled. First, many of the girls never appeared. They preferred that I appear, enter guilty pleas, and pay their fines. Second, there were those who had been re-arrested, surrendered back into custody, and had a motion filed to exonerate their bond. Third, there were those who failed to appear, which meant the bail bondsman might have to pay the court the full amount of their bonds if they weren't found and returned to jail.

This last situation led her to the most interesting question of all.

She noted how much quicker and easier it would be if I entered a plea "in absentia" for all the girls, rather than having to hunt some of them down or pay off their bonds when they failed to appear. She asked why I didn't file my motions on all of them.

Although I knew she was as bright as she was beautiful, I couldn't help teasing her a little about using such big Latin phrases like "in absentia." I explained that I was able to use my cop-out sheets only in certain courtrooms, and only when certain judges were on the bench. I explained how most of the alternate judges were lawyers, which meant they were 'wannabe' judges who got to play judge for a day when regular judges were sick, on vacation, or attending seminars.

These wannabes routinely refused to allow anyone other than a fellow licensed attorney to appear in their court or enter a plea on behalf of absentee defendants, even if the defendants signed a document like my cop-out sheet, giving a non-lawyer, like myself, their power of attorney to do so.

I explained that I didn't want to waste my money retaining attorneys to handle cases that easily were being dismissed daily by the regular judges with a simple twenty-five dollar fine. I had only two alternatives: hiring the attorneys, or re-arresting and surrendering these clients (mostly repeat customers) in hopes that their new case, the one for failing to appear in court, would come up in front of the right judge the next time; one who allowed cop-out slips.

Then, she shocked me right out of bed. She said, "You have a third alternative lying right here next to you. I can fix them."

I asked what she meant. She said, "First, I need to know how you're able to pay the fines. And is that money coming out of your pocket, or from collateral these clients give you?"

That's when I let her in on my little scam. I told her about the extra two hundred I collected on every misdemeanor case, how I used part of it to pay fines, and how I pocketed the rest for my time and trouble appearing in court on their behalf.

If I had to personally re-arrest a good client and return her to jail instead of hiring an attorney, I'd have to refund her entire two hundred dollar collateral. If the defendant was a "one timer," I could pay my bounty hunter, but that meant I'd get nothing for my time and trouble. Or I could take time away from writing bonds and look for the skips myself. Using an attorney or a bounty hunter because an arrogant asshole wannabe judge refused to accept my cop-out-sheets cost me money.

When I finished my tantrum, she repeated her initial comment: "I can fix them."

This time she explained exactly how she could do it.

She said it was her job to type up the judge's decision on each case. She did this from handwritten notes taken by the head clerk who attended court whenever it was in session. Her notes were usually written in shorthand to expedite the proceedings. At the end of each session, she'd hand off all the case files, which included her shorthand notes, to Misty.

It was Misty's responsibility to transcribe the shorthand notes, then destroy them to ensure that none of them accidentally turned up in another case file. She also processed the fines and related payments made on behalf of each defendant. This ensured that the amounts on the ledger matched the transcribed case notes before she entered them on the daily deposit list.

Since all this was done on the "honor system," and no one checked Misty's transcribed notes against the handwritten copies, she could alter the content of the handwritten notes in any file while transcribing them into the minutes. Those altered notes became the official notes of record.

As an example, she could easily change a non-appearance notation (a failure to appear) into one reflecting an actual appearance by stamping the judge's signature on her transcribed document and destroying the shorthand notes written by the head clerk.

She also mentioned that her boss, the head clerk, kept a rubber signature stamp for each judge in her safe, including ones for the alternates and substitutes; each morning she'd give Misty the appropriate stamps for that day's presiding judges. The stamps were the ones needed for the morning and afternoon court sessions. Misty was required to keep the stamps locked in her desk drawer, including during lunch, bathroom, or regular break times, and to return them to the head clerk at the close of business each day. This was to ensure that no one else could use the stamps to alter any file while Misty was away from her desk. Before leaving the office, Misty also provided her boss with a list of the cases she'd processed that day, together with a corresponding copy of the daily deposits.

She said, "If you could provide me with a signed cop-out slip for each of your defendants who fail to appear each day, I'd place them into their court file; type up the minutes to reflect his or her entry of a guilty plea; note the regular amount of the fine for each offense, which I can take directly from the court's printed fine schedule; and note the correct payment being made on my daily deposit ledger. Just give me a signed cop-out slip and the fine in cash for each "no show" at some point during the day they were scheduled to appear."

During the 1960s and 1970s, court clerks maintained a schedule of fines. They were posted in the clerk's office and provided to each judge to use to ensure consistent fines for each crime throughout the court system–i.e., driving under the influence, first offense: $50; second offense: $100; drunk in public: $25; assault: $75; assault with intent to do bodily harm: $250; prostitution: $50 first offense and $100 for each offense thereafter. (Some girls got arrested twice, or even three times, in the same night if a police officer wanted to harass them.)

This list was reviewed each month by a panel of local judges and adjusted as they deemed necessary. Then, on the first day of each month, the court clerk would prepare the new list, which reflected any changes made by the judges' panel. The clerk posted a new copy in the window of the clerk's office, and distributed others to the jail commander and the judges.

The jail commander also provided a copy to all jail personnel and booking officers. This eliminated the need to call a judge at all hours, day and night, every time someone was arrested and booked into jail.

Misty and I moved our plan into action, taking one or two cases each day for a week, then laying off for a week to evaluate any fallout. The plan was working better than expected, so I began to automatically collect the full 10 percent premium on each defendant's bond, as well as an additional two hundred as collateral or expense money, which I told the girls I'd use to make the charges go away without then needing to appear. If they baulked, I said they could take their chances and appear the next morning on their own. At least 80 percent elected to let me do it, which put a lot of extra cash in my pocket.

I'd now convinced myself I no longer needed to use an attorney and could afford to split the collateral deposits with Misty instead. I was happy to give her the money rather than to some sleazebag lawyer. After all, she and I were the only ones that knew what was happening, and when the only two people in on a scam are participating in the financial rewards, it makes for a very controlled environment, at least from a white-collar criminal's perspective. In addition, I trusted her more than anyone else. Let's face it, I was in love with her.

As months went by and we progressed further into our relationship and into this business arrangement, we became comfortable enough to expand the scam program to include all types of charges. We began using cop-out slips on other bonds where judges would regularly authorize payment of a fine to defendants who showed up in court and issued warrants for those who failed to appear. Misty could process a fine on any of the cases where my defendants didn't show, as long as

I could give her a cop-out slip and cash for the fine during her lunch hour the same day.

There were other agencies writing bonds in Reno, including some of Mickey's new agents. These other agents may have had backdoor payment arrangements with other court personnel, but there were always enough regularly handled cases being processed to deflect suspicion away from any of us. I wasn't sure which competitors were paying people off or how they were doing it, because Misty was the only clerk handling all the morning and afternoon arraignment files. I knew, however, that if Misty's daily deposits balanced against my files, we were always in the clear.

As additional insurance against getting caught, we intentionally let some of my cases slip through. This meant if I didn't appear on their behalf or return them to custody within ninety days of their failure to appear, I had to pay the court in full. But these were usually from out-of-state clients who sent me the entire bond amount, knowing they were never coming back, and didn't want me coming after them. Misty and I also let a few locals slip through where the bonds were insignificant in size and the judge didn't issue warrants for their arrest.

We did this to protect either of us from getting caught; or at least giving us some cases to reference if we were ever accused of any complicity or wrongdoing.

After months of carefully working to protect what we had going, I still found myself explaining how important it was that Misty and I publicly maintain the appearance of being casual friends, rather than lovers. I didn't want Misty to lose her job; or worse, go to jail for working my little scam and earning a few bucks on the side. Every day that we worked together, we made our professional relationship as fun and exciting as our personal one. We made sure that if we got caught messing with or losing court files, it would look like an honest mistake, not an intentional act of dishonesty on her part or mine.

In reality, unless she got caught in the act of changing a file, it would have been almost impossible for us to get caught, as the court received all the fine money, and I was the one representing the defendants through the use of properly executed (although sometimes forged) cop-out sheets. It would be my word against a set of handwritten court minutes that no longer existed.

I seldom asked Misty to "lose" files, meaning she would "accidently" shred them, which could happen on any given day by any of several employees, especially in a court that processed as many case files as the Reno Municipal Court.

My main objective was to make as much money as I could while minimizing any risks. I took every precaution I could think of while being able to help Misty make some real money without getting caught, and not having it look like I was exchanging money for sexual favors.

We continued to secretly see each other every day; sometimes overnight, and sometimes for just enough time to share a few laughs and a little intimacy. We would have dinner together at her place or mine as often as we could, and always topped it off with some great sex for dessert, and again the following mornings whenever Ricky stayed overnight with his dad.

We also had some special moments during her lunch hour. She'd walk through the back alley behind my office, tiptoe into my apartment, catch me napping, jump into bed with her dress on, while her panties and bra were stuffed in her purse. She'd wake me up, kiss me and rub her cold hands inside my shorts. Then, after we both climaxed, she'd hop off, clean herself up in my bathroom, kiss me goodbye, and head out the back door singing, "Hi ho, hi ho, it's off to work I go."

Other days, when we had files to work and fine payments to arrange, she'd put on her tennis shoes, tell everyone she was going for a power walk during lunch, and sneak over to my office to power me up for another ride. These times, while I was closing the shades and locking the office door, she would take everything off except her shoes. Don't ask me why. I guess she wanted to be ready for a quick escape in case we set the bed sheets on fire!

We made love in my office almost every day for months; and both of us were making more money than ever before. Life was good. In fact, it couldn't have been better.

But one day, out of nowhere, it all started to unravel, and not for any reason you would imagine. We didn't get caught fixing or losing files, using forged cop-out slips on my skips, arguing over money or getting sloppy and complacent in covering up our personal relationship . . . although a few people asked us both why we didn't date, especially since we seemed to like each other when they spotted us talking or walking around the courthouse.

It was none of the things that normally cause people to drift away or relationships to fall apart. It was something I never could have imagined: She wanted to become a high-class call girl.

She dreamed of becoming one of the escort girls who were on call for the casinos when one of their high rollers came to town. From where I was standing (or lying), she had everything it took to be one: looks, figure, class, sexual experience, and a full appetite for the good life.

She told me that although she was making enough extra money from our little business arrangement, she wanted to make much, much more. In fact, she wanted the best of everything money could buy, and everything life had to offer. She believed she was sitting on a million-dollar asset and wanted to put it to work making money before she got too old.

After hearing all my conversations and seeing how much money some of the "low class" hookers were making, she said, "I can't even imagine how much I could make as a high-class call girl." She knew in her heart of hearts that she would make big bucks—if she could only get started with the right people. Then she dropped the first bombshell. She said, "Who better to help me meet them than you?"

"Hey, slow down." I reminded her that I wasn't a pimp, nor was I some ugly bad guy willing to ask or maybe force her to do something, anything, with anybody, for money. "If you're serious, I'm the one who's going to end up with a broken heart. How about getting married to some nice, hard-working guy like me, instead?"

I asked her to marry me; that's how serious I was about our relationship, and about her. My proposal went right over her head, lost somewhere in her new dream.

For clarification, it's important that I explain a little more about hookers. Even in the late '60s and early '70s, there were four types of hookers. There were those who walked the streets and would fuck any guy with fifteen dollars in his pocket and a half-assed backseat in his car. These hookers usually took their money and bought a heroin fix or a snort of coke from a street dealer. Either of these drugs would get them high enough to get back on the street looking for their next trick.

Then there were those who worked in a whorehouse and would go with anyone who walked in and picked them from a lineup. All the available girls, meaning those not busy in their rooms with other customers, would get up from the bar or the couch, wearing almost nothing to show off their potential, and warmly greet each new customer. The house set their rates:

$50 for one quickie climax; $100 for some extra time; $500 to spend the night in the house or with two or more girls; $1,000 if you wanted them to go with you for a night out on the town and all the sex you could handle. The houses had security guards walking the halls in case a customer tried to get more than they'd paid for.

The girls shared their money with the house, then gave the balance to their boyfriend or pimp. They seldom kept anything for themselves. Instead, they let the boyfriends or pimps spend it on them, to try to feel loved and wanted.

Third on the list were women who sat in the casino bars waiting to be picked up by some drunk with a handful of chips and a hotel room key. They'd maybe get a hundred bucks up front, and then steal another hundred or more off the gaming table while their trick was playing heavy and getting drunk on the club's free booze. Then, the poor bastard takes one or more of them to his room and gets it on once or twice if he's lucky before passing out. This is when a hooker helped herself to a few hundred more, or maybe all he had, including his jewelry and credit cards.

The smart ones took only a few hundred more and left. The others usually were hassled by casino security after the customer complained. Then they were either thrown out with a pleasant request never to return or were arrested by the local police if security learned they'd rolled the guest for everything he had. Since these customers never returned to testify against the girls, the charges were usually dropped, but the girls knew better than to return to the casino.

Fourth on the list were the high-class hookers, the real "call girls." These escorts were usually matched with a high roller by casino managers. They had personal managers (more like pimps in three-piece suits) who handed out business cards to casino managers and pit bosses while explaining that their stable boasted a more celebrated variety of hookers, those with style, brains, good looks and class.

At the casino's request, the personal manager made sure the escort was dressed to the hilt; she arrived at the hotel by cab; and she had the necessary security clearance to take the High Roller elevator directly to the client's room. There, she knocked and said something like, "Hi, Mr. Schmuck, the casino boss said you were looking for me."

A night with these girls (back in the sixties and seventies) could run as high as $2,000 to $2,500. But more often than not, the escorts earned these fees when the high roller wanted the girl(s) to accompany him to dinner, hold his hand for luck while gambling, or spend the entire night tending to anything else he might want or need. The girls split their purse with their managers, who, in turn, provided a small token of appreciation to the casino bosses or bellmen for setting up the score. Usually, the pit boss and/or bellman also got a nice tip from the "trick" if he or she liked their date. (There were male hookers servicing the needs of female high rollers as well.)

Anyway, back to Misty. A few nights later, while we were once again lying in bed, she said, "I know you know someone who can help me get started with accommodating the personal needs of the rich high rollers that come to party and gamble in the downtown hotel casinos."

She made it clear she wasn't interested in a pimp; nor was she looking to sit around casino bars hoping to get picked up. Because she had been looking through and working on my files while fixing cases behind the scenes for months, she knew every kind of hooker, and how or why many got arrested. From overhearing many of my calls, she'd also learned that no one bothered the escort girls; none ever got arrested. The casinos liked having them available at a moment's notice but didn't want them hanging around the clubs.

I told her I knew a couple of guys around town who managed these girls and set them up at the casinos as escorts. These "special escorts" would do anything for the right price; if a high roller liked them, he would request the same services from the same escort every time he came to Reno.

By the time I finished the sentence, my heart had fallen through the floor—because Misty got up and strutted back and forth across the room shouting, "I knew it! I knew it! I knew you could help me."

I said, "Listen, I want you to marry me, today, right now. I mean it. I can't see myself without you." I couldn't get my head around being with her if she went through with this crazy idea. "If you become a hooker, even a high-class one, it will be the end of our relationship."

Then it dawned on me: Our relationship would be damned if I helped her; and in her mind, I would be damned if I didn't. I was stuck in a no-win situation.

She begged me for days, maybe even weeks, to introduce her to one of the managers, while trying to convince me that this wouldn't interfere with our relationship.

She said, "The most that would happen is I'd spend a few nights each week working. And, if I had to stay over with one, it would be different, because I'd only be doing it for money; not like us. No matter what, when the date is over, I'll always come back to you."

I finally realized she was determined to do this. I broke down and agreed, but only because I wanted to make sure she didn't get mixed up with the wrong people. I set up a meeting with someone I knew and made it clear that I could not and would not do anything else. She'd be on her own from there.

Tommy was a class guy. He managed some of the best-looking, brightest, most interesting "women of the night" in the Reno–Sparks area. He set up their dates, collected their money in advance, watched over them in the casinos and bars, and acted as their bodyguard if or when they needed one. He never took them to bed, and took only his share of their money, never a penny more. He offered to hold or bank their share for safekeeping, and even invest it for them, if they wanted. He was a professional and ran his escort operation as a legit business. From everything I knew and heard, he was more than a few steps above the rest.

Introducing him was the best I could do to ensure Misty's safety and provide her with an opportunity to do what she thought would make her happy. I knew she was serious when she said it wouldn't hurt our relationship. And from her standpoint, it probably wouldn't have. But in my heart, I knew it would mean the end of everything we had together. If she decided to do this, there was no way I could be with her again. I knew the little sparkle of innocence in her smile would be gone forever, and she would no longer be the girl I fell in love with. She would always be just another potential client, another high-class working girl.

I guess I'd thought that in the end, she'd give up and say, "On second thought, that marriage offer sounds pretty good, if it's still open!"

I was wrong. She went with Tommy, and we said our goodbyes. It was the hardest thing I ever did. I thought my life had hit rock bottom. Little did I know, this was just the beginning of my downhill slide.

CHAPTER

#16

My emotions took a nosedive. I could hardly get out of bed to take a bail call, and when I did, I usually ended up at one of the casinos playing 21 until I lost the entire premium from the bond, including the portions I owed Mickey and the insurance company. At one point, I lost so much I couldn't meet my monthly obligations on either the bail business or my properties without having to hit my cash reserves. It was time to get my head out of my ass about the loss of my love life and start thinking about how to avoid the fast track to financial ruin.

I needed a quick fix of cash, and the only thing I could think of was . . . going to Mom. Although she was comfortable financially, she had nowhere near what I needed in ready cash. But she did have the ability to help me in a way you would never guess. I failed to mention something important about Mom: She counted cards. This sweet little Catholic lady who went to Mass every morning was a card cheat for the casinos. It was her secret little gig; one that helped keep her employed as a blackjack dealer for more than thirty-five years.

Every casino had a set of rules to ensure against losing to some drunken cowboy who rode in off the range, or some rich kid in from California. These in-house rules allowed pit bosses to rotate dealers randomly, from one table to another, whenever needed to protect the house. They also used "shills"—players on the casino's payroll, who sat in to play at any given table or any given game with house money. Shills were sometimes used to make the casinos look busy on slow days, but their main job was to break a gambler's lucky streak by playing at the same table, because this would disrupt the flow of cards.

Rotating dealers and shills became a regular thing on every shift, in every casino. They would routinely move shills at random about every twenty minutes or so to relieve dealer boredom and give dealers an opportunity to get off their feet for a while, which did help. But the main purpose in rotating dealers was to curb a customer's winning streak.

Dealers in for the long haul, especially women like my mom, ended up bow-legged from having to stand at the table games in high heels six or seven days a week, over twenty or thirty years.

In the '60s and '70s, all the clubs used single decks on their blackjack tables. Dealers could reshuffle the cards as often as they felt necessary, or when a pit boss signaled them to do so. It depended on how many players were at the table and how lucky they were.

Over Mom's thirty-plus years of dealing single-deck black-jack at the casinos, she became quite the card cheat. She could tell you, within 98 percent accuracy, if the card she was about to deal was a face card, a ten, or something smaller. If a high roller needed what she thought was the next card up, she'd reshuffle the deck in an effort to break his luck. This little trick almost always broke the streak and changed the odds in favor of the house. As a result, Mom was always their "go to" dealer when high rollers were winning big.

When a pit boss found himself with a losing table, especially to a high roller, he'd put in a shill or two if the table had room. If that didn't work, he'd change dealers as often as he could to try and break the gambler's concentration and his winning streak. But when things got really tough, they'd put in an experienced dealer like Mom.

Mom's saving grace in front of God, or at least she thought so, was going to Mass each and every morning, and never winning back more than the house lost. She also had the pit bosses remove anyone she recognized from her table, especially friends of mine or my sisters, because she didn't want to send any of them home broke.

Although she could have used her talents to make extra money on her days off by playing at other casinos, she never used them for personal gain. My case was different. I'm sure she rationalized away any guilt by convincing herself that the casinos had taken my premium money at a time when I was emotionally unstable. In her mind, it was okay to help me win it back.

Anyway, I asked her for help, and she agreed. But she made me promise never to tell anyone, especially my sister or brother. She also determined when it was time to quit. No matter how much we were winning, I had to finish the hand, tip the dealer, and walk away from the table. It was her intent to win back all the money I lost, but she had no intention of getting caught or losing her job in the process. She made sure I agreed to these rules every time we went to play.

Every afternoon, we would go to lunch at a different club, play 21 for about twenty minutes, win about $500 and quit. I'd play while she stood behind me and watched. She could see my cards and tap me on the back very discreetly . . . once to hit and twice to stand. Before we went into a casino, she always went over the plan.

"Lefty," she'd say, "sit down at any table with two or more players; if you win the first hand, you let it ride two more times. If you lose, double your first bet, and then triple it, if you lose again. If you win on the third hand, draw it all in and start again with your original bet. If you win on the first hand, let it ride two more times, and then draw it all back and start with a fresh bet."

She had me take the seat closest to the center of the table. This gave her an opportunity to watch all the other players and the dealer without raising suspicion, especially from the house security's eye in the sky.

From her position, she could easily count the cards; usually, by the third hand, she knew exactly what cards had been played and what was left in the deck. She said most dealers never reshuffled until after the third hand, unless the table was full.

"Play tables with two players, or maybe three if necessary," she instructed me. "Three, including you, is perfect."

Thanks to Mom, it took less than a month to pick up about $12,000, a little over what I needed to get out of the hole I'd dug for myself. We never won more than $500 at any time, from any casino, but we did frequent a few of them at different times during the month. We never sat at a table if she knew the pit boss or the dealer. On those occasions, we would leave after my mom said hello while I played our first and only hand, win or lose.

We hit a lot of different casinos, large and small, during that month, and not just in the Reno and Sparks area. We went to Carson City and South Lake Tahoe as well. Lunch, especially one that included a scenic drive, was always a nice break for Mom. I made sure we stayed away from Harrah's casinos. The last thing I needed was to have my mom caught hanging around someone—me—listed in their black book.

When I was whole, she made me promise not to lose more than fifty bucks of my own money ever again. "Lefty, the only reason I helped you," she said, "is because you were feeling miserable about your breakup with Misty. Don't ask me to do it again."

Mom was one of the few people that even knew Misty and I were dating regularly.

To this day, I've kept my promise, with one exception. The day after Mom died, I dusted off the card-counting skills I learned from her and went to a little club in downtown Carson City to see if I could pull it off on my own. The answer was a resounding no; two security guards caught me, took me out the back door, and confiscated all my winnings, plus every dime I had in my pockets, which fortunately wasn't much. I was told: "If you ever come back here, it'll be the last place you ever visit in this lifetime." It didn't take a rocket scientist to get the message.

I went back to hanging out in all the topless bars and men's clubs around the Reno–Sparks area, looking to drown my sorrows by crying on the shoulders of any girl that would listen. Buying a few drinks was cheaper than gambling,

As I mentioned, the hookers liked staying in my rental units because of my strong set of house rules. "Quiet" was at the top of the list, followed by "no tricks or johns in the room—only boyfriends, pimps, or husbands, and no parties." They understood that if they broke the rules, I could evict them immediately. This was the primary reason I rented the units and apartments only for thirty days or less at a time. After thirty days, the law required that landlords needed a court hearing before forcibly removing or evicting anyone. Thirty days or less meant I could throw their asses out the minute they broke a rule. It worked for me!

At this point, I kept my bail bond office/living quarters in the ninth apartment, but I began to work on converting the motel office into a new combination rental office/bail office and using the manager's unit above it for my living quarters. I tried to convince myself I was doing this to maximize my rental income, but the real reason was because being in my old unit brought back memories of Misty.

I tried to keep busy while staying away from the municipal court clerk's office as much as possible, since Misty hadn't quit her day job for obvious reasons. She needed a legitimate cover in case her mom or ex-husband asked where she was getting all her money. I also tried to limit my contact and call on her for help only when I absolutely needed it. But this lack of contact resulted in having to surrender more of the girls, and spend a lot more time chasing skips, rather than asking her to fix cases like we used to. I'm sure she would have continued to work with me, but my heart wasn't into seeing her. I knew if we interacted too much, I'd start asking questions about how Tommy was treating her, which would have poured more salt on my wounded heart.

It happened that when I moved my attention away from Misty, I spent much more time working the other courts and jails around the sheriff's department. This diverted my interests away from the municipal court and police department. As a result, I began writing more felony bonds, which were much larger and required defendants to appear in justice or superior courts with an attorney, rather than in municipal court with my cop-out slips.

This switch in direction not only increased my bail bond premium revenues and collateral deposits, it increased the number and size of my forfeitures. Because the superior court judges required attorneys to appear with their clients, I could no longer use my cop-out sheets. This is when I hooked up with Dennis Harper. He became my personal attorney, as well as one of my best friends, at a time in my life when I really needed one.

Dennis had just quit his job as a prosecutor with the Washoe County District Attorney's Office, hung out his shingle, and was hanging around the courthouse looking for clients.

He was a few years older than me, but we knew a lot of the same people, so we started talking during the court recesses and breaks. We became friends. Because I needed a lawyer to handle my dealings with the courts, I began referring as many of my clients to him and his office as possible. Whenever I could, I made his representing them a condition for posting someone's bail.

My reasoning was twofold. First, Dennis could ask for continuances and postpone the entry of forfeitures for our mutual clients. This, in turn, gave me more time to locate those on the run. Second, he would meet with the judges in chambers or in local pubs for lunch to arrange a dismissal, a fine, or a significant reduction in my bond forfeitures—the ones I couldn't locate—and return in time to avoid having to pay the full bail amount.

Felony bonds were always really large. For example: $25,000 for armed robbery; $20,000 for burglary; $10,000 for possession with intent to sell drugs. Marijuana and heroin dealers topped the list of arrests at the time. Coke came later. Picking up these skips posed a huge risk of injury to me, my bounty hunters . . . even the police. So paying a little something to a judge for assistance in reducing my loss, rather than getting killed or seriously injured, was always the better choice.

This was about the time I went back to using attorneys to handle my payoffs, bribes, or compensation for their special assistance; call it what you will. Dennis's relationship with the judges—a result of working as a prosecutor for the D.A.'s office—made him a natural to handle these. I never knew how much, if any, the judges were receiving, or how much Dennis pocketed; as long as I got off on the cheap, I couldn't care less.

Larger forfeitures meant I needed more help, both to locate the defendants and make the arrests. I called the police or the sheriff's office for backup when I felt the defendant, or those harboring him, would be armed or dangerous. Many times, they were. But most of the time they were too drunk, too loaded on heroin, marijuana, or booze to put up much, if any, resistance.

These large bonds meant I was holding a lot more collateral, and my contract with the defendant stated clearly that I could use their collateral to pay off the forfeiture or recover all the costs involved in apprehending and returning them to jail. I figured my time and expertise into all my calculations, and I didn't come cheap! I always got receipts from Dennis and any of the skip chasers I used that charged more than I regularly paid. Most of the time, when I added my cut onto the bill, there was no collateral left to return.

When I'd started working for Mickey, we seldom dealt with drugs or drug dealers, so chasing skips was relatively easy, at least in Reno and Vegas. But when the drugs from L.A. and San Francisco started showing up on our doorstep, writing bail became a much riskier business, both from an underwriting and an apprehension standpoint. I decided to look for someone with a few brains and a lot of balls to help me out; someone who could think like a person on the run and also interact with those involved in the drug culture. I was looking for someone who dressed and talked the part of a hippie, biker, drug dealer and thief, all rolled into one.

At first, I hooked up with a two-time loser named Bruce Jennings who had spent time in prison for armed robbery. Bruce swore up and down that he was through being a bad guy and wanted a straight job. Becoming a bounty hunter didn't require a license unless you were carrying a gun, which ex-felons like him weren't permitted to do anyway, so I hired him.

He turned out to be an okay guy for the first three months or so. But then he found a lady friend named Sandy. She was wealthy, owned a little ranch, and raised peacocks for a living. They would invite me to her ranch for lunch or dinner every so often. One day, she called to say Bruce had gotten arrested for armed robbery. So much for him swearing off crime. I knew I couldn't use him to chase skips or anything else anymore. And I wasn't about to post his bond and let him try to con me into picking up a few skips in exchange for his premium.

But when Sandy called and offered to put up her ranch for collateral, I wasn't about to let her call one of my competitors. She said Bruce would pay me as soon as he got out, but that I would have to take him to a friend's place to get the money. Normally, I would have asked the friend to bring the money, but since I trusted Bruce to have my back when picking up skips, I didn't think it was a setup.

He was released shortly after I posted his $20,000 bond, and Sandy brought him to the office as agreed. She told us she had to go home and feed her peacocks, otherwise she would have been happy to take him to his friend's place for the money. I knew the story was bullshit, but I wanted my money before I let him out of my sight. So I agreed.

Once in my car, he said, "Look, I need to meet my friend at his favorite hangout. It's a bar on the Mt. Rose Highway, about a third of the way to Incline Village. He's waiting for us; we should hurry before the place gets packed. He says he doesn't want to be seen handing me a bunch of cash. Actually, I think he doesn't want to be seen with me, period. I would have asked him to pick me up, but he's already loaning me the $2,000 I owe you, so I thought asking for a ride would be too much. Anyway, Lefty, thanks for helping me out. Let's get going."

What I didn't know, and Sandy failed to mention, was that she'd brought him a gun when she picked him up at the sheriff's office. When we got to the bar, Bruce asked me to wait in the car, because he'd only be a few minutes. Since it was winter, he suggested I keep the car running to keep warm. About five minutes later, he returned with two small white-cotton moneybags; the type used to collect coins from the bottom of the old slot machine cabinets as customers played the machines. He got into the car and said, "Okay, let's roll," as calm as could be.

Back at Sandy's place, he paid me the $2,000 in cash for his bond and gave me one of the coin bags he'd taken from the bar. He said it was a little something extra for trusting him. I was tired from driving and from working all day, so I passed on their offer of a drink, drove back to my office, and hit the sack. The next morning, while I was fixing my first cup of coffee and listening to the news, I learned what really went down between Bruce and his so-called buddy the night before. The Mount Rose Bar, the one I took him to, had been robbed at gunpoint.

That idiot had used me as his wheelman without giving it a second thought. Luckily, no one in the bar at the time was able to identify my car; and none mentioned seeing a second person. They did, however, describe Bruce to a tee. When the police showed up at Sandy's house, she told them he took all her cash, and left her holding the bag on his bail bond.

Fortunately, it took them only a couple of days to locate and arrest him. This time, the judge revoked his original bond, and held him without bail on two additional charges of armed robbery, since he'd allegedly robbed his girlfriend at gunpoint. I say "allegedly" because I think Bruce told her what to tell the police so they wouldn't arrest her as an accomplice or for aiding, abetting, or harboring a criminal. He also said she should tell them I had dropped him off earlier and he'd caught another ride to the bar. This was to ensure that neither she nor I would be implicated in the robbery.

As a result, my previous bond on him was later exonerated, and Sandy and I were off the hook. She dumped him quicker than a load of peacock shit, and so did I. He was later found guilty and sentenced to five years in the Nevada State prison. Fortunately, I was never questioned or implicated, so by the grace of God and Mom's prayers (which I'm sure nudged Him a little), I dodged another bullet.

This was the first close call in my early career as a bail agent. Knowing there would likely be more to come in future years, I etched this lesson deep in my memory bank. In addition to losing my first bounty hunter, I could have been implicated as an accomplice to an armed robbery.

A few days later I rented one of my units to a topless dancer named Kitty and her new boyfriend, who happened to be an ex-biker. He rode around town on his Harley Chopper, carried a Bible, and went by the name of "Preacher." Kitty and Preacher moved into the unit right above my office. By his looks and actions, Preacher could have been the poster boy or spokesperson for any of the notorious top-ten biker gangs across America, like the Satan's Raiders, the Mongols, the Black Pistons, or the Outlaws.

He was the perfect guy to back me up. His real name was Dusty Martin. He was a nice looking, 200-pound ex-member of the Raiders, with long black hair and a full straggly biker beard. The club nicknamed him "Preacher" because he carried his Bible everywhere, especially to gang fights. Dusty allegedly spent the night with another biker's old lady shortly after joining the club. This resulted in him having to leave town in a hurry—so fast, in fact, that he mistakenly grabbed a bag filled with the club's drug profits on his way out the door. But "mistakenly" may not be accurate.

Somehow, Dusty ended up in Reno shacked up with Kitty. Living close made it simple for him to stop by on his way upstairs to say hi and shoot the shit. We exchanged some war stories, him on his biker adventures, and me on my Vegas trips. He began and ended each visit by reminding me he was around if I needed help picking up my skips.

When Kitty left for work, he'd invite me to go out for something to eat, or maybe down a few brews while watching the girls dance. Misty was out of my life, but not quite out of my mind, so I was always ready to hit the clubs and seek sympathy from anyone who would listen.

We became friends. I started calling him Dusty instead of Preacher because I thought some of his past buddies might come looking for him one day. I began using him to help locate some of my more difficult skips. He was pretty good at finding them, but not exactly professional when making arrests, so most of the time I went along to ensure that he didn't cuff the wrong person or kill the fugitive in the process of an arrest.

I never told him that. Instead, I said he needed a car in order to return fugitives safely after making the arrests. His normal response to my excuse was, "You don't have to worry, the worst I could do would be to drag 'em behind my chopper if they try to escape." That pretty much validated all my earlier concerns.

One day, he asked me to help him sell his chopper and buy a car. Although he wanted a clunker, he hit me up for a loan. He needed the difference between the money he received from the sale and whatever he'd need for the car. It was like paying him in advance for picking up skips, he said, so why not?

One day, he confided that he'd heard some of his ex-gang buddies were looking for him and he expected them to turn up in Reno soon. Within days of telling me, they not only showed up in Reno, they roared up to my office on their choppers.

The leader of this small (but very loud) hunting party walked into my bail office like he owned the place. He plopped down in a chair, put his boots up on my desk, and asked, "Where's the Preacher?"

I responded with, "At a local church, I suppose." Not too bad for a quick comeback, but it didn't go over very well.

He got up, leaned across the desk, put his ugly face close enough for me to smell his beer breath, and said, "Tell the Preacher we're coming for him, only next time we'll get him. Keep in mind, asshole, if you help him, we'll take you along for some of the fun too, you little smart ass."

That proved it: This guy really didn't like my sense of humor.

The next time they came, and a few times after that, they kept missing him. That's because he ran upstairs and hid in the attic above Kitty's apartment whenever he heard the roar of motorcycles in the street; sometimes he stayed up there for a few days to ensure they were gone. After a month or so of dropping in whenever they damn well felt like it, I told them, "I heard the Preacher sold his bike to the local Harley dealer, bought a train ticket, and headed back home to Michigan." I even gave them the dealer's name and phone number so they could verify what I was telling them. I figured this would be the last time I'd ever see them, because the guy Preacher sold his chopper to was bigger than all those guys put together and would happily kick their asses if they accused him of lying.

I was right. They stopped coming to Reno, and Preacher stopped hiding. Although I'd heard rumors, I never asked them why they were looking for Preacher. And Dusty never volunteered to tell me. Whatever it was, it clearly wasn't bad enough to send them all the way to Michigan to get him. After that, the Preacher and I spent a lot of time together chasing skips, watching the topless dancers, and catching a bite of lunch or dinner whenever Kitty was busy.

He tried to keep me from drinking too much when he could, but I was still using alcohol to forget about Misty. My poison was always the same: a boiler-maker, consisting of a straight shot of Jack Daniels either dropped (glass and all) into a full glass of beer, or downed straight, with a beer chaser.

By this time, I was making more money than I ever had working with Misty. I was arranging collateral kickback deals while Preacher was helping on forfeitures and Dennis was making all the necessary court appearances and monetary contributions to the clerks and judges as needed. But although things were going better than ever financially, I was having a hard time getting over Misty. I was touring the topless joints and men's clubs looking for potential bail customers and new tenants to try to keep my mind off her and her career choice. I noticed which of these bars and topless dance halls were becoming prime hangouts for the new drug dealers and users popping into town by the dozens, especially on the weekends.

Although they were all potential customers for my new bail business, I shied away from renting my units to them. The last thing I needed was a bunch of narcs raiding my apartments and closing them off as crime scenes for God knows how long, because they'd confiscated drugs on the premises or kicking them out because they used their rent money to shoot-up or snort their stash.

Even though I refused to rent units to these new players, I was still their first call after being arrested. They knew me, and I knew how, when, and where to contact their friends for help when they needed it.

So drowning my sorrows started to turn into a good thing. I was writing more and more bonds. Many of them were large and presented a much higher risk of forfeiting. I knew it wouldn't take many of them going bad to put me out of the bail business for good, so I was taking everything I could get my hands on for collateral on their bonds; everything except their drugs.

CHAPTER

#17

One of the first felony bonds I wrote after terminating my working relationship with Mickey was for ten grand. I told myself while I was writing it that it was time to start making some fast money on my own. After all, I had a lifetime of "street smarts," a significant amount of underwriting experience, and years of Marine Corps hand-to-hand combat-training, all of which made me think I was tough enough and smart enough to kick some ass and chase my own skips. If I was ever going to get the edge on my older, more experienced competitors, I was going to have to take more risks and write larger bonds. This meant dealing with druggies after all.

That's when I began writing drug bonds on a regular basis and making more money than ever. But I also watched my forfeiture notices pile up. I started getting small ones on the users, usually $1,000 for possession of marijuana. The quality of my underwriting on these bonds was still good, but my clients were going to la-la land a bit too often. Most of them didn't skip; they got wasted on drugs and missed their court dates. Bringing them into court, arranging for a new date, and reinstating their bonds—for a small fee of course—was easy, just too time consuming.

Although I'd learned early on that larger the bonds usually meant shiftier clients, I took extra time and more security when writing them. One day, I slipped and wrote a $10,000 bond on a guy named Joey Romelli. He was not only a user, but a small-time marijuana dealer who hung around topless bars selling drugs to the girls and their customers. He graduated to selling heroin, so I knew I should never have bailed him, but he was so convincing when he said, "Honest, Lefty, I'm innocent. I just need a chance to get out of here and prove it to you and my family. I'm sure they'll cosign for me if you talk to them. I made a big mistake, and you know better than anyone it's impossible to do anything from inside a jail cell. Let them know I can help with my own defense if I'm out on bail. I promise you won't regret it."

Later that day, I persuaded his parents to guarantee his appearance, had them sign a deed of trust on their home for collateral, and wrote his $10,000 bond for possession and sale of heroin—hard drugs, the worst stuff.

This wasn't the first $10,000 bond I wrote, nor was it the first one to forfeit. It was, however, the first one I received through my own agency; one I was totally responsible to pay if I didn't find him in time.

It also turned out to be the largest one I apprehended without backup from Mickey's professional bounty hunters. I was going it alone on this one, with Dusty as my only backup . . . and betting on the fact that I would remember everything Mickey's guys taught me so I wouldn't kill or get killed.

Just thinking about how I felt that morning when the postman delivered my first large forfeiture notice is almost enough, even today, to turn my guts upside down and cause diarrhea, vomiting, or both.

My postman was a whole other trip. Every weekday he'd plop his fat middle-aged sweaty ass into one of my office chairs and pretend to shuffle through his beat-up leather mail pouch hoping to find a registered letter from the court clerk's office; one announcing that another asshole client of mine failed to appear. He knew exactly where the letter was, but he made a big deal out of stalling. "Gee whiz," he'd say. "I know I put one of those fancy registered letters in my pouch this morning. You know the ones I mean."

Yeah, I knew the ones he meant—the ones that made me sweat bullets watching him reach for them. Hell, he'd even go through his bullshit routine on days when he didn't have one, just to watch me squirm.

As a courtesy, I referred to my customers as "clients"—until they failed to show up for their court appearances. Then they became "assholes." That's because once they failed to appear, I had to jump through all the hoops even if they'd simply overslept and missed court. Unless I could find them or produce a body (dead or alive) within ninety days, I would have to pay the full amount of the bail. In Joey's case, it would be the full $10K. Or, I'd have to pay Dennis to try to work magic on the judge or the clerk; either way, it would cost me.

On this day, not knowing if Joey had made it to court, I was sitting on pins and needles awaiting the postman. After exchanging some niceties like "Good morning" (which it wouldn't be, thanks to him), I ripped open the envelope and read the certified notice just as quickly as he handed it to me, in hopes that it was some little bullshit $100 bond.

"Shit! Shit! Shit!"

The butterflies in my stomach swarmed like bees. It was the forfeiture I was dreading: the $10K bond I had written on that piece of shit, Joey.

As I pulled Joey's papers from the filing cabinet, I told the mailman to get his ass out of my office. Although I saw where Joey's parents had signed the agreement and put up a deed on their home to guarantee his appearance, I knew they were in no position to cough up $10,000 within ninety days . . . which meant I might have to pay it, if or when the time came.

What an asshole! How could Joey do this to his parents? Their home was the only thing they had to show for a lifetime of hard work, yet they trusted him enough to use it as collateral to guarantee his appearance.

I murmured, "Maybe I'm the asshole." After all, I was the one who had convinced them to co-sign in hopes of collecting my $1,000 premium, and I was the one who'd have to pay the court $10,000, then chase these hardworking people all over hell to collect it if I didn't find Joey in time. Why? Why didn't I listen to my gut? I should never have written this bond in the first place.

Mickey always said, "Kid, never become too focused on the premium instead of the potential loss. Especially when the co-signers have property, but little available cash. If you see the cosigners or the defendant struggling to pay the premium, picture them struggling to pay the loss when he skips. Better yet, picture yourself struggling to pay the loss. Then decide if you want to write the bond or need the premium that badly."

This bond was Mickey's scenario to a tee. Had I still been working for him, he'd be kicking my ass all over the office then send me out on my own nickel to look for the jerk. I was thankful he wasn't here. But kicking my own ass around the office in preparation for spending whatever money or time it would take to find the jerk didn't make me feel any better.

I either had to fund an investigation by some regular bounty hunters or do it myself. Either way, it was going to cost me, but doing it myself, with as little backup as possible, would cost me a hell of a lot less.

There was no way I could sit back and wait for the little S.O.B to surrender on his own volition. Even though Joey had been an old school friend of my sister's, and he got his folks to put up their home, druggies like him don't waltz back into court on their own. They know how the system works. Going to jail is the worst thing that can happen to them, because after twenty-four hours without a fix, they're fucked: that's when withdrawal begins. They're left with two choices: kill the demons by drying out in jail, or start hiding and keep using, because jails don't provide drugs.

Knowing that Joey was having those thoughts made me realize my butterflies felt like a walk in the park compared with his. Losing money has got to be easier than going through drug withdrawals. You can always make more money.

I knew I had to bring him in sooner rather than later because he'd be using more drugs now due to his paranoia. Besides, the risk of losing $10,000 became greater as each day passed. My only real option was to go after him myself, especially considering his parents' questionable financial means.

Because drugs were involved, and Joey's behavior would be unpredictable, there was no way I was going after him alone. One misjudgment on my part could turn my first felony arrest into my last. I needed someone to watch my back. Someone I could trust. Someone I could afford given the circumstances surrounding my shitty decision to write this bond in the first place.

I had the perfect guy in mind: Dusty, the Preacher.

I knocked on his door. "Hey Dusty, I really need your help," I said.

He knew from my tone of voice that something was really wrong. He opened the door and started downstairs before I explained what was up. As usual, he was wearing his motorcycle boots and black leathers. I couldn't help but wonder if he slept in that same getup, but I held my tongue. Some things are better left unsaid, especially when you're in need of help.

A few days and a few cash payments to some informants and drug addicts later, we got a solid lead on Joey. Word was he was hiding in a newly established safehouse for junkies like him who were on the run from the cops or from their suppliers.

Dusty and I drove by the house. It was small, probably two bedrooms at best, with a detached single-car garage. Both the house and the yard were in poor shape; except for the three cars parked in front, and the one in the driveway, anyone would have thought the place was abandoned.

Dusty said, "From the looks of it, there's at least three people inside." Since it was almost dusk, and all the windows were covered, this was a wild guess.

"Hell, who are you kidding? There could be a hundred guys in there," I responded. "Regardless, chances are, most of them are shooting up, or already loaded. Either way, we're going in."

No way was I letting this asshole get away. I parked as close to the front of the house as possible without being noticed.

Dusty said, "One of those assholes could be peeking out of a hole in the shades. We better be ready for just about anything."

I got out of the car, opened the trunk, reached for our crash gear, and slipped Mickey's gift on my left hand. Those brass knuckles always gave me a feeling of strength and confidence.

"Okay, listen up. We've got one chance to catch this little prick, so let's not screw it up. You take one of these sledge-hammers and go around to the back door. I'll give you a fast count to fifty so you can set up back there, then I'll smash in the front door. As soon as you hear me busting in, you smash your way in from the back. The people inside won't know how many of us are coming in or have a clue as to what's happening. The ones that aren't too spaced out will think we're cops, which will add to their confusion and give us the edge."

As we moved closer to the house, I continued talking. "Some of them will try to make a run for it. Let's hope our boy is hallucinating, passed out, or too fucking stupid to try to escape. Most of the rooms will be dark, given that the shades are down, so check the mugshot I gave you to make damn sure you'll recognize him; don't be afraid to bash in a few heads if anyone gets in your way! Remember, everybody inside will probably be on drugs or dealing. And most are fugitives. They won't know or care if we're the police or other druggies after their stash. They'll be rushing to get themselves and their drugs out. Don't let anyone leave unless you're sure it's not Joey. Check under the beds and in the closets in every room. We don't want him hopping out a side window after we've moved on to another room."

Dusty headed toward the back to take up his position, while I walked toward the front door. As I finished counting, "forty-eight, forty-nine, fifty," I smashed my way through the front door with my sledge and began pushing over the portable pot burners. This sent spoons loaded with liquefied heroin flying all over the room. I knew exactly what Joey looked like and started pushing the business end of my sledgehammer into the guts of anyone standing in my way, man or woman.

As we busted into the house, most of the junkies, those still able to move, were trying to scoop up the smallest amounts of spilled drugs off the floor or to finish shooting up with a loaded syringe. Dusty and I threatened our way from room to room until we found good-old Joey boy. The little prick was trying to escape through a bathroom window. We dropped our sledgehammers, pulled him back into the house, and simultaneously began hitting and kicking him into submission. Thanks to my knuckles, this didn't take long. Dusty began pushing Joey's head into the toilet to wash off some of the blood, and make sure he was still breathing—which he was. We handcuffed him and continued kicking and punching him and anyone else who got in our way as we headed out the front door.

We threw him in the trunk of my car, went back inside to retrieve our sledgehammers, kicked over a few more pots just for the hell of it, and gave each other a high five for a job well done. We hopped down the front steps, jumped into the car, threw the hammers into the back seat, slipped my knuckles into the glove box and headed to the city jail.

Since we had an unwilling passenger kicking and screaming to be let out of the trunk, I drove the speed limit to ensure that we didn't get busted for kidnapping by some rookie cop. I took the long way, in hopes of getting our adrenalin under control before we got to the police station. When we got close, we parked on a side street, opened the trunk, took poor little Joey out, straightened him up a little and wiped off any remaining blood. After we were satisfied that he was somewhat presentable, we replaced his handcuffs, this time with his hands behind his back, and placed him securely in the back seat. We threw the sledgehammers into the trunk and drove off.

When we arrived at the booking desk, Joey started squealing like a pig. "These guys kicked and beat me! They threw me in the trunk of their car. I want to file a complaint. I want them arrested for assault, or kidnapping, or something."

The duty officer came out and asked what was going on. I said, "Can you imagine, this little fugitive piece of shit is accusing us of hitting and kicking him, when, in fact, he was resisting arrest and attempting to escape out the bathroom window of a drug house. We only used necessary force to stop him from escaping, and to secure him in the car for the trip to the station."

Then Dusty began telling the jailers his pre-rehearsed story. "Yeah, poor Joey here tripped over an extension cord from a hair dryer and fell headfirst out of the bathroom window into the middle of a rock garden. His fall, coupled with the fact that he landed flat on his face, knocked him out cold. That's probably why he's having difficulty remembering much of anything."

As usual, our comments were being entered into the booking officer's arrest report amid a lot of muffled laughter from everyone within earshot, except for the duty officer, of course.

The next morning, I filed a motion in open court, asking the judge to set aside Joey's forfeiture, and exonerate my $10,000 bond, which he granted. The judge asked the court recorder to make a note in Joey's file reflecting that "as a result of the bail bondsman's efforts, a fugitive from justice was arrested and returned to the custody of this court in a timely manner. Bond exonerated."

Not only did I get Joey's original $10K bond exonerated, I also collected $3,000 from his parents, which they happily paid. When all was said and done, I saved some grateful parents $7,000 and taught them a good lesson. They promised not to trust their son, or sign anything for him until they got him professional help to beat his drug habit.

I paid Dusty a grand, and after reimbursing myself for the informant fees and out-of-pocket expenses, I pocketed a cool $1,500 over and above my share of the original $1,000 bond premium. At that moment, it seemed like enough money for my time and trouble. But before we caught Joey, when I was sweating bullets about paying a $10,000 loss, I gladly would have given his parents back their premium and my $1,500 bonus, and not written his bond. But like Mickey always said, "If you're not willing to take the risk, become a plumber."

This case was a good example of how the bail bond business really works. I spend twenty-four hours a day, seven days a week, including holidays, getting deadbeats and some straight guys out of jail. Then, when one of these pillars of the community fails to appear, you spend every bit of extra time you have over the next ninety days hoping you find them, or hoping they get re-arrested by the police before that time is up. This, by the way, are the only two legitimate ways the court will exonerate your bond. And if you don't find them, the police doesn't arrest them, or your attorney doesn't figure a way to make it all disappear, you end up paying the full $10,000.

However, since some of my clients tried to screw me by running off after I help them get out of jail, I didn't give a rat's ass who located them, or how they turned up. You know, *Dead or Alive*! Either way, I was off the hook. As far as the extra money I collected on these cases, that's what I called protection money—payment for protecting co-signers, friends and family, those good people trying to do the right thing by helping a friend or family member get out of jail. They don't deserve to lose tens of thousands of dollars just because they had faith in my client's innocence, or his promise to show up in court. But they should lose just enough to teach them a lesson. If that doesn't sit well, try this: It's blood money. I earned my money for being on call 24/7, 365 days a year, not for sweating blood. But that's exactly what happened to me every time some asshole client failed to appear. I would start sweating blood.

CHAPTER

#18

During my many tours through the topless joints, I met a lot of girls. Some worked in the clubs; others hung around for the music and fun. Then there were those looking to give some old drunk a quickie in exchange for enough money to buy a quick fix of coke or heroine. They all knew me, or at least knew what I did for a living. So they never hit on me because they knew I was strictly business, and I never messed around with potential customers.

But most of the girls wanted to be friends, in case they or their boyfriends needed my professional services. Two of them, hookers from a whorehouse in Lovelock, attached themselves to me like glue every time they came to town. All they wanted was companionship; someone to show them around town on their nickel, not mine, which I never allowed or accepted. I never wanted to be indebted to a potential client.

The girls just wanted to go dancing, shoot pool, have dinner or get a little drunk. They never wanted sex. They got enough of that at work. Every three weeks, when they came to town, I took them around to all the clubs. We usually had a lot of laughs, but mostly we all appreciated the break from our normal routine.

I had a policy to never ask the girls their real names, except when one of them needed a bail bond or wanted to rent one of my units. That's because the police always booked individuals under their real name, and their customers knew them only by their working names. I used a girl's real name when she rented one of my units to ensure her privacy. If she wanted friends to visit, she would be the one giving them her unit number, not me. This went for all the girls, including those working the streets, clubs, and topless joints. As a result, I had first names only for these two, which was more than enough. One went by Bambi, because someone told her she looked as innocent as the fawn in the popular children's movie. She was petite, slim, and cute as a button. She had little freckles on her cheeks and nose and was very playful, so the name really fit her.

The other girl, Marlene, was a tall blond, and built like some of the showgirls from Vegas. But since we never got intimate, I never knew if what she had going for her was real or silicone. She was a little older than Bambi, acted more mature, and was more attractive, but she couldn't dance a lick, on stage or off. Although she gave the impression of being a hard ass, she was a soft, sensible person.

She had a boyfriend old enough to be her father. His name was Tony. I never knew, nor did I need to know, his last name. He owned and managed one of the gentlemen's clubs on Lake Street. It was a place where a guy who was willing to spend a chunk of money could find a girl and a private booth in a dark corner. You never bought sexual favors from the girl, you bought her champagne. But you always got what you paid for. The more you spent on drinks, the more you got, if you get my drift. That's how Tony got his cut from the girls, and the police couldn't arrest him for pimping, because he was only selling drinks. What the girls did in those booths was their business.

Tony was an Italian Mafia-type guy—one of the "Bada Bing Bada Boom" kind from New Jersey. A real stand-up guy who occasionally needed my services, not for himself, but for a few of the bodyguard-bouncer boys from his club. They'd occasionally get arrested for beating the shit out of a customer who manhandled one of Tony's girls, or tried to get more than the amount of champagne they'd bought. Most of the charges against his bodyguards were dismissed for lack of evidence, or the victim never showed in court to testify against them.

Over time, Tony and I became fairly good friends. I said he was a stand-up guy because he'd co-sign for a lot of his guys, and if any of them ever failed to appear, he'd send some of his other boys out looking for them; or he'd pay off their bond if one of them needed to get lost.

Tony introduced me to Marlene and Bambi. He knew I was on the mend from my latest relationship, so he liked the idea that I only wanted companionship. This made me a safe date for them. He also knew I could handle myself pretty well, so they, too, would be safe.

Bambi and Marlene lived with Tony when they were in Reno, so they never needed a place to stay or to rent. Although I got the feeling that Bambi wanted to be more than casual friends, I tried never to spend more than a few hours with them on any given evening. Most of the time, I'd get a legit bond call and drop them off at Tony's on my way to the jail.

When Bambi occasionally started getting a little too serious about us, I'd excuse myself from the table, call my answering service from the payphone, and ask the switchboard gal to page me in about ten minutes so I could get away without hurting her feelings. These two girls were a great break from thinking about Misty and feeling sorry for myself, but I wasn't interested in getting involved again, nor did I want to disrupt my friendship with Tony.

One day, I ran into one of my tenants as she was crossing the street. A quick glance revealed multiple bruises covering the exposed parts of her arms, neck, and face. She looked like she'd been run over by a bus. I found out later she'd run into her boyfriend's fist.

I started asking around to ensure that he was, in fact, her boyfriend, and that he wasn't breaking my tenant rules. If he wasn't with her, I wanted to make sure he wasn't causing problems with any of the other tenants. The answer was always, "Not that I know of," or, "I'm not really sure if he's even staying in one of your units, Lefty." But from their tone, it appeared that everyone I talked to was afraid of him or didn't like him. I let it slide, but I started paying closer attention to what was going on and tried to spend as much time as I could around the units.

A few days later, the same girl came running across the street crying and yelling, "He's got a gun! He's going to kill me!"

As she ran up to my porch, I came out of my office, grabbed her by both arms, looked her in the eyes and said, "Go upstairs to Kitty's apartment—NOW!" As she headed for the steps, I said, "Close and lock the door behind you, and tell Kitty not to open it, come out, or let anyone else in, until I come and get both of you."

She did exactly as I said. I was standing outside on the top step of the porch. This placed me about 18 inches above the sidewalk. I stood and waited with my hands at my sides, but clearly visible from the street. So if he headed my way, he would see I was unarmed.

When he appeared, I watched him closely as he staggered in my direction. He was yelling, "Where are you, you little bitch? I'll find you." By his gait, I could tell that he'd had way too much to drink—or snort. He was carrying a gun in his right hand and moving toward me, but definitely not in a straight line.

The next part came easier than I expected. When he made it across the street I'd positioned myself in the middle of the top step. As he moved within range, without saying a single word, I kicked him as hard as I could, square in the nuts. He doubled over and grabbed himself with both hands, while struggling to hold onto his gun. I reached out, grabbed his shoulders, and, while pulling his upper body forward, I smashed my knee into his face. The force not only broke his nose, it literally flattened it all over his face. At the moment of impact, I let go with both hands, and sent him flying flat onto his back. He was out cold, but I wasn't finished.

My adrenaline was rushing full speed as I walked over, picked up his small-caliber pistol by the barrel and placed it back into his right hand. I put his index finger on the trigger, put my index finger over his, aimed the gun down the front of his leg, cocked the hammer and pulled the trigger. He didn't even flinch when the bullet ripped off the upper corner of his shoe, about where his little toe would have been. From where I was kneeling, it looked like the poor guy had accidentally shot himself in the foot.

I rolled him over on his side, just far enough to reach his wallet. I took it out of his pants, rolled him back, checked his front pockets, and took the key he had from the girl's unit. My goal was to ensure that, before I called the police, I erased any connection he might have with me, my units, or the girl upstairs.

I returned to my office, washed my hands, and changed my clothes as quickly as I could to ensure that I had no blood or gun residue splattered anywhere on me. This took about two or three minutes. Then, I called the police.

They immediately dispatched two officers. I saw them run out of the police station and head toward my office, guns drawn. In the short time it took them to reach the building, I was able to run up the stairs, yell for Kitty to open the door, and told her to "hide these," as I handed her the guy's wallet and his keys.

"The police are on their way, so, whatever you do, don't answer the door if anyone knocks. I don't want them to know you're home. Don't go near the windows or let that girl out of your sight until they're gone; and for God's sake, don't make a sound. I'll be back to explain everything later."

The police reviewed the scene, called for an ambulance, and began questioning me. I explained, "I heard someone ranting and raving; I looked out of my window and saw him. He'd apparently been drinking or was high on drugs, and he started walking toward my building. That's when I saw he had a gun in his hand. I lost sight of him for a minute, which is when he must have tried to climb the front steps, lost his footing, fell forward, and hit his face on the railing. This likely knocked him dizzy and he fell backward onto the sidewalk. His gun discharged, and he may have accidentally shot himself in the leg or foot, since there's blood on the sidewalk."

One officer asked me if I'd ever seen him around, or if he was a client.

"No, I've never seen him before; I have no idea where he came from."

About that time, the ambulance arrived, and the medics began bandaging "John Doe." After a few minutes, he started to wake up, so they sedated him while they finished bandaging his wounds. About the time they finished, I completed my statement for the police, and asked one of the medics for an update on his condition. They said he was lucky; his nose was broken in a few places, but it would heal; however, he had managed to shoot off part of his little toe. We all kind of laughed, including the cops, as he was loaded into the ambulance, which took him to Washoe Medical Center.

The police thanked me for calling, and for the information. They said they'd follow up with him whenever the doctors determined he was well enough to make a statement; probably in a few days. They said I could check with them if I was interested in knowing who he was, where he was from, and where he might be living. Since he was the only one involved or injured, they didn't feel it was a high priority, or required any immediate follow-up, so they returned to the station to file their report.

When they were out of sight, I went upstairs and explained what went on. I asked Kitty if the girl could move in with her for a few days while I packed up her boyfriend's stuff and took it to him at the hospital. Both girls were topless dancers working at the same club, and Kitty had an extra bedroom, so it seemed like a reasonable request. Later that day, Dusty and I cleaned out the guy's stuff. Dusty took the girl's belonging's to Kitty's and I took the guy's stuff, including his wallet, to my office.

The next day, I went to the hospital to visit "Mr. Doe." I went early enough to ensure that I arrived before the police, so I continued to use Mr. Doe, even though I knew his real name from looking in his wallet. Entering his room, I could tell he was still in a lot of pain, but able to talk. He asked who I was, and if I knew what happened. I told him the same story

I'd told the police—with one exception. I told him who I was, and I explained that he was no longer welcome at my place, nor was he welcome in or around the club where his now-ex girlfriend worked.

I gave him his stuff, including his wallet. He said he remembered having a lot more money in it; but must have lost it gambling and drinking. I knew better. I'd removed three hundred dollars and planned to give it to his ex-girlfriend when I returned to the office. I was sure it was probably hers, anyway.

He understood about not returning to her place, and said he was leaving for his parents' house in Southern California, as soon as he could check out of the hospital.

Because the police hadn't shown up yet, and they hadn't placed a police hold on him, I offered to take him to Western Union so he could pick up the money he'd asked his family to wire him in care of their office, and then to the Greyhound bus depot to catch his bus. He accepted. His parents had already arranged to take care of the hospital bill, so checking out went fast.

I thought, the quicker he's gone, the quicker we can all put this behind us. Keep in mind, he didn't remember a thing, since he was too drunk and too battered to even talk.

I guess his girlfriend wasn't the only one that dodged a bullet from that event. I lucked out too. It appeared that no one saw what happened; at least, that's what everyone told the police. The cops simply closed the case because no one else was involved, and their suspect, or victim, had already left town.

The next day, the girl came downstairs to thank me for helping her. I learned her name was Sherri. She said Dusty and Kitty explained everything, including her boyfriend's quick decision to leave town, so she thanked me for that as well. While Dusty knew every detail about what happened that day, I wasn't sure if Kitty or Sherri knew about the depth of my participation in his decision to leave.

I gave her the three hundred I'd lifted from her ex-boyfriend's wallet. This brought a tear to her eye just before she kissed me on the cheek. She said Kitty had asked her to move in with her and Dusty, since they had the extra bedroom, and it would cut their monthly expense. Dusty didn't object, so she agreed.

CHAPTER

#19

Between looking for new clients at the topless joints, using Dusty to help chase bad guys, and Sherri living upstairs I found myself running into her often. She was still a little shaky over the frightening incident. Naturally, Dusty, Kitty, Sherri and I started hanging out together whenever we could, strictly as friends. We also started to party a lot.

Sherri and I had no interest in getting involved and didn't give a shit about doing anything except developing a pleasant, but platonic, relationship. We were looking to help each other through the rough spots and get our lives back on track, nothing more . . . no heavy lifting. At least, that's the way I felt.

After about three months, Dusty decided to ask Kitty to marry him—or that was the storyline he was trying to peddle. The truth (according to Sherri) was that Kitty told him, "Marry me, or move out." Although he provided her with an engagement ring, they couldn't agree on a date for the wedding. That didn't stop them from talking about it every day.

I think all their marriage talk made Sherri start thinking about her future as well, and she began to focus more and more attention on me. It was more than I wanted, and I had no problem explaining that to her. I think she was lonesome for some intimate affection, and I was not interested, or willing, to provide it. So we continued to remain friends for the time being.

One night, about six weeks later, when both girls were off work, the four of us went to dinner, did a little dancing, and ended up having a few too many cocktails. Before we knew it, we were on our way to a wedding chapel in Carson City. Dusty and Kitty finally decided to tie the knot. After weeks of arguing about a date, they said, "Let's do it right now . . . you two can be our witnesses!" Since Sherri and I were tired of listening to them argue, we were happy to oblige. Nevada is the perfect spot for spontaneous weddings, as marriage licenses are provided on the spot.

The next thing I knew, I woke up nude in my own apartment, and in my own bed, with Sherri wrapped in my arms, naked as well. As I jumped out of bed and tripped onto the floor, I yelled, "What the hell happened last night?"

She laughed and said, "Don't you remember? We were witnesses at Dusty and Kitty's wedding, and they were witnesses for ours!"

I started to laugh. "Very funny. Now tell me, what happened?"

She repeated the story. I grabbed my clothes and hopped upstairs to confront Kitty and Dusty. I was still hopping around the corridor, trying to put my pants on, when Dusty opened the door. "What the hell's going on out here?" he asked.

I screamed, "What the hell happened last night?"

He laughed, repeated Sherri's story, and handed me our marriage license, which he and Kitty had held onto for safekeeping.

"No way! You let me get married, you asshole? Are you nuts? Shit! This can't be happening. I can't be married to someone I hardly know, and especially to someone I definitely don't love."

He said, "Too bad! You are, whether you like it or not. That's what you get for persuading me to marry Kitty."

I went back downstairs and asked Sherri to please get dressed and go upstairs to her apartment. After she left, I headed straight for Mom's house hoping to find some sympathy and advice on what the hell I should do next.

Mom, who was like Mother Teresa—but without the nun's habit or any miracles to her name—proceeded to recite the holy vows of matrimony, including "until death do us part." I knew she wanted me to settle down, and I was sure she decided this might be what she'd been praying for these past few years. Little did she know my new wife was a non-Catholic topless dancer in one of the local clubs.

She said nothing close to what I wanted to hear. I needed time to weigh my options. Packing my bags and skipping town was the first thing that came to mind, but I ruled it out. After all, I was only twenty-seven, and had amassed a small fortune in real estate and two bail businesses. I started to evaluate the pros and cons of what happened, first from a personal perspective, then from a professional one.

The personal plan came easy. Although Sherri appeared to be a nice enough person, I needed to show Mom that my new wife was no saint. In fact, she was a topless dancer who flopped her tits in the faces of local drunks hoping they'd tuck dollar bills into her panties. Then I could tell Mom we'd been drunk when we got married, and that she wasn't the girl I loved, nor was she the one I wanted to marry. But I stopped there, because the girl I loved and wanted to marry had dumped me to become a high-class hooker. This was something I hadn't told anyone, especially Mom, and I wasn't going to now.

After some serious thought, I decided that telling Mom all this right after breaking the news that I was married would start her thinking I'd been possessed by the devil, and she'd probably call one of her Catholic priest friends to perform an exorcism on me.

After about ten seconds of seriously considering offering Sherri a few hundred bucks, or even a thousand bucks, to ease her pain, and given the fact that my new wife and I weren't married in the church, or by a Catholic priest, I thought I might even be able to make Mom smile by telling her all this. Instead I decided to consider what I believed to be my only reasonable alternative: I began weighing the pros and cons of this sham marriage from a business perspective.

The cons came to mind first. I was married to someone I liked as a friend but did not love. She was someone I would never have considered marrying under the best of circumstances, let alone doing it when I was drunk. But she was attractive enough, especially if I could convince her to dress for success and abandon the hot pants.

She also appeared intelligent enough to help me collect rent and answer the bail phones; God only knew how much help I needed. Taking the bail calls, completing the paperwork, and chasing skips for my two bail agencies every single day was hard enough, but factoring my twenty-four apartments into the equation made it more than any one person could handle.

So after assessing my professional situation and considering the possibilities of finding someone who wouldn't steal me blind or turn me in for misappropriating collateral or fixing files, I came up with a plan. It wasn't one of my better plans, but it sounded good at the time.

I'd almost finished remodeling the living quarters at the Jet Motel. I decided Sherri and I could move in there. I'd intended to eventually move into the manager's apartment anyway. Now I could rent out my current office/apartment across the street. And since I'd been thinking seriously about hiring someone to help me collect rent and answer the business phones, why not train my new wife, and keep the money in the family?

Despite this plan, I remained stunned by my recklessness. Yesterday, I was young, single, and well on my way to financial security. Today, I'm married and have absolutely no idea where I'm going or what I'm doing. But this option seemed to be the best I could do, at least for the time being.

It's not that Sherri was a bad girl, or that being a topless dancer was unacceptable. Nor did I care about being her third husband (after she admitted she'd been married twice before). I just didn't want to marry anyone other than Misty. So without having discussed the situation or attempting to arrive at a better option, my new wife and I settled into our refurbished apartment above the motel office.

Sherri learned faster than I expected. She took care of collecting and banking all the rents and did an even better job of answering the two bail phones and keeping the incoming call registers straight for each office. She put my old professional answering services to shame.

With Sherri running the office, and Dusty doing most of the preliminary work on my fugitives, I kept busy promoting the bail business. Although my life had taken such an unforeseen, unplanned, and personally unsatisfying turn, all my business ventures, the apartments, the motel, and my two bail operations were exceeding my financial expectations.

A year later, Mom told me she was tired of taking care of the three-bedroom house my dad and his brother had built, but failed to finish, before he split. Now, living alone, she realized the house was way too big and expensive for her. So I made her a deal she couldn't refuse. I bought the house, for the full appraised value. My attorney drew up the real estate documents at no charge, and we didn't use a realtor, so Mom received more cash than she'd expected.

Before we closed escrow, she and I shopped around and found a brand new, two-bedroom, one-bath condominium with a fireplace in the living room, a nice-size kitchen, and a separate little laundry room. It was just what she needed, and less than a mile from her current neighborhood. She could shop at the same stores and pray in the same church. It turned out to be a great deal for her, because her new homeowner's association took care of the yard and outside maintenance. This meant she only had to worry about the inside, but since I bought her new furniture, and the builder provided all built-in appliances, she ended up with zero worries.

As a bonus, my buddy Roy bought a unit in the same complex and agreed to keep an eye on Mom. He said, "It's no big deal, since the front entrance to my place is across the sidewalk from hers. Hell, if I'm lucky, I might even get a free breakfast from her every now and then, like I did when we lived next door in the old neighborhood."

I, on the other hand, ended up with an old, three-bedroom house with one-and-a-half-baths and an acre of grass. It required a lot of tender loving care and hands-on work. I know it sounds like I made a bad deal, but it gave me something to do. It was an opportunity to take periodic breaks from the business, the office, and an unwanted marital situation. Even though my wife tried everything she could to make our marriage as nice for me as possible for the first year or so, I wasn't happy. And by this time, Sherri was so entrenched in the business that I couldn't afford to get an annulment or a divorce and start looking all over again for someone to help me.

Since I was just about finished fixing up the inside of the house, I started buying new appliances, new carpets, painting the place inside and out, and landscaping the entire acre lot. I was eager to rent it out to a young couple I'd recently met. They had numerous friends and business associates and entertained regularly; they often invited us to dine and dance with them and their many acquaintances.

Soon after renting out my mom's house to Jill and Marty, I began making even more money. Not because my attitude changed about bumping elbows with the social set, or the new referrals I got from some of them, but because Sherri was taking care of the paperwork and deposits, and Dusty was working most of my skips.

Their help provided me with time on my hands; time I used to work on future business plans—until one day, out of the blue, Sherri told me she was pregnant! I couldn't believe I was in for another life-changer.

Although we were not in love, we still had sex occasionally, but my heart was never in it, and neither was hers. The thought of having a baby never crossed my mind. I guess I assumed she was taking the necessary precautions to ensure against it. To this day, I believe she allowed herself to get pregnant as a form of insurance against losing the comfortable lifestyle she had going.

I had to shit-can all the future plans I had been working on, and start factoring in what to do, if anything, with an expanded family.

It was also time for Sherri to start coming clean about her past.

I'd learned about her previous marriages right after our marriage, which didn't help my attitude with the situation. But had I known then that she also had full custody of a daughter (she'd left the child in her mother's care) from one of those marriages, I'm sure I would have filed for an annulment.

I felt trapped and needed someone to talk to. Someone, anyone, other than my wife.

CHAPTER

#20

Mom told me to "do the right thing." She said I might not like it, but my baby-to-be had a half-sister; I needed to talk to my wife about raising them together.

Being married was bad enough; being too drunk to see it coming made it even worse. But this? Had I been sober, I guarantee you things would have been different. But now, I was not only married, but I was also an expectant father. This was the scariest thing that had ever happened to me. It made chasing fugitives feel like a walk in the park. The thought of having to face the responsibility of a child was overwhelming. And because I wasn't sure I was ready, willing, or able to handle a child, having the responsibility for two children was utterly unimaginable.

Don't get me wrong. Being a father could turn out to be a blessing. The problem wasn't becoming a father, it was my wife. She wasn't the person I would have chosen to be the mother of my baby. What's more, I was still coming to terms with the bombshell that my wife already had a child from a previous marriage and that she had pushed that child onto her mother while she went out and partied. I couldn't believe how bad this situation and my life had become as a result of one stupid, drunken night on the town.

After some soul searching, I determined that Mom was right. There was no way I could leave the baby's half-sister with her grandmother after our baby was born. Nor could I get an annulment or divorce; I couldn't break up my family.

First, I had to step up and stop whining. Then I had to hunt for a new home, one large enough to accommodate my new family. There was no way the four of us could continue living in a one-bedroom manager's apartment. The final and hardest thing on my list was finding a replacement for Sherri—not as a wife, but as my business assistant. I refused to give her an excuse to skate her responsibilities as a mother again, this time for two kids, by saying we needed to hire a nanny because she had to continue working.

Although I had months to locate and train someone, I felt it was going to take much longer to trust that special someone with access to all the information and personal contacts outlined in client case files, not to mention information on court corruption schemes, the misappropriation of collateral, and padding of my fugitive apprehension billings.

Sherri and I found a new three-bedroom, three-bath home in a recently developed subdivision close to Mom's current condo in Sparks. These were new homes, and financing was easily available, with low monthly payments. Qualifying was a breeze, thanks in part to the cash flow from my rentals and some fancy manipulation of collateral deposits. Closing took thirty days, and we moved in shortly after. Since both our extended families lived in the Reno–Sparks area, it wasn't necessary to save one of the bedrooms for company, so we converted one of the two smaller bedrooms into a nursery for the baby, and the other into a bedroom for the baby's four-year-old sister.

From all outward appearances, we looked and acted like a happy little family, but we weren't. Being pregnant and having to take responsibility for her other daughter was hard on Sherri. And commuting back and forth to the office, the different jails, and back home at all hours of the day and night was an intolerable drag on me. In addition, Sherri's daughter, Ann, had a hard time adjusting to being away from her grandma, especially at bedtime. Sherri's adjustment to having Ann around 24/7 was also tough. By the time our baby was due to arrive, we were all ready for a break from each other.

When Sherri went to the hospital, her mother, Florence, took Ann back to her house, and I went out and got drunk with Roy. Sherri's labor lasted almost forty-eight hours; she spent an additional three days in the hospital recovering from a tough delivery. I couldn't stand sitting around the hospital day and night, waiting for the arrival of our child, so I had the answering service page me on false bail calls. This gave me an opportunity to come and go as I pleased, while Sherri's mother stayed with her, and Ann stayed with "Grandpa" Floyd, Flo's boyfriend of eight years, and eventual husband-to-be.

The first night, while Sherri was in early labor, her mother hung around the hospital. She planned to say until the baby arrived. Roy and I went out and hit some of our favorite joints. Before long, we bumped into one of his old girlfriends, who introduced us to her new roommate, Nikki. Nikki was attractive, single, had no boyfriend, and looking to have fun. After dancing and drinking for a few hours, I suggested renting a two-bedroom suite at Harrah's new hotel to continue our party with a little more privacy. Everybody was in.

After a night of unbelievable ecstasy with Nikki, one like I hadn't had since the night before Misty dumped me for her new career, Nikki woke to the beep of my pager, rolled over and kissed me, handed me the phone and headed to the bathroom. When I called in, I learned I was the proud father of a daughter, and that my wife was looking for me.

I told Nikki I had to run to the hospital to see my new baby, but I wanted to see her later. She said, "No, just go and be a good father." I left after telling her how much I enjoyed her company, and that I'd be back.

After visiting with Sherri for a few hours and arriving at the name Ella for our new daughter, I left the hospital in search of Roy. When I found him, he said Nikki didn't want to see me again; she didn't date married men. I said, "Take me to your girlfriend's house so I can talk to Nikki." As we drove up, Nikki came out and told me she wasn't interested in breaking up a family and asked me to leave. I told her everything: how I'd ended up married, how unhappy I was, and what a stupid mistake I'd made. Nothing worked. She went back in the house without saying goodbye, and she left for Sacramento the next day. I never saw her again, but I never forgot her, or that night.

In late 1972, just after Ella's first birthday, we decided to move into a new home. This one also had three bedrooms, but the rest of the house was much larger. It had a family room connected to the kitchen and a nice fireplace. Now, counting mom's old house, which was still rented to the young couple, I owned three houses, nine apartments, a 15-unit motel, and two bail bond businesses. Not bad for a twenty-eight-year-old kid with no college degree.

But then, out of nowhere, all my real problems began. Sherri's mother got in a big fight together, and after almost ten years with him, she walked out. With no money, and nowhere to go, she landed on our doorstep, baggage and all.

Sherri moved her four-year-old into the nursery with the new baby and gave the newly vacated room to her mom. Shortly after Flo moved in, the two started acting more like sisters, rather than mother and daughter. They went shopping, exchanged clothes, and God only knows what else.

Sherri started buying her mom similar hot-pants outfits, and the two started going out on the town while I was working. They left the kids home with a neighborhood babysitter. Every so often, Roy and I would run into Sherri and Flo downtown. After a while, Roy and Flo became an item. She was a nice looking, forty-five-year-old woman, and he was a young buck looking to be tamed. What a pair.

This started out well but ended terribly. When I asked Sherri and Flo to stop going out, they started drinking at home. It got to the point where they were buying half-gallon bottles of vodka by the case and getting shit-faced from noon on, almost every day.

That's when Roy told me he wanted nothing more to do with Flo, and he stopped coming over. One day, shortly after Roy stopped coming over, I came home to find the two women passed out on the couch. Ann, the five-year-old half-sister, had been left to care for the baby. That was it. I went upstairs, grabbed all of Flo's clothes from the closet and the dresser, and tossed them out the window, onto the front lawn. I went downstairs, called Floyd, and asked him to come and get her. Then I woke them both up, grabbed Flo by the arm and tossed her out on the lawn with her clothes.

I said, "Floyd's on his way to pick you up, so gather your clothes before I throw them in the trash."

Back in the house, I told Sherri, "I've had it with you and your drunken lifestyle, not to mention your total neglect of our daughters. If you say one word, I'll load you and your clothes into Floyd's car and you can live with them permanently."

From that day on, Sherri's mom lived with Floyd—until he passed away from liver failure some years later. And I know for a fact that Flo never wore hot pants again.

Sherri stopped drinking and started acting like a real mom, but our relationship with each other, and my relationship with her mom, were never the same.

Beyond all this drama at home, I began having problems at work. To begin with, two of Mickey's Las Vegas bail agents, his two buddies I trained back when they were looking for new, "legit" careers, were arrested in an FBI sting operation. They were charged with bribing a Las Vegas municipal judge. The two, together with a third agent from a different Las Vegas bail agency, were caught paying a local judge to exonerate bonds that the three were responsible to pay off.

I later learned that all three agreed to surrender their bail licenses and testify against the judge in exchange for immunity from prosecution. While good news travels fast, bad news travels even faster. The insurance commissioner's office in Carson City and the municipal courts in Reno caught wind of the scandal.

When the news hit Carson City, the commissioner started his own investigation—into the entire Las Vegas bail industry. During the inquiry, his investigators stepped on the toes of some guys sent from back East to keep public awareness of crime at a minimum. Rumor had it that shortly after they all met, the investigators were too intimidated or too scared to move forward with any additional complaints. Rumor also had it that one of the informants in the pending FBI investigation mysteriously disappeared and had not been heard from since.

However, when news regarding the same cases hit Reno, the city's chief municipal judge started making waves about the "illegal" practice of cop-out sheets being used by bail agents to enter pleas and pay fines for defendants who failed to appear or were told their appearance was unnecessary. He ordered all city judges to cease honoring cop-outs and instructed all court clerks to start sending copies of all notices of forfeiture to the insurance companies, as well as the bail agents, on every case—not just those where defendants had willfully failed to appear.

Since my office used more of these forms than all the other bail agents combined, my agencies were in serious financial jeopardy. The judge's order meant I'd have to surrender every client who failed to appear, because I could no longer use my pre-arranged cop-out agreements on their behalf.

It also meant that after surrendering them, I'd also have to return their $200 deposit, because I failed to meet the terms of our deal. The worst part was that if I was unsuccessful in surrendering any client in a timely manner, I'd have to pay the full amount of their bond rather than the normal $25 fine. I'd be required to pay $1,000 to the court on every client I was unable to find, or I'd forfeit my license until they were all paid.

I protested the immediate implementation of this policy through my lawyer, Dennis Harper. His plea at the municipal court level fell on deaf ears. So I asked him to apply for a restraining order against the municipal judges in district court, which he did. We thought it was a longshot, but to our surprise, it was granted. It forced the municipal judges to honor the standing practice of accepting pleas and fine payments from bail agents on all bonds posted prior to the date of the restraining order, thus limiting the implementation of the municipal court's new policy to future bonds only. As this was a blanket order, it covered all bail bond agencies operating in Reno, not just mine.

After Mickey heard the news, he called and said we needed to talk. He suggested we meet in private, maybe at his house, because he thought his office might be bugged. Although I found his comment about bugging a little unnerving, I agreed and immediately drove out to his ranch.

After chasing his wild turkeys away from my car, the ones he'd trained as watchdogs, Mickey thanked me for coming out, invited me into the kitchen, and offered me a beer. He asked whether I'd heard the latest about what was happening in Vegas. I said I had, but I'd been too busy trying to salvage my own ass in Reno, so I hadn't paid much attention to anything else, especially as far away as Vegas. That's when he dropped the first bombshell.

He told me that the FBI or the Department of Justice, he wasn't sure which, was acting in unison with the Nevada Department of Insurance regarding allegations involving Las Vegas bail agents and their attorneys attempting to bribe court officials.

He said that two out of the three agents involved were his: Duke Porter, the one I had trained, and one of Duke's buddies. (I assumed it was Corey.) And even though I no longer officially worked for him, my bail agencies continued to transact business directly through his general agency. He felt we'd both be called on the carpet to explain the actions of these individuals.

"I feel it's in both our interests to provide a unified position, rather than starting to point fingers at each other in an attempt to shift blame," Mickey said.

These thoughts had already been racing through my mind. Mickey was my friend, my coach, and my most trusted mentor. He knew that even though I let him down once, I'd never do it again, even if it meant taking a fall for him. I needed to know just how bad things were; if anyone else was involved besides Duke and his helper, and what Mickey was suggesting we do next.

That's when he dropped the second bombshell.

"Look, kid, at this point, the investigations are limited to Vegas, as are the indictments and arrests that undoubtably will follow. But in light of the court decision regarding the elimination of cop-out sheets in Reno, they must be getting insider information from some asshole in Vegas. Some little prick within the inner circle of that investigation must be trying to make a name for himself by passing information about what they've uncovered down there to someone in Reno. It's probably some asshole buddy he met at one of those worthless court employee conventions. I'm guessing that jerk-off informed the chief municipal judge here in Reno, who immediately started to clean up the local court's act. The judge is concerned that the practice of using cop-out sheets, on its face, could appear as corruption. Fortunately, the way things are going, the Feds appear to be after the judges in Vegas, more so than the bail agents. That's probably why the judges in Reno are concerned.

"If we, or more importantly, you, push it any harder," he continued, "it could broaden the investigation here in Reno, which could sink the entire business on a statewide basis. We need to tread lightly and coordinate our actions against the local court."

As for Las Vegas, Mickey felt Corey could be next, because he was sure he and Duke were both involved.

From the way Mickey was talking, it seemed like after he and I split, he'd paid little or no attention to what was going on in his retail agencies, especially those in Vegas. He was more interested in developing his wholesale general agency business, sponsoring agents throughout Nevada and Northern California, while taking a percentage off the top from each one of them. Being a general agent meant that Mickey was acting as a "reinsurer" for smaller individual bail agents. His new position didn't require much work. He merely sat in his office, waited for the mail, had his staff process the agents' weekly reports, deposit the money, send the agents more blank bonds and pay the insurance companies their share. And then Mickey pocketed his share. This is exactly what he was doing with me, just on a much more profitable basis, since I was the largest producer in his stable of agencies throughout California and Nevada.

The fact was, Mickey enjoyed the G.A. business so much that he'd turned over his own retail agency in Reno to one of his buddies; the agent he hired to replace me after my fall from grace as a result of my relationship with his stepdaughter.

His lack of interest in what his retail agents were doing is what got us into this mess, and now it was all he could do to weather the storm and save his ass. His license, his agencies, and his new general agency were all on the line, and so were mine.

As fate would have it, we both came out unscathed. The criminal investigations were limited to Las Vegas, thanks to the bail agents who took immunity and testified against the judge. Earlier on, I believed the Feds would come after the bail agents and offer the judges the deal. I was wrong. When push came to shove, the Feds went after the judges who'd turned a blind eye to what was going on or were participating in the corruption of the justice system. Either way, it gave the bail agents a chance to skate on criminal charges.

However, the financial losses that hit the Las Vegas agencies as a result of this one case were felt by many agencies throughout Nevada. After years of posting bonds based on their ability to pay off clerks and judges, rather than underwriting them properly, in an effort to regain financial control of their businesses, many Nevada bail agents were now faced with paying tens of thousands of dollars in forfeited bonds, in addition to apprehension costs and the investigative fees they paid out attempting to hunt down flaky clients all over the country.

In fact, to ward off bankruptcy, many agencies across the state had to terminate their secretaries, bounty hunters, and relief agents. Others were forced to closeup shop and look for jobs.

One day in early 1974, Mickey called with some more bad news: He was right about Corey. The financial pressures Corey faced because of what happened to the bail business forced him back into his old career of burglarizing homes, as he tried to meet his financial obligations to the courts and his family.

He started traveling out of state, hitting homes of the rich and famous in Arizona and California. On one of those trips, he was shot and killed by an Arizona homeowner while attempting to break into the guy's house. The homeowner was supposed to be out of town, but Corey's information, or misinformation, proved fatal.

As for me, Dennis won the first round in our case against the municipal court. The superior court judge in Reno issued a temporary stay order. This automatically reinstated the existing cop-out sheets already on file in municipal court, but only on those cases where the surety bail bonds were posted prior to the date of the municipal judge's order to reject them. Everything the agents wrote after that date fell under the new rule.

Thanks to Dennis, the superior court judge set the hearing dates far enough in advance to ensure that most of the pending municipal cases would be heard prior to his having to make a ruling on my suit. This made the issue on the existing bonds moot, because we always filed our cop-out slips and paid the defendant's fines within forty-five days of their arrest.

My suit really pissed off the municipal court judges, which placed me, and the long-term future of my two bail agencies, in financial jeopardy. I knew they would start ruling against me on any and every motion for extension of time whenever I needed it to find my skips. I also knew they wouldn't give me credit for expenses paid out on my failed attempts to find fugitives.

Padding the expense reports I attached to many of Dennis's motions and finding additional skips through the extensions of time were important parts of my future financial success; especially since the use of cop-out sheets were no longer an option. Losing all three options meant the loss of a large portion of my ill-gotten gains, leaving me to rely entirely on writing only low-risk bonds, taking full collateral, collecting premiums, and listing expenses that would be regularly scrutinized by the Department of Insurance.

Because I really pissed off the municipal judges, their friends in the clerk's offices, the local police, and many of the city officials, my future in the retail bail business, at least in Reno and Las Vegas, was dubious at best. It didn't take me long to decide on a course of action: I had to sell my bail businesses and reinvest the proceeds into more income properties, then let the turmoil surrounding the bail business cool off.

I was forced to begin reevaluating my options. I'd retain my bail agent's license, so I wasn't giving up on a business I knew was made for me. I just needed time to regroup and reorganize, financially and personally.

CHAPTER

#21

I'm sure it was Mickey's obsession with securing his new G.A. venture that led to his lack of supervision over the Las Vegas agents, which, in turn, led to many of the industry's statewide problems. But it was also his preoccupation with his current cash flow that got him involved with helping me find a buyer for both of my bail agencies. My two agencies were the two largest in his group, and he needed to protect the profits he was reaping from them.

Over the years, Mickey made many friends on both sides of the law—and all sides of the financial spectrum. It was this exposure to a vast variety of contacts that led us to our primary target. His name was Bernie Adams. He, along with Mickey, was a member of the local Harley Davidson Seniors Motorcycle Club.

Bernie was a perfect prospect. He was a nice guy and a good businessman. He was as honest as the day is long. Considering everything that was happening around me, Bernie was a breath of fresh air.

The days of bail agents making big bucks in Nevada with limited legislative or regulatory supervision were over; or at least stalled until the headlines and investigations died down. Bernie had already made his fortune in the construction business; he was looking for something a little more interesting and exciting. The bail business provided both of those to an extreme. He was already somewhat familiar with bail bonds, as he'd bailed out quite a few of his construction workers through Mickey's office over the years.

Selling my agencies was more of a necessity than an option, and I wanted to stay involved in the industry. Mickey sensed that; he was devoted to helping me find a buyer. He was motivated in part because he needed qualified help to manage his new insurance company and his ongoing managing general agency. But he also knew that before I could give any thought to getting involved in the bail business again, I had to sell off my agencies and rearrange my real estate holdings to ensure my family's financial future.

I needed to liquidate or close out all my outstanding bonds, and Bernie had to agree to assist in that process. This didn't mean he had to pay any of the losses associated with my previous bail bonds. But he needed to process all the correspondence from the different courts and notify me when one of my clients failed to appear and needed to be rescheduled for court, or let me know if and when I needed to apprehend and surrender one of them. It also required that he document all new court dates and provide me with all correspondence associated with my bonds.

Holding, returning, or liquidating collateral for use in satisfying any outstanding financial obligations incurred in connection with one of my bonds remained my primary responsibility. This meant I would be working alongside Bernie for at least another year. As long as I didn't have any significant losses, or was unable to locate my skips, I would be okay. I decided to spend a lot more time chasing down my own skips and deadbeat clients.

Although Dusty did most of the legwork on my skips, we worked as a team when it came to the actual apprehension and surrender. I'd always had his back and he always had mine. But now that Bernie was writing the bonds and collecting the income, and my income was limited, I told Dusty I would be doing the legwork on my own cases and would call him whenever I needed backup. This arrangement worked out fine until the day I decided to go after Taylor Manning, a guy I'd frequently bailed. Manning had always shown up for court when I was running the office, but now, since I was no longer there to help him, he decided it was okay to skip out on his old bonds and stick the losses up my ass. He was wrong, and I intended to show him just how wrong he was.

When I reviewed his file, I noted our history of doing business together. The first bond I wrote for Manning was for assault with intent to commit bodily harm. He'd beaten the shit out of a guy who owed him a bundle. This resulted in the police marking him as "Potentially Dangerous." However, at trial, the judge dismissed the case because the prosecutor couldn't locate his witness. The second bond was for possessing a firearm as an ex-felon. This happened when he was stopped for speeding. The cop found the gun in the trunk. The judge dismissed the case because the arresting officer had no probable cause for the car search, and therefore had needed a warrant.

Because both cases were dismissed, I didn't think I needed to pay someone to tag along while I made an arrest for a simple failure-to-appear on a drug charge.

I found Taylor at his girlfriend's place with a group of friends. They were hanging out in the backyard celebrating a birthday. From the looks of things, they'd been smoking grass, drinking, and popping pills for the better part of the afternoon in hopes, I guess, of reaching some new heavenly high.

When I told Taylor to come with me, a buddy sitting next to him decided I should leave, because they were busy having fun. As Taylor stood up, hoping to show off in front of the girls sitting on the grass behind him, I stomped on his bare foot with my boot as hard as I could, and simultaneously punched him square in the face with my trusty brass knuckles. He fell backward, hard and fast, right into the laps of the girls he was planning to impress. They didn't look very impressed, but they sure looked shocked.

A third guy sitting at the table wanted nothing to do with me. He froze in place as he watched his buddy fall backward onto the girls.

I moved to one side, grabbed my client by the back of his shirt, and proceeded to drag his fat ass out of the gate. I'd learned much earlier that users always protect their stash first, so perhaps the partygoers were relieved when I escorted Taylor out, leaving them with a bigger supply. I didn't expect trouble from anyone left behind.

Taylor was nearly comatose from whatever he'd taken. He was slurring his words and wobbling as we walked, so I relaxed my guard. This resulted in a few tactical errors:

Mistake #1: Thinking that taking custody of a fugitive with little or no trouble meant that handcuffing him wasn't necessary. Wrong.

Mistake #2: Plopping him into the back seat alone, without backup to watch or control him was okay. Wrong again.

Mistake #3: Using a two-door vehicle to transport him to jail was fine. This turned out to be downright stupid.

Talk about falling asleep at the switch. You'd think this was my first rodeo! Any one of these mistakes could have gotten me arrested for assault or, if we fought and he'd died, involuntary manslaughter. Worse yet, since I didn't pat him down or frisk him, I could have ended up dead if he'd had a weapon.

As it was, Taylor came to and became more aware of what was going on. He decided he wanted out of the car. He began pushing the back of the driver's seat forward, forcing me against the steering wheel, while he tried to reach the handle on the driver's door in an all-out effort to open it and escape. He pushed hard enough to pin me against the steering wheel and get the door open, but he wasn't quite able to get out.

Meanwhile, the car was moving, and I was attempting to keep it in the right lane. The only things I could think to do were to try and pull the car door closed with all the strength I could muster, or stop the car, get out as fast as I could, and beat the shit out of this idiot before he had a chance to stand up.

As I was pulling the door closed, I caught the fatty side of his hand between the doorlatch and the jam. He started screaming bloody murder. "My hand, my hand, it's caught in the door!" he yelled as he slumped over in pain.

Instead of stopping the car and releasing his hand, I decided to leave it slammed in the door while I took a leisurely drive to the jail. By the time we got there, he'd passed out again, only now it was from the pain in his hand, not the drugs he'd been using. At the jail, I opened the door, released his hand, cuffed him to the door, and went looking for help to bring him into the booking area.

Once we got him inside, the jailers called for medical assistance and began booking him on the failure-to-appear warrant the judge had issued when he hadn't shown up in court. They started questioning me about the injury to his hand. I said he got it caught in the car door while attempting to escape, so they added a charge of assault with intent to flee to his booking sheet.

On my way out of the station, I stopped by the Narcotics Division and dropped a little hint about the party house I'd busted. I told them the approximate number of guests in attendance and the quantity of drugs on display. It was the least I could do, considering Taylor failed to appear on my bond, and his buddies didn't give a rat's ass about whether I lost money.

When I returned to the car, I started to review my actions. I realized I hadn't even patted him down for a weapon. Had he been carrying a gun, a knife, or another weapon, things could have ended up much differently. I got lucky that day, or Mom's prayers for my safety were working. Either way, I vowed to do a better job of following my self-imposed rules regarding the apprehension of fugitives.

I still had over a million dollars in outstanding bonds, and I was concerned that the amount of my reserve savings Mickey was holding, coupled with the substantial amount of collateral I was holding on these bonds, might not be enough without doing my own skip chasing. I worried that the loss of steady cash flow from my bail agencies would force me to sell some of my properties in order to meet my contractual obligations to Mickey and the insurance company.

To protect my properties while still meeting my obligations, I entertained the thought of having Bernie deposit the monthly payments from the sale of the agencies directly into my reserve account with Mickey, as additional collateral on my contract. Then I'd have my attorney add a provision that allowed all the funds, both from the sale and from the reserves already on deposit, to be returned to me upon the liquidation of my outstanding liabilities under my contract, and in the event of my untimely death, placed into a trust fund for my daughter.

CHAPTER

#22

Within days of closing my deal with Bernie, Sherri's mom called and said that the son of a good friend had been arrested on a high-profile fraud case in Reno, and my help was needed to get him out on bail. His name was Dino Thomas, and he owned a local business called The Auction Barn. It was the only auction house in northern Nevada. Dino's booking sheet listed fifteen counts of possession for sale of stolen property. In addition, the police file stated that Dino was allegedly using his auction business as a front to dispose of stolen artwork, jewelry, and other valuables. His bail was set at $15,000—$1,000 for each of the fifteen counts.

My mother-in-law, Flo, said his family didn't have the money to bail him out, that he and his wife had a young daughter who was about the same age as ours, and that they really needed help. I told Sherri I couldn't help, because I was selling my business. When Flo talked to Sherri again, she begged her to help. In turn, Sherri called and begged me to help.

I'd never considered myself a softy, so don't ask me why I agreed to post this asshole's $15,000 bond. To this day, I have no idea why I did, given the fact that I had never met him or his family, nor did I have previous business dealings with him. Doing something this stupid without collecting any part of the $1,500 premium he needed for bail was something I seldom, if ever, did. To top it off, the only collateral I took was a promissory note from his parents for both his $15K appearance bond and the premium. And, since they couldn't find two nickels to rub together or a pot to piss in, the notes were worthless, and I knew it.

Shortly after Dino was released on bail, I asked Dennis Harper to represent the jerkoff free of charge. Boy, what a mistake.

After a short meeting with the district attorney, Dennis was able to get all the charges against Dino dismissed for lack of evidence, and the $15K bond I wrote was exonerated. I was out only a few hundred bucks in bond cost to Mickey, so I was feeling a lot better about my good deed. However, due to all the bad publicity on TV and in the local papers, Dino's business was ruined, and the lease on the Auction Barn building was cancelled by the landlord.

This happened in late July 1974. In early September, Sherri got another call from her mother. This time, Flo told her that Dino's family was still down and out because of the wrongful arrest, that Dino's reputation and his credit rating were ruined, and that he, his wife, and their new baby had to move in with his parents.

Dino's mother wanted to know if I would loan Dino $3,000 so he could host his annual Christmas toy auction in late fall. His plan was to host the event to raise enough money to pay his bills, feed his family, and pay me the $1,500 bond premium he still owed. Plus, it would hopefully get him back on his feet.

I told Sherri *No!* I'd set a rule long before I met her, never to loan anyone money for any reason. I wanted her to relay that message to her mother and the rest of them. Although the thought of getting my $1,500 sounded pretty good, my gut told me not to push my luck with this guy. And being in the bail bond business, it was never my goal to project a Good Samaritan image.

Well, the group came back again. This time, Sherri was leading the chorus while everyone else played hearts and flowers, trying to convince me that this should be my one and only exception—not only because it was a good deal, but I'd be helping a young family get back on their feet.

"Please, Lefty! Think how you'd feel if the tables were turned, and we needed the help?"

I finally gave in to their pressure, but not until I set a few guidelines I thought would protect me. But I was dead wrong. My actions just dug the hole deeper.

First, I refused to just hand Dino $3,000 in cash; I was sure that with that kind of money, he'd simply skip town. Second, he had to make all the arrangements, from securing the purchase of the toys to selling them. That included selecting the hall, since The Auction Barn was closed, and arranging all the advertising.

I made it perfectly clear to everyone involved that my only role would be that of a loan broker; I'd simply follow along behind him and pay any start-up expenses, up to the $3,000 limit of the loan. This way, I would be assured that he didn't pocket the cash. In addition, I told him that Dusty, my bounty hunter, would be riding along with him when he went to pick up the toys in Los Angeles.

When the time came, I gave Dusty the thousand dollar cashier's check to pay for the toys and told him, "Look, I don't care about the toys. Just don't come back without that punk, no matter what it takes. Hurt him if you have to, but make sure you bring him back."

While they were gone, I used the balance of the $3,000 to pay for the TV and newspaper advertising Dino had arranged, as well as the rental of the Holiday Inn's largest banquet hall, which was where the auction would be held. I remember thinking, "One night soon, all this bullshit will be over." Wrong again.

Upon their return I had Dusty and Dino unload all the toys into my two-car garage for safekeeping and paid Dusty to help keep an eye on them and on Dino until the day of the auction. I was satisfied I'd done everything I could to provide this punk asshole with an opportunity to get back on his feet, while having a high level of certainty that I'd recover my money. The rest was up to him.

Sherri and her mother were walking on eggshells, worrying about the money, so they took some security steps of their own. Their plan was to act as cashiers during the auction to ensure that I received my money before Dino, or his family, got one penny.

The auction went off without a hitch. He sold every toy in the place and raised a pretty penny over and above my $3,000. He paid me back, and even gave me $300 to cover the cost of his bail bond; the part I had to pay the insurance company. I waived my remaining $1,200 profit, trying to show my nicer side. And, even though everyone thought I should at least receive interest on the initial $3,000 I'd loaned him for the auction, I refused that as well. All I wanted was to have everyone, including my wife and my mother-in-law, leave me alone and never ask for any financial assistance again. Everyone agreed, and we all left on good terms.

It wasn't until mid-October that I learned the toy auction had been a scam. All the toys Dino purchased and advertised as new were broken and distressed merchandise customers had returned to large retailers like K-Mart, Sears, and Walmart. The stores, in turn, returned them to their distributors for credit. The distributors then offered the toys to reclamation companies for pennies on the dollar. After paying virtually nothing, these companies specialized in questionable repairs, rewrapping, and reselling goods to secondhand thrift stores and guys like Dino on the cheap without any guarantee or warranty.

This punk auctioneer purchased the toys for pennies more, and he knowingly sold them as new, thinking no one would be able to tell the actual condition of the toys until they reopened them. Since the plan was to host a Christmas toy auction, he thought no one would find out until late December. By then, he would be long gone.

It almost worked, except for the fact that some of the five hundred to six hundred customers that purchased toys at the auction were planning to resell them. While preparing them for resale, they discovered that many toys were unsellable because they were supposedly repaired and repackaged. Many customers attempted to locate the auctioneer in hopes of getting a full refund. When that failed, they went to the Washoe County District Attorney's office complaining they'd been swindled and were looking for satisfaction.

Some of the small retailers (some that spent as much as $600 on this junk) were rightfully pissed. They were expecting to make a nice profit from their much-anticipated Christmas business. Instead, they lost their investment and their anticipated profits. Those who weren't satisfied with filing a civil complaint for fraud elected to hire their own lawyers. The lawyers, in turn, hired private investigators to track down everyone involved in what came to be known as the "Christmas Toy Scandal."

Word spread quickly, which brought out an additional number of individual purchasers yelling fraud. The Civil Fraud division of the Washoe County District Attorney's Office became involved. And, based upon the large volume of publicity surrounding the case, the D.A.'s office felt compelled to release statements concerning things like the number of investigative man hours they were devoting to the case, and the discovery that the auctioneer had a business partner. This business partner was a local, well-known businessman and property owner within Washoe County. They said they were preparing a 40-count indictment for civil fraud against all parties involved within the next few weeks.

Because my attorney and I had numerous dealings with the D.A.'s office vis-a-vis my bail bond businesses, they gave us an opportunity to come in and explain my position. During our meeting, they outlined the evidence their investigators had gathered to date: receipts for payment of TV and newspaper ads, rental of the U-Haul that picked up the merchandise, a copy of the cashier's check used to pay for the toys, a receipt for rental of the meeting hall, and numerous receipts from customers marked "paid in full," all signed by my wife or my mother-in-law. As they put it, "We feel we have a very compelling case reflecting your participation in a scheme to profit from the fraudulent sale of broken and distressed merchandise that was disguised and sold as new."

I tried to explain the circumstances surrounding the thing, but they were only interested in letting me know that our meeting was more of a courtesy than anything else, as their office would be filing a 40-count civil fraud lawsuit against Dino and me. They thought I should hear it directly from them, rather than reading about it in the paper. They asked if I knew where they might find Dino. That's when I said,

"Look, I haven't seen or heard from him since the night of the auction, and I have no reason or need to ever see him again. That is, until now, but you can bet your ass I'm going to find him." I got up and stormed out the office without as much as a goodbye. Dennis followed, expressing our thanks for the heads up. Dennis always believed in ending any meeting on a polite, if not necessarily positive, note. In the hallway, he said that my last comment concerning Dino might be construed as a threat and added, "You better hope nothing happens to him, or you'll be first on their list of suspects for an assault or murder charge."

"Dennis, you worry too much," I replied. "There are lots of people looking for the little punk—some who don't like what he's done to little kids, and some who don't like what he's done to me. All I can say is, I wouldn't want any of them looking for me! Don't worry; I won't do anything stupid. We'll just hang around and wait to see what condition he's in when they find him, if they find him."

After I called Sherri and filled her in, she called her mother, who, in turn, called Dino's parents. They had no idea where he was; he'd disappeared a few days after the auction, leaving his wife and baby behind with them. I didn't believe any of this. They knew what was going on, and they were afraid of what I, or some of my friends, might do if anyone found him. They were right to worry.

Fortunately for Dino, I had a few more important things to worry about, like saving my financial ass. So rather than look for him myself, I checked in with a few of my friends to see if they had any leads. I reminded them that I'd make it well worth their while if they found him.

I continued to work on closing out my old bonds and managing my properties, but problems surrounding the toy auction kept creeping into my thoughts. In late November, I went to Dennis's office to talk about all the upcoming trials and to see just how much shit the little asshole had gotten me into.

"Well, in addition to the forty individuals who filed complaints and want the D.A.'s office to make sure you hang in the town square," Dennis said, "there's about sixty more planning to file individual lawsuits against you for the recovery of their money, plus the profits they lost from future sales, plus punitive damages, to ensure you never try this again. They all think you knew, or should have known, that the auction was a scam from the beginning."

Then he mentioned the children. "Listen. Come Christmas, I'm sure more people will be coming out of the woodwork saying their kids were emotionally traumatized when Santa Claus either forgot them, because their parents lost all their Christmas money at the auction, or he left them a bunch of broken toys under the tree. They'll all be looking for a financial windfall from the guy with the deep pockets—namely, you."

Although he knew I was innocent, snagged into this deal by my wife and mother-in-law, the fact remained that I was the big, bad bully bail bondsman who tried to use Santa and Christmas as a cover to rip off innocent families; I was the Grinch who stole Christmas, leaving a lot of little kids crying on Christmas morning. At least, this is what the D.A.'s office was saying in its civil fraud indictment against me. Almost all the private attorneys began using this tactic to sell their cases to prospective clients and juries in more than sixty other individual lawsuits.

That's when I learned that the deep pocket theory of civil justice actually works: the one where all the ambulance-chasing attorneys really do go after the person or company with the most to lose, not necessarily the person or entity that's truly guilty. Why bother with the asshole who's guilty when they have someone like me? This line of thinking not only held true with the new deputy prosecutors in the Washoe County D.A's office, but those across the country as well. Their main interest is not reaping justice, but likely getting all the positive publicity and enlarging their track record of convictions or civil settlements to further their careers.

The pictures of me these nickel-and-dime ambulance chasers were painting were not pretty ones. I was pissed. I didn't do anything wrong in this particular case, and I refused to admit that I had. And in my eyes, attempting to settle any of these cases without my day in court was the same as admitting guilt.

I was young at the time, and stupid enough to think that if I defended myself against every one of these ridiculous charges, people would begin to see that I'd been duped as badly as they'd been. Because I was on a first-name basis with the Washoe County District Attorney from my bail-related dealings over the years, I felt confident I could win his support as well.

Over the next year or so, I did just that. But then I lost the D.A.'s fraud case, which I never thought possible, as well as a dozen or more of the individual cases. Together, they indicated a definite error in my thinking. That's also when I began to see there was no sense in continuing the battle, so I asked Dennis to begin negotiating settlements with some of the more reasonable victims. While he was doing that, I started liquidating as many of my assets as necessary to ensure I could meet all our settlement efforts.

You may think that having been found guilty by a jury of my peers meant I was guilty, especially when it happened numerous times. But wait until you hear some of what went on in open court. You might feel a little differently.

Every juror on each of the cases heard testimony at trial about how I conducted my bail businesses. This had nothing to do with the toy auction. Nevertheless, the victim's attorneys conducted a character assassination, and I was their only target, pure and simple. No one, not even the judge, said a word when witnesses testified about how I kicked doors down, intimidated little old ladies, and picked up fugitives and left them in the trunk of my car for days before surrendering them to jail. And let's not forget about how I raided a fugitive's home with guns drawn in front of his small children and made them watch while I put handcuffs on their daddy. Or the one where we beat the shit out of some guy after we found him hiding in the closet, then dragged him out of the house in handcuffs while his elderly parents cried out, "Please don't hurt our son."

The best one I heard was when an elderly woman, who had never seen me before, sat in the witness chair pointing a finger at me, and began telling the jury how "He put a gun in my face and yelled out to my son, who was hiding under the bed, that if he didn't come out with his hands up and surrender he was going to shoot me for aiding and abetting the escape of a fugitive." She continued, "When my son came out, that man handcuffed him, took him out to his car, put him in the trunk, and drove off without saying one word to me about where he was taking him. I was terrified and crying the whole time."

Although some testimony may have contained a certain amount of truth concerning my behavior as a bail bondsman, again, it had nothing to do with the toy auction, or my alleged involvement in sponsoring it. Every time someone came up with more of this bullshit, my attorney objected, calling all of it uncorroborated cheap shots and character assassination to sway the jury. He stated that all this testimony was irrelevant and prejudicial, but the judge kept overruling him and telling him to sit down. No one really cared except me.

There were a few judges who periodically agreed with Dennis and occasionally ordered the jurors to disregard all such comments. But it always came after the witnesses finished embellishing their stories. As the expression goes, it was like closing the barn door after the horse got away. The jurors heard enough to rule for the victim in every case and provide each of them with significant punitive damages as well.

As a result, some people who had purchased $600 worth of toys won judgments against me for $16,000 counting punitive damages; people who bought more, got more; people who bought less got a little less. But they all won.

Being in the bail bond business, I'd always saved for a rainy day, because I never knew when the police would make more arrests, or when I would be posting bonds. Nor did I have any idea when one of my clients would skip, leaving me with a large potential loss that might require paying some bribes or paying bounty hunters. I set aside money from every bond I wrote to handle most emergencies. But the judgments from these toy-auction cases far exceeded any rainy-day scenarios I could have imagined. These claims were piling up fast and furiously; they were coming more like hurricanes than rainy days.

Settling these cases and paying all the court costs and their attorney fees far exceeded my personal savings and the equities in all my properties. The more cases I lost, the more properties I sold. And the more I sold, the less income I took in and the tougher it was to meet my financial obligations or take care of my family. This was the first time I found myself running out of money, as well as options to make more.

When I began to accept the fact that I was going broke, I sat down with Dennis to make plans to file for bankruptcy.

He said anything I sold or transferred within the six months preceding my filing the bankruptcy papers could be reversed by the bankruptcy trustee. I had to make arrangements to protect whatever I could. I especially wanted to protect the special relationships I'd developed with the surety insurance companies and my reputation within the bail industry. Mickey knew the bail business was in my blood, and I knew in my heart that if I was ever going to recover financially from this mess, I needed to go back to it, in whatever capacity might still be open to me.

As we were winding down our meeting, I told Dennis I'd work on a plan to openly liquidate all my property in order to continue settling the upcoming claims. At the same time, I'd work out a separate plan to protect my reputation in the industry by making sure Mickey had enough assets to protect him and the surety insurance companies against any and all losses resulting from the bonds I wrote prior to the sale of my agencies to Bernie.

In the meantime, I wanted him to start working on the bankruptcy papers, because we had to orchestrate the necessary documents while the toy-auction trials were still going on, and my real estate assets, although dwindling, would be sufficient to keep the wolves away from my bail reserves for now.

As fate would have it, that same afternoon, I got a call from Mickey. "Kid," he said, "I think we should meet and talk a little about your future. I know you're losing your ass, and so does the rest of the world. All anyone needs to do is read the papers or listen to the news."

I agreed. "Thanks Mickey, I'll come over in the morning for breakfast; a free meal would be helpful." The two of us laughed, agreed to meet, and hung up.

I had no idea what he had in mind, or what he could possibly say or do to help. But listening couldn't make my life any worse. The next day I arrived bright and early for my free meal. The minute I walked in, Elaine ran over, threw her arms around me, gave me a big hug and said, "Don't you worry, we're going to fix this."

I was shocked, considering the situation with her daughter. But I knew in my heart that she wasn't really mad at me; she felt a little guilty for having played Cupid. Her reaction was so warm and sincere, I almost felt like crying. These were the first two people, outside of Dennis and my best friend, Roy, who had offered to help since this mess erupted.

I told them about my meeting with Dennis, and our decision to prepare for bankruptcy. I said my primary concern was to protect them and the surety company from losses because I was hoping to get back into the business on some level when this was over.

Mickey stopped me.

"It happens that Elaine and I want you to come work for us. We want you to run our general agency, but not until we, and I do mean 'we,' get a handle on this mess. We want to make sure that your financial problems don't spill over into the runoff of your previous business. If they did, I'm sure both Central States and Blue Lakes Insurance companies would object to Elaine and I having someone who cost them losses due to their own forfeited bonds running one of their largest bail general agencies."

I agreed wholeheartedly and told them about my plan to transfer all my reserve deposits into Mickey's name, in exchange for releasing me from all potential losses on more than a million dollars in bail bond liabilities. And, because my reserves totaled only a little over 10 percent of the pending liabilities, we would draw up papers transferring all future payments from Bernie's purchase of my bail businesses into Mickey's name as well.

I also agreed to continue working with their bounty hunters—I needed to do everything possible to prevent my bail losses from exceeding the amount of security the agreements were providing. Based on my previous track record of writing solid business, Dennis and Mickey felt this would provide the bankruptcy trustee with a plausible justification for approving this financial transaction, even though our goal was to complete the transaction prior to the court's six-month rule regarding the transfer of assets.

In addition, my reputation with the surety companies would remain solid, as I was no longer responsible for any losses on the bonds I'd previously written.

We also agreed that Mickey should release the remaining second-mortgage liens he was holding on my properties—first, because the bail agencies were worth much more to Mickey, and second, because Dennis wanted to show our good faith by continuing to liquidate all my remaining properties in order to satisfy my financial obligations. He felt this would prevent the bankruptcy trustee from setting aside the deal between us and trying to place an attachment on my reserves.

When the discussion was over Mickey said, "Well, kid, as I see it, you're asking Elaine and me to take on all your bail liability in exchange for a few bucks and your promise to help us close out all your bonds. That's a tall order, considering you're also asking us to give up the second deeds of trust we're holding on all your properties.

"I'm sure my attorney will ask if Elaine and I have lost our minds. But he doesn't have all the inside information we have, and neither does the bankruptcy trustee. You're one of the best bail agents I've ever known. And I can trust you with my life, if ever necessary. So as far as I'm concerned, we have a deal—on one condition. You have to start working for us. You'll have the freedom to take off whenever you need to work on your toy shit, or your bankruptcy, but Elaine and I need you now."

Mickey understood that his risk in this business transaction was zero, both for him and for the insurance companies. If anything, he stood to make a lot of money by the time it was over. Hopefully, down the road, he'd share some of his windfall with me.

With Mickey's agreement, I started reviewing the necessary paperwork to file for bankruptcy. The best part of having to list all my assets and liabilities was the fact that I no longer needed to list any of the assets, liabilities, obligations or income from my previous bail bond businesses, since I no longer had any loss reserves accounts, nor would I be receiving proceeds from the sale of my bail businesses to Bernie. If everything went as planned, I would walk away from this mess with my bail license, my business reputation intact, and a job managing Mickey and Elaine's growing general agencies, thanks to Dennis, Mickey, and Elaine.

Luckily, none of the attorneys representing the remaining litigants alleged fraud. It required a lot more work to prove, and they figured I'd be settling with them soon enough. They were wrong. After I filed bankruptcy and listed the remaining wolves at the door, it was too late for them to adjust their filing by alleging fraud. These last few unsettled cases were just a group of hangers-on trying to make a fast buck off my misfortune. After the bankruptcy trustee sold off the remainder of my assets, they each got a few bucks, which is exactly what they deserved.

Earlier, Dennis had instructed me to list every financial obligation I had, including the cases I'd settled during the previous six months. He said I also needed to include the remaining judgments, as well as all remaining personal bills, no matter their size, down to my last utility bill. All told, they were in the tens of thousands of dollars. Then he said I should list my current assets, which by this time amounted to only a few hundred dollars, since we'd lost our homes in foreclosure; our only car was an old '60s Chevy station wagon, which I'd purchased to drive back and forth to my new job at Mickey's office.

Six months later, I was totally broke, and totally free of debt, with one exception: The bankruptcy court would not dismiss the $44,000 fraud judgment awarded to the State of Nevada from their civil fraud case. So it was business under the table as usual to avoid that jerk prosecutor from attaching anything until I could negotiate a settlement.

CHAPTER

#23

Our home foreclosure was completed around the time I filed for bankruptcy. At that low point, with no money and nowhere to go, I moved Sherri and the two kids in with Mom. Sitting in a 900-square-foot, two-bedroom, one-bath condominium with three adults and two kids, was when reality hit me like a ton of shit.

All this misery was because I'd tried to help some little asshole get back on his feet. To this day, it's still hard to believe that I lost two cars, three homes, nine rentals, a fifteen-unit motel, thousands of dollars a month in personal income from my rentals, and the entire proceeds from the sale of my two bail businesses. In addition to losing everything, including an excellent credit rating, I left the courtroom still owing $44,000.

If that weren't bad enough, the State's Attorney had his investigator follow me to court the morning of my bankruptcy hearing to see where I'd parked. At the direction of his boss, he called a tow truck and waited with the driver until I came out of the courthouse. They wanted me to watch them tow my old, beat-up Chevy. It was my only means of transportation, and the State's Attorney knew it. He also knew the judge ruled I could keep it. But in his eyes, it was a personal asset subject to seizure and sale, with the proceeds going toward reducing the state's remaining judgment against me. Dennis found out later the State's Attorney sold it for less than it cost the state to tow it. I lost the car, and not one penny was credited toward the $44K judgment. It was the attorney's way of letting me know I would never own another thing of value in the State of Nevada while he was a prosecutor—or until the $44,000 was paid in full.

As I turned to walk away, thinking I had finally hit rock bottom, the State's Attorney served me with a copy of the garnishment papers his staff had served on Mickey and Elaine while I was in court. This little prick would now receive 25 percent of my net wages after taxes, the maximum allowed by law at the time.

Even after I'd gone through over eighteen months of hell and lost everything I owned, the attorney's personal hatred toward me remained. He was attempting to send me a message: All he wanted, over and above the money, was to run me out of town, and he wasn't going to leave me alone until he accomplished his goal.

Well, I'm a strong believer in fate, and as fate would have it, Mickey and Elaine came to my rescue once again, and once again changed my life.

While dealing with the liquidation of my assets and the bankruptcy filing, I'd had been working with Mickey as his manager and right-hand man. In my capacity as manager, I had an opportunity to meet, deal and negotiate with many of the bail agents throughout California and eleven other western states. I'd also had weekly conference calls and some personal meetings Hal Cummings, the senior V.P. and operations manager for Blue Lakes Insurance Company. This was a small surety insurance company owned by a guy named Brian Reid. Brian was also the national managing general agent for Blue Lakes' bond department. He'd given Mickey his first general agency contract, and thus the opportunity to exclusively solicit and contract bail agents throughout the Western United States.

Mickey had a long, prosperous relationship with Brian long before Brian became president and sole owner of Blue Lakes. They'd met while Brian was the national general agent for Central States Insurance. Over the course of their business relationship they became the best of friends.

About two years into their friendship, and six months after I started working for Mickey again, Brian opened his western regional office for Blue Lakes in Los Angeles. This office serviced Mickey's bail general agency, as well as other general agencies and independent bail bond agents throughout the West. They provided criminal surety bail bonds, and also processed all types of civil surety bonds through independent insurance agencies. These included sales tax bonds, notary bonds, contract performance bonds, swimming-pool contractor bonds, and contract completion bonds.

Brian's current V.P. and western regional manager, Vance Parker, had just decided to run for the California State Assembly seat in his home district. At Brian's urging, along with a sizable campaign contribution, Vance decided to resign his position with Blue Lakes and devote all his time to his campaign.

When Mickey heard about this through Hal Cummings, he called Brian to learn about the L.A. bond office. Brian said they processed all their bail and civil bond business for the Western US through this office, with the exception of Mickey's business, and they were looking for a new V.P. and western regional manager. Mickey immediately tossed my hat into the ring—without even asking me.

But first, he told Brian every negative thing that had happened to me—and why he was giving me the highest possible recommendation. He said I was a stand-up guy, someone he could trust, and someone with the knowledge and experience to deal with both bail and civil agents, especially those currently reporting business through his own general agency.

As a result of Mickey's efforts, Hal called me to set up a meeting with Brian. He said Brian had heard a lot about me, and that Mickey and Brian thought it was time we met. Hal never let on that our meeting was actually an interview for the V.P. job, and neither did Mickey. I was to meet Brian and Hal in L.A. the very next week, all expenses paid.

Hal met me at the arrival gate and escorted me to the Hyatt Hotel for lunch with him and Brian. They had arrived the night before on the company plane from their home base in Hill Crest, Indiana.

After telling me everything they'd heard about me from Mickey, they explained the real reason for our meeting, that I was being interviewed for the western regional manager's position. They told me the number of employees working in the office, the number of agencies reporting through the western division, the volume of business they were processing, and the fact that the position required moving to L.A. within the next thirty days, if I was interested. I sensed their urgency and eagerness to close the deal when Brian asked if moving to Los Angeles would be a problem.

I said, "I appreciate being considered for the job, and moving wouldn't be a problem if I were selected. The job would be a great opportunity for me and my family. However, I owe Mickey and Elaine my loyalty for what they've done for us over the past two years, and I can't leave them high and dry. Before I can give you my answer, I'll need to talk with them. I understand your need to fill the position immediately, and if I'm unable to give you an answer within your timeframe, please know I'm grateful for just being considered for the job."

Brian replied, "Mickey knew exactly how you would respond to my offer, and to my timetable for filling this position. That's why he and Elaine have already approved your immediate departure. So, with the concern for them out of the way, can we assume your answer is yes?"

I was overwhelmed. But before I could utter a word, he said, "Someone from our HR division will contact you within the next few days to go over all the company policies, our family health insurance plan, expense accounts, auto allowance, and compensation paperwork; plus, they'll assist with your housing needs in L.A. In the interim, HR will arrange for you to stay here at the LAX Hyatt, since it's next door to the Airport Plaza complex, which is where your new office is located."

Hal suggested that we schedule my introductions to the L.A. office staff, as well as a review of the office complex for my second trip, since they'd not yet discussed their management transition plans with Vance Parker, the current western regional V.P. That was their next stop.

As our meeting ended, Brian suggested I bring my wife along on my next trip, suggesting she might want to look into housing and other needs. Then he handed me a slip of paper and said, "You might want to look this over before our next meeting, in case you have questions or concerns. Have a safe trip home. We'll meet again soon."

Then it was my turn.

"Thanks again for the opportunity. I'll do everything in my power to ensure your company's success out West."

As they stood up to leave, Brian corrected me, "You mean *our* company. You're a big part of it now."

After they left, I glanced at the paper he had given me and noted the first line. He offered me four times the money I was making with Mickey, plus a percentage of the gross revenues from all increases in production. It also outlined the auto allowance I'd receive, and reiterated the fact that the company would be providing health insurance for the entire family, as well as an open-ended expense account for travel, entertainment, etc. Last, but not least, the letter mentioned the company would cover all my relocation costs, and said if I needed anything else, or he'd left anything out, I should contact Hal, and he would arrange it.

When they were out of sight, I pinched myself to make sure I wasn't dreaming. My head was spinning. I could hardly wait to get home and tell everyone the good news. So rather than staying overnight in L.A., I took the next available flight back to Reno.

When I broke the news to Mom, she was just as excited as I was. But when I told Sherri, she went quiet. I explained that this was the only way to get our financial life back on the right track. I suspected her mood had to do with leaving her mom behind, so I said she could return to Reno to visit her mom whenever she wanted. Even that didn't seem to make a difference, so I let it go for the time being, hoping she'd eventually come around.

I called Mickey and set up a meeting for early the next day to thank him and Elaine for everything they had done to secure my new job, and to discuss a suitable departure date. When we sat down together, I saw that they were just as excited as Mom and me. They said I could leave the next day if I needed to, and presented me with three-months pay, in cash, as a going-away present. I actually broke down and cried, and I said I'd never forget them. Mickey laughed and said, "Kid, you'll be processing all our business for years to come; you won't have a chance to forget us."

On my way out he said, "By the way, Bernie called. He said Tony from the Men's Club on Lake Street heard you might be leaving town and asked Bernie to give you a message. So be sure and stop by Bernie's office and pick it up."

I hadn't talked to Tony since the day I sold my bail businesses and introduced him to Bernie. I couldn't imagine what he would possibly want or need from me.

Bernie came out of the office and handed me the note. "Tony said this was very important and personal, and to make sure you got it before leaving town. He asked that I not open it, because it's private" as he handed it to me. "You can see it's still sealed."

I thanked him again for his help with my bankruptcy, the sale of my agencies, and the note from Tony, and I drove away.

I stopped at the Halfway Club on the way home, ordered a pizza and beer, hopped into a booth and opened Tony's note.

"Hi, Kid. I've always liked you and respected the way you took care of the girls and conducted our business. Since I heard you were leaving town to take a new job, I wanted you to know, I always thought you got fucked by that piece-of-shit auctioneer. So I had a couple of my boys look around to see if they could find him. Word had it that he abandoned his wife and new baby, moved to Battle Mountain, and took up housekeeping with one of the working girls from up there. I never liked what he did to you or those kids at Christmas. I asked the boys to take him for a scenic ride

*through the desert on their way back. Unfortunately,
they lost him somewhere out there, if you get my drift.
Hope you sleep a little better knowing that what goes
around, comes around. Good luck with the new job.*

Best Wishes, Tony

*P.S. I strongly suggest you burn this note when you're
finished reading it.*

I knew a lot of people were looking for Dino, but I had no
idea Tony was one of them. Nor did I know if everything he
said in his note was true, or if he just wanted me to feel better,
thinking Dino got everything he deserved. Either way, I did
start sleeping better. I wondered how Tony knew about my
new job, but then I remembered he called me "Kid," which
meant he picked everything up from Mickey.

Hal called the day after I got home. He said the current
V.P. was leaving within a week; I should meet him in L.A. the
following Monday and bring my wife.

On Monday, Sherri and I flew to L.A. We met the staff,
viewed the office, had an early dinner with Hal, and flew home.
Sherri was impressed with everything, but her attitude and
her willingness to discuss what was bothering her remained
unchanged. I put it on the back burner again, thinking things
would work themselves out when we got settled in L.A.

Rather than wait a few weeks, or a month, as Hal had
offered, I decided we should leave for L.A.as soon as we could.
First, I had to take care of some last-minute things.

I needed a car for my new job, and a credit card to cover
my business-travel expenses. I also needed to get the state prosecutor off my ass by somehow settling the $44,000 judgment

and the wage garnishment he was holding over my head. Even though Mickey had explained my situation to my new boss, the last thing I wanted was to have the prosecutor contact him. That's when I decided to attack the biggest problem first.

I contacted Dennis, told him I was leaving Nevada for good, and asked him to arrange a settlement with the prosecutor regarding my debt with the State of Nevada before I left. I said to make the asshole an offer he couldn't refuse: Take $4,000 now, which was all Mom could borrow, together with my promise never to open a business in Nevada for the next ten years. "If that isn't enough," I added, "tell him to stick the judgment up his ass, and good luck trying to find me or collect any part of my debt in the future."

Of course, I asked him to rephrase my offer in a more sophisticated and legal manner, emphasizing the fact that my mother would be the one borrowing the money.

Whatever Dennis told him worked. He drew up the necessary papers and paid the $4,000, which Mom actually borrowed from the bank so the State's Attorney couldn't trace it back to me. The bankruptcy judge approved and signed off on the settlement agreement. This meant I was finally out from under the fucking toy auction and that prick prosecutor. The toy ordeal had brought me to my financial knees and taught me a valuable lesson. But it didn't put me down for the count or out of the bail bond business.

The rest was easy. I gave Mom back her $4,000 from the cash Mickey and Elaine had given me and had her use the rest of the money from them to lease a new Buick two-door sedan in her name, with me as an additional driver. I would use my new auto allowance to make the payments. In addition, she co-signed on my new credit card application. But, because of my bankruptcy and Mom's limited income, the bank was only willing to extend a $500 line of credit on the card. This meant I'd have to make payments weekly, depending upon how much I traveled. Or I could pay for my airfare through the travel agency on the ground floor of my new office building, so I'd have availability of a credit card during my travel through the West.

Having solved all the immediate problems that might hold me back, I rented a small U-Haul for a one-way trip to L.A. and packed what few worldly possessions Sherri and I had left. In less than a week, Sherri, the two girls, and I headed out of town on our new adventure. Despite everything I'd been through, I still felt pretty good about life. I came out with my business reputation intact, and with a promising career in a business I loved. And I secured the opportunity to rebuild my financial net worth. Not too bad for a thirty-one-year-old punk.

Little did I know it was too early to start patting myself on the back. While I was able to satisfy the financial issues surrounding my life, there was one enormous, personal, life-changing item lurking in the shadows.

CHAPTER

#24

Off we go, into the wild blue yonder . . .

Go West, young man . . . and all that bullshit.

We were officially on our way to Los Angeles. I was driving the U-Haul and Sherri was following behind, driving with the kids in our new Buick. We got a late start, so when we reached Modesto, we decided to stop for the night. We checked into the Holiday Inn, had dinner, put the kids to bed, talked for a while, then decided to turn in and get some sleep.

At around 2:00 a.m., Sherri woke me. She was crying and mumbling about wanting to go home. To ease her mind, I said, "We are going home. We're going to our new home in L.A." That's when she stopped mumbling and hit me with it: "I want to go home to my boyfriend. We've been having an affair for the past six months. He just divorced his wife and wants to marry me as soon as I'm free."

I think I said something like, "Holy shit! Are you kidding me? I need some air."

I put on my clothes and headed out the door. I walked around the parking lot thinking how I'd just spent the worst two years of my life trying to dig myself out of a financial disaster that was a direct result of her and her mother; or at least by way of their interfering in other people's lives. Now, after spending all that time trying to save my family and our future, she was off fucking some idiot and making plans to dump me. I guess that made me the idiot, didn't it?

After about an hour of thinking, talking to myself, and wallowing in a lot of self-pity, I returned to the hotel room. I told Sherri we should finish the trip to L.A. and discuss her return to Reno once we got settled—if she still wanted to go. She reluctantly agreed. Neither of us could get back to sleep, so we woke the kids and checked out.

Once in Los Angeles, we went directly to the temporary three-bedroom apartment the company had rented for us on a month–to-month basis. As soon as we got settled and returned the U-Haul, Sherri started asking when she and the kids could fly home. I said she would have to wait until I officially signed in with the staff, finished my office tour, and completed a personal interview with each one of the members, because I was planning to fly back to Reno with her. I booked our flights for the following Friday. That way, I could spend the weekend in Reno, and Sherri and the kids could spend time with family.

When we arrived late Friday night, she and the kids went to stay with her mother, and I went to stay with Mom. She was at work, so I waited until the next morning, when she came home after morning mass, to fill her in. That's when she made a comment that sent my life in another direction.

She said, "I don't care if you get a divorce, but you're not leaving my granddaughter with THAT WOMAN. You give that little tramp her divorce in exchange for full custody of my little Ella. You understand me?"

"Mom," I said. "I don't know the first thing about taking care of a four-year-old kid, let alone a little girl. I now live and work in Los Angeles and have no friends or family to help me out. How in hell am I going to be a good father while traveling all over the United States working to protect my new job?"

She interrupted me and said, "After everything you've been through these past few years, I'm sure you can work this out. Lefty, I know that everything will work out, as long as you do the right thing and keep your baby. Nothing in life is worth more."

Until now, business and making money was all I thought about. Although I loved Ella immensely, I spent little time with her because I was doing everything I could to save our financial future.

I knew Mom was right, but I had no time to think about it, because Sherri started pressuring me. She was back with her boyfriend, and I had to return to L.A. on Sunday. Before I left, Sherri kept calling me at Mom's. After I returned to L.A. alone, she started calling collect, sometimes two and three times a day. All she could talk about was getting one of those quickie Nevada-style divorces. She was frantic that she might lose her boyfriend.

After a few sleepless nights wondering if I could raise Ella on my own, I laid it out to Sherri: "You can have your divorce. You can keep whatever money we have in our checking and savings accounts as of today, and I'll pay to have any furniture or personal belongings you want returned to Reno. I'll also pay whatever current bills we have, including the full cost of our divorce. You can have full custody of Ann. In exchange for all this, my one and only request is that you grant me full custody of Ella. Keep in mind, since we are each taking a child, there will be no child support. You pay everything for your daughter, Ann, and I pay everything for our daughter, Ella. I'll also pay for Ella to visit you and Ann one month each summer, and you pay for any additional trips if you want her to come and see you."

I couldn't believe it; her response took less than ten seconds.

"It's a deal. How long will it take?"

I flew back to Reno that Friday, met with Dennis, arranged for him to file our divorce papers the following Monday, and flew back to L.A. Sunday as scheduled. When I got in my car, I pinched myself twice; I couldn't believe I was about to start my new life as a single parent and would be facing another life-changing challenge. This time, however, it would be as a single father, with my little girl.

Since Sherri and I had spent most of our lives in Reno and had worked out the child-custody arrangements, Dennis said the court proceedings should only take a few minutes. So I flew back to Reno the following Friday, signed the divorce papers, and stayed over on Monday to make sure I got my filed copy.

After celebrating the end to that chapter in my life with my two best friends, Dennis and Roy, I called a cab, and picked up my daughter at my ex-mother-in-law's place. From there, we went to say our goodbyes to Mom and my sister. On the way over, I began to worry that I might have taken on more than I could handle, and I began to worry about Mom as well. Sis met me at the door, hugged me, and promised to take over caring for Mom. Then it was Mom's turn. She could see the concern in my face. She hugged me, told me to stop worrying, and assured me that no matter how things worked out, my little girl would always be better off with me.

After a short visit and some quick farewells, Ella and I left on our new adventure. I thought for sure she would be upset about leaving her mother and sister behind. Instead, she held my hand, smiled and said she was excited to be with me, and excited to be on our way to our new home. What a fantastic moment.

On the plane back to L.A., I thought about the past six years with Sherri. Although I never loved her, I liked her well enough. She'd had a tough life. Like me, she'd come from a broken home. Although her affair and our divorce were unexpected, she did give me Ella, and a chance for a new life.

CHAPTER

#25

My new job was now in full swing. I found a new two-bedroom apartment in Redondo Beach, a coastal community close to LAX and about fifteen minutes from my office, and I bought Ella one of those white fluffy canopy beds for her room. I'd just turned thirty-two, with a bright, yet challenging, future ahead, and my only responsibility, other than the new job, was taking care of Ella.

Mom was right: Taking full custody of Ella was not just the right thing to do, it was the only thing. That first weekend we bought new beds, went grocery shopping, did our laundry and played games. Then, on Monday, I faced the toughest and most immediate challenge, which was finding a way to balance my job responsibilities with those of being a single parent.

My first day on the job, I took Ella along to the office since I hadn't yet made satisfactory arrangements for daycare. Mom must have been praying in overtime, because my number one problem was solved that same day.

Teresa was the office receptionist, as well as the all-around backup for the other five employees. It happened that she was the last employee I met with that morning.

She was twenty-eight and attractive. She had a science degree from the University of Oregon and had earned teaching credentials in California. For two years she taught science and health to high school kids in the Watts area of L.A. At the time, she was separated from her husband, who was living in another part of L.A. She had full custody of their daughter, Bonnie, who was eleven months younger than Ella. Teresa's parents and sister lived in Las Vegas, so our family situations were somewhat similar, especially when it came to needing childcare during working hours.

It was approaching lunchtime when I finished the last of my meet-and-greet sessions with the employees, which just happened to be with Teresa. So the three of us, Teresa, Ella, and I, returned to the reception area.

When I saw that everyone else had gone, Teresa explained that each staff member took a turn staying behind for lunch to cover the phones, and today was her turn.

"Well, I said, "I planned to buy lunch for Ella and me from the hotel restaurant next door; can I get you something?"

She said thanks and that she'd watch Ella while I was gone. When I returned, we all sat down to lunch in the breakroom, and before we took a bite of food, she asked, "What are your plans regarding daycare for Ella?"

I said didn't have the slightest idea. And with my family living in Reno, I wasn't sure where to begin looking.

She immediately picked up the phone and called Mattie, the owner of a daycare center called the Little Red School House. Teresa explained my situation and asked if Mattie could accommodate another little girl. After a few moments of silence Teresa said, "Thanks, Mattie, I'll let him know. We'll all see you when I pick up Bonnie."

I could tell from her smile that we were in. If this place was good enough for Teresa's daughter, I knew it would be perfect for Ella. Problem solved.

I once again gave thanks for the power of Mom's prayers. My concerns about caring for Ella during work vanished in less than forty-eight hours; it seemed almost too good to be true. But in retrospect, I shouldn't have been so surprised. After all, Mom was praying for her granddaughter, not necessaries for me.

After lunch, Ella and I returned to my office. She went back to her new coloring books, while I just stood at the window, watching planes taking off from the airport and thinking about how lucky I was, not just for my job, or my fresh start, but also for meeting Teresa. I knew there was something special about her, and I wanted to get to know her better.

When everyone returned from lunch, I asked Sandra, the office manager, for her perspective on each employee to learn as much as possible about each one and their job duties. When we got to Teresa, Sandra must have sensed something because she said, "Teresa already has a boyfriend, so don't get any ideas."

Competition never really bothered me in business or in my private life. But thanks to Sandra, I found out all I needed to know.

After work that afternoon, Ella and I followed Teresa to Mattie's place in Manhattan Beach, which was on our way home, and even closer to the office than our apartment. The Little Red School House was actually Mattie's home. Teresa introduced us to Mattie, and then to her own daughter, Bonnie. The kids hit it off right away; they ran off and started to play. I took care of paying Mattie and explained our schedule.

She said her monthly fee allowed us to come and go anytime between 6:00 a.m. and 6:00 p.m., Monday through Friday. She understood that between L.A. traffic and work schedules, it was best to allow parents some flexibility.

With my number one problem solved, I decided it was time to do something positive for myself. During my years of marriage to Sherri, which included the past two miserable years of stress, I'd gained forty-five pounds. I went from 185 lbs. of muscle to 230 pounds of fat. As a new hire and single parent, I needed to be in better shape. Even though my clothes helped camouflaged the extra weight, I needed to make the best impression I could on everyone around me, especially my boss, the bail agents I'd be working with, and my fellow employees; not to mention Teresa.

The next day, I joined the Men's Executive Health Club located in the building between my new office complex and the Hyatt Hotel. My daily routine started by dropping off Ella at Mattie's around 6:00 a.m., then driving to the club for a two-hour workout. The facility was fantastic; I could shower, shave, change into a suit and tie, then walk a few hundred feet across the parking lot to my office building. I exercised faithfully, pushing myself as hard as I had when I was in boot camp, and stuffing myself full of protein every weekday, even when I traveled for business or had lunch with clients. After just a few of months, I was back to 185 pounds of solid muscle.

During this same period, I decided to move to Manhattan Beach. When a cute two-bedroom house came available a few blocks from Teresa's house, I jumped on it.

Our relationship started when I asked her to babysit Ella overnight the times I had to go out of town on business. Then I occasionally asked if she could pick Ella up when I was stuck in downtown L.A. with clients. The girls became great play partners. In fact, they began to want sleepovers—first Bonnie at our house, then Ella at Bonnie's. Sometimes I'd stop and pick up food on my way home, and the four of us would have dinner together.

In today's workplace, a budding relationship between the boss and a female employee might raise eyebrows or uncomfortable questions. But things were simpler fifty years ago. People didn't think poorly of two young, single people developing a workplace friendship, especially when one was dating someone on a steady basis, and the other one was dating on a hit-and-miss basis, with more misses than hits.

I offered to babysit Bonnie whenever Teresa needed someone as a way of reciprocating for her watching Ella. As time went on, the four of us started doing more things together on weekends and evenings. We would either take the kids to the neighborhood park, go to the beach for a picnic, out to lunch, or just out for ice cream.

At one point Teresa suggested we take the kids by train to the San Diego Zoo for the weekend. "We could spend the night and come home on Sunday; that way, we could maybe even see the aquarium," she said. Our relationship was strictly platonic, so she added with a smile, "We'll get separate rooms, of course."

I said, "Great! Let's do it."

My life was never the same after that weekend.

We were able to get separate rooms with an adjoining door, so we could keep an eye on the kids playing together in one room, while we sipped some wine, talked, and listened to music in the other one. After the kids fell asleep on the bed in the other room, and the music changed to something soft and easy, we began snuggling on the couch and exchanging small kisses. The next thing I knew, we were in bed.

After that weekend we tried to maintain the platonic relationship we'd developed over the past few months in and out of the office. But we began showing signs of jealousy. Whenever I asked her to babysit, she'd ask where I was going, who I was going with, and when I'd be home. Every time she and her boyfriend went out, I asked the same questions. It was obvious that our attraction for each other was rising to a new level.

While my private life appeared to be going extremely well, I found my new professional life more problematic. Vance lost his California Assembly race and was trying to get his old job back with Brian Reid. Hal called to tell me Brian had decided to decline Vance's request, assure me that my performance had already exceeded their expectations, and said if I continued to do my best, my job was secure. They had no intention of bringing Vance back; Vance had made his choice, and now Brian had made his.

Vance relocated to San Diego, took a position with Cal Western Insurance as vice president and manager of their new bonding department and began establishing them as a formidable competitor. Within weeks, Vance convinced Cal Western to let him expand their new bonding business to include surety bail bonds. He started an aggressive campaign to solicit bail and civil bond agents away from Blue Lakes.

Although unable to capture a significant share of Blue Lakes' business through his past relationship with many of our agents, he managed to create a lot more work for me when it came to competing for new prospects.

Despite his attempt to get his job back and send me back to Nevada with my tail between my legs, we hit it off well on a personal level. We were the two new kids on the block. Our companies, Blue Lakes and Cal Western, jointly represented "the new competition" for the old guard. As a result, the old timers, who felt they had an adequate share of the market, hated Vance and I equally for trying to horn in on their business.

Although Vance and I were still competitors and used the same marketing tactics to attract agents away from the old-guard companies, we worked more as friendly adversaries. We stopped hitting on each other's agents and focused all our efforts the old guard.

Our tactics—offering their agents contracts that provided them with a larger percentage of the premiums as commissions on their bonds, increasing their underwriting authority, and giving them the ability to write larger bail bonds without having to wait for approval from the company's underwriters—were starting to cut deeply into the old guards' market share. They didn't like it, especially when it came to giving the agents a larger underwriting authority.

When bail agents work to get clients out of jail, time is always of the essence. Delays in approval to write a large bond could cause the agents to lose their customer to a neighboring competitor.

Implementing these three tactics meant the old-school companies had to pay their agents a greater commission up front, give them authority to write larger bail bonds, or lose their entire business. Failure to compete with us on these two points was costing them a ton of money.

Instead of giving in and providing their agents with new contracts, they sent their thugs around with the intention of stopping us. Rather than shaking in our boots, we hired a couple of our own thugs to escort us to our appointments with their agents. When the old guard realized we weren't going anywhere, they attempted to intimidate their agents into staying. They warned them that when we went bankrupt (this was inevitable in their eyes) they'd gladly welcome their agents back but said their new relationship would require a much more expensive contract rate and a much lower underwriting authority.

No matter what these old timers said or did, their agents kept calling us for new contracts and our businesses continued to grow.

In December 1976, I decided to have a Christmas party at my place for the entire staff and their significant others. Since Teresa and I were the only ones with little kids, I asked how she felt about arranging to have the kids stay overnight at her ex-husband's place, or maybe at Mattie's, since we had no idea how long the party would last. She agreed and said she would take care of it.

The party was a great success and lasted into the wee hours. After everyone else left, Teresa helped clean up while we talked. One thing led to another. Before we knew it, she decided to spend the night. The next morning, she rolled over, kissed me, and said it was time for us to start dating on an exclusive basis. This meant it was time for her to give up her old boyfriend, and I had to stop pretending I had other dates.

From that day forward, between working, taking care of the kids, and sleeping together whenever possible, we spent most of our time together. The only thing we didn't do was live together.

Since Teresa was still going through her divorce, we decided that living together would not be emotionally beneficial for the kids or financially beneficial for her. At the time, knowing that we were in love and committed to each other was enough for us.

After almost a year of struggling to recover from my past and having fallen head over heels in love with Teresa, I began to feel like my whole life was finally back on track. In fact, it was better than I could have ever dreamt possible.

Six months later, on the Fourth of July, while I was still daydreaming about how perfect our relationship was, and how perfect my life was becoming, the phone rang with a call that shocked me back to reality.

CHAPTER

#26

Hal called that afternoon around three o'clock.

"Lefty," he said, "you probably should sit down before I start." He paused. "Brian and nine other members of our senior staff were killed early this afternoon in a terrible midair collision between two of the company's planes."

I remember that call like it happened yesterday. It was one of the few times I found myself speechless as feelings of despair and hopelessness all but engulfed me.

The only words I could think of to say came out in a whisper: "How could this happen? What were they doing?"

Hal said the employees had accepted Brian's invitation to attend the Fourth of July Air Show in Jasper City, Indiana. Brian thought everyone would enjoy watching him fly his biplane in the aerobatics portion of the show, so he offered to cover all the costs, including their air transportation to and from the show. Everyone traveled in the company's passenger plane, while Brian flew his biplane.

Hal said, "I can't believe it. I would have been on that plane had I not watched Brian perform many times before. I figured I'd leave a seat open for one of the younger executives."

Brian was not only an excellent pilot; he was an experienced stunt pilot. He had hundreds of hours of experience flying his biplane and the company plane.

At the end of the show, everyone returned to the company plane for the trip home while Brian climbed into his biplane. Although no one could say for sure, it was the consensus that Brian wanted to make the return trip a little more exciting for those on board the company plane by flying his biplane in loop d' loop patterns around theirs.

About four miles northwest of the company's home field in New Castle, Brian made a fatal error in judgment. Some of the witnesses on the ground near the crash site said he was flying his stunt plane upside down around the company private plane when the tip of his wing collided with the wing tip of the company's plane, sending both crashing to the ground and killing everyone on board both planes.

Only two members of the senior staff at Blue Lakes had declined Brian's offer to go: his wife Tracy, who'd helped Brian start the company, and Hal. The remaining employees were devastated. Not only had they lost friends, associates, and a great boss, they had to deal with the uncertainty of their jobs and the company's future.

This was especially true for Teresa, me, and the rest of the West Coast team, since we were over 19 hundred miles away, and our office was the newest part of the Blue Lakes operation.

Most everyone in the company knew that Brian and Tracy were the sole owners. Hal instructed me to tell everyone, including all the bail agents doing business through the West Coast office, that the company would continue to operate during this time of mourning, and that Tracy and I would make the necessary arrangements to ensure the ongoing success of the company. Hal asked me to do everything I could to keep my section of the company's ship afloat, then he hung up.

When we returned to work on the fifth of July, our office was flooded with calls from bail agents across the Western states. They were all sorry to hear about the unfortunate accident and the loss of Brian Reid, but they were more concerned about the impact Brian's death would have on their ability to continue to use Blue Lakes as a reinsurer for their bail bonds.

Many were concerned that they would lose thousands of dollars in business while searching for another company should Blue Lakes go out of business or be temporarily suspended from transacting business by the Department of Insurance. My staff spent the first few days after the crash holding everyone's hand and assuring them that "It's business as usual at Blue Lakes," even though we had no idea what would happen next.

Every day that went by without news from the home office made it harder for us to continue reassuring the agents. We used the obvious excuses like funeral arrangements and internal restructuring of staff as justification for the lack of news from back East.

After almost a week of being left in the dark, things seemed to normalize. That is, until Hal called to say he was flying out to meet with me, and not to tell anyone inside or outside the office know he was coming. What I thought would be a phone call with news I could share with everyone turned out to be a cloak-and-dagger message I was restricted from sharing with anyone.

I wasn't about to keep his trip a secret from Teresa. I needed someone I could trust to consult with, and who better than the person I loved most, and the person whose life would be impacted as much as mine?

She and I discussed everything that night, including the possible closing of the office, and what we would do next if faced with unemployment. But until we knew what Hal had to say, there was nothing we could do except wait it out.

CHAPTER

#27

Hal's plane was scheduled to land at LAX just before lunch. Since no one knew he was coming, we arranged to meet out of the office. I reserved a table at the Hyatt Hotel. The moment we sat down, I asked him straight out, "Are you here to close the office?"

He said, "No, so let's order lunch first, then I'll explain everything."

After the waitress left with our orders, Hal got right to the point. "Brian's wife wants to sell the company and she's hired an independent insurance executive who specializes in reorganizing and selling insurance companies to help.

"He wants to restructure the company and phase out lines that are less profitable or less favorable for selling or merging Blue Lakes. Although they didn't say it, their goal is to maximize their profits from the sale, regardless of the impact on the employees, especially you and me. She's appointed this guy to the board of directors; they'll appoint him as interim chairman and president."

Hal continued, "He's reviewed the company business plan, and current lines of business. As you know, our main book of business is surety bonds, the largest part of which is bail bonds.

"The new president believes that few, if any, companies would want to buy Blue Lakes whole. Companies either file for bankruptcy and the bankruptcy trustee sells their licenses to the highest bidder, or the board sells off each outstanding line of business together with the qualifying licenses for each. In our case the board plans to sell the company in pieces to the highest bidders. So they'll try to sell the bail business to one of our current competitors and retain the qualifying licenses for sale at a later date. Most every prospective buyer for the surety bail business already has staff in place, together with the experience necessary to manage the business, so they won't be needing us.

"In the meantime, Blue Lakes will be using us to maintain a 'business as usual façade' long enough to relicense our agents with the new owners. Everyone benefits from our hard work—except us."

As I listened, I knew Hal hadn't come just to paint a picture of doom and gloom. He must have a reason for telling me all this, but I wasn't sure what it could be.

That's when he said, "Lefty, this is bullshit! I'm not going to stand by and let them do this without a fight. I've been sharing this information with a friend, one of Blue Lakes' largest general agents from New Orleans. His name is Marty Dupree. In addition to being a G.A., he's also a lawyer, with a successful law practice specializing in insurance.

"He and I have made a tentative deal, which is why I'm here. He's been working to acquire his own insurance company and is looking to close a deal on one in particular that has qualifying surety licenses in numerous states. The company has no outstanding liabilities, policies, or business. It's what the insurance industry calls 'a clean shell company.'

"We plan to steal Blue Lakes' bail business, rather than buy it. We want to steal away enough to make the remainder worthless to anyone else but us. At that point, we make the Blue Lakes board a reasonable offer to take over the remainder.

"As it stands," he continued, "one third of Blue Lakes' business is being conducted in the South, through Marty's general agency. Another third is conducted in the Midwest, and processed through Blue Lakes' home office, in other words, through me. The remainder is being written through your office here in California. So I've come to offer you an opportunity to join us, with the possibility of becoming an equal partner."

My head was spinning. it was a lot to take in, especially when I'd thought we'd be closing the office.

"If you accept," Hal said, "Marty and I are prepared to pay you the same salary and benefits you're currently receiving. And if you're able to deliver a significant portion of Blue Lakes' current western regional business to the new company within the first year, you'll also receive a one-third ownership interest in the new company. To help ensure your success, we want you to bring your entire staff along at the same salary and benefits they're now receiving. We don't want you to leave anyone behind to help them help pick up the pieces. You'll have full authority to relocate your office anywhere you want and make all the decisions as though this were your own business.

"The eleven western states represent about a third of Blue Lakes' business, so if you're successful in moving it all to the new company, and maybe sign some additional business as well, you could end up with 33 percent ownership in our new company.

"I'm going to need your answer before my plane leaves tomorrow. I realize this doesn't give you much time to talk it over with anyone. But if you do, I must have your word that you won't share this information with any employees or bail agents associated with Blue Lakes."

I said simply, "I don't have any questions now, but you have my word; regardless of how this plays out, I'll never tell anyone about our meeting today."

We shook hands, and I said I'd give him my answer at breakfast the next morning, before he checked out of the hotel.

I went directly back to the office, knowing full well that I'd had my fingers crossed when I made my promise. There was no way I was leaving Teresa out in the cold. This decision was too important to our personal relationship, as well as our future employment; I didn't want to make this decision without her.

As for discussing this with the other employees, or any of the bail agents, I planned to keep my word, even though it was the second hardest part of my promise. I really wanted to call Mickey and ask his advice, but his relationship with Brian, and presumably Hal, was how I got my job with Blue Lakes, and if Mickey told Hal I discussed our plan with him, Hal would know I broke my word, and therefore couldn't trust me. In fact, I think he was testing me, because he'd probably already told Mickey.

So Teresa and I were on our own. Just knowing how we felt about each other gave me the strength I needed to make the call, but I wanted it to be a team decision. I would be giving Hal "our" answer.

When I told Teresa, she wasn't as surprised as I'd expected. I could see that she knew exactly where we stood and what we should do before I finished explaining the plan.

She gave me a kiss. "I want you to know, we'll be together no matter what you decide. But keep in mind, all of us will most likely be unemployed just as soon as Blue Lakes sells the bail business anyway; especially if they sell it to one of our competitors. Hal's proposition isn't necessarily our best option now, but it's our only one."

I met Hal the next morning and told him, "I'm all in."

I added, "I'd like to meet my new friend and future business partner, Mr. Dupree, as soon as possible, to ensure that we're all on the same page and discuss which of my employees stay with Blue Lakes, and which come with us, from his perspective. I'll also want to reaffirm all their salaries and benefits, and so on. I wouldn't want to mislead them about leaving Blue Lakes and then not receive the same compensation. And of course I'll want to hear about earning my interest in the company. I realize we don't have a company yet, but we need to start setting the perimeters of our plan."

Since time was of the essence, he said they'd find an opportunity to meet within the next few days.

CHAPTER

#28

During a short conference call the next day, the three of us decided L.A. would be our best option for secrecy, and picked the following Thursday for convenience, since Fridays were always taken up with questions and answers from our staff and the agents.

I felt like Thursday would never arrive. The excitement of possibly owning one third of an insurance company was almost more than I could grasp, especially after all I'd been through.

Thursday did arrive, and Marty and I met. I was surprised that we were about the same age. I'd imagined he would be in his mid-fifties, like Hal or Mickey, not in his early thirties, like me. On one hand, I was okay with him being younger, thinking he and I would have more in common. On the other hand, I was somewhat skeptical, worrying that he might not have the resources to secure ownership of an insurance company.

I thought it wise to ask, point blank, how he was going to pull it off. He assured me that Gulf Coast Insurance, the shell company he'd been working on, held a sufficient number of qualifying certificates throughout the US to adequately appoint all the agents needed to pay back the loan from his father's bank.

That answered one big question: His father was behind him, and his dad was not going to let us fail.

Marty said he had enough personal assets and income from his current general agency to provide the new company with adequate startup capital to meet the salaries and expenses necessary to strip Blue Lakes and satisfy the concerns our bail agents might have about the new company's ability to provide them with a stable market. What's more, we'd also provide a more knowledgeable and secure group of employees than those left at Blue Lakes after we split.

I felt good about everything I was hearing, but Hal seemed skeptical. He worried that the company Marty was about to acquire didn't have enough state qualifications and certificates to weaken Blue Lakes' position in the national market. This would leave Blue Lakes in a position to sell off the remainder of their bail business to an existing competitor. If that happened, our competitors, including Blue Lakes, would be able to paint our company as an unproven, financially weak regional marketer rather than a strong national carrier.

Hal's concerns rattled Marty. He abruptly ended the meeting. He said he'd return to New Orleans to discuss Hal's worries with his dad, the bank, and the Louisiana Department of Insurance, to see if Hal's anxiety was shared by others.

After Marty left, Hal expressed serious concerns about Marty's proposed purchase, now only days away. "Gulf Coast Insurance is a perfect fit for Marty and his general agency because it's already licensed in all the southern states, which gives him the ability to protect all his current agents and their cash flow. That's the main reason he is buying it.

"But bullshit, even the name suggests limitations on our marketing ability. And it's insufficiently licensed for a nation-wide marketing or business plan. If Marty continues down this path, I'll withdraw from the deal. My plane leaves for Indiana in about an hour, so I have to go. Why don't you let Marty know what we just discussed, and how I feel. That'll give you and him some time to think about what you'd do if I withdraw from the deal before we talk again."

Hal left to catch the shuttle bus to the airport.

Back at work, I told Teresa, "Everything's up in the air. I'll fill you in later, but right now I need you to do some research. Find as much information as you can on Gulf Coast Insurance, especially in what states they're qualified to write surety bonds. I don't want to rely on information I got from a guy I just met, while the guy I've been working with for almost a year is skeptical about the plan."

Since we were not anywhere near the computer age, she called the Louisiana Department of Insurance. Within minutes, she learned that Hal was only partially correct about Gulf Coast's limitations. However, Marty's information proved out. The new company was cleared to do business in California, as well as the other states in our western region. So Hal's piece of the business puzzle was the only region not fully covered. No wonder he was skeptical; I would have been too, if the tables were turned and my territory was left open.

I was sure Hal had offered only half the facts about Marty's proposed plan to get me to join him in persuading Marty that our deal was off unless he found a different company. I realized that if I didn't agree to join Hal in rejecting Marty's plan, hell would freeze over before he would include me in any of his future plans.

But I also realized that Hal was for Hal, which meant it was every man for himself. I decided to call Mickey before I called Marty.

Mickey wasn't surprised to hear from me, since Hal had told him about Brian's death and his concerns about Blue Lakes' future. He was surprised, however, to hear that Hal didn't have the balls to take a chance on the deal with Marty, even with the new company's limited coverage in the Midwest.

I said, "I'm still giving serious thought to going with Marty. He made me a hell of a good offer, and I don't think I have a future with Blue Lakes, or Hal, now that Brian's gone. Plus, I can't trust Hal to keep me on at Blue Lakes since I know about his breach in loyalty to the company.

"So, Mickey, if I go with Marty, can I count on you to move your business to our new company? At least until you get your own company, the one you've been working on. Or is your loyalty still with Hal and Blue Lakes?"

His reply was simple and to the point.

"Kid, I'm surprised you asked. You know Elaine and I see you as family, and family comes first. My allegiance was to Brian, not Hal, and it's always been to you. You can count on us. And if anything goes wrong with this deal, you can always come back and take over our business. I'm getting too damn old for this, anyway."

That was just the boost I needed, and I couldn't wait to share it with Teresa, who knew about Hal and was also concerned.

I called Marty and told him what Hal said after our meeting.

Marty responded, "I'm sure you were as surprised as I was about Hal's concerns. Lefty, I'm still moving to close the deal with Gulf Coast and the Louisiana Department of Insurance.

I plan to have the meetings we discussed earlier concerning my father, the bank, and the Department of Insurance, but this time, I'd like to fly out and meet with you privately. I'm not trying to go behind Hal's back on this, but I'm sure his comments haven't provided either of us with a high level of confidence. I'd like to update you about my recent discussions, including those with him."

"Marty, I can tell you right now, I'm all in, as long as my part of our deal hasn't changed. I don't think we should discuss any of this over the phone, and we should keep our meetings confidential, regardless of which way we go. I look forward to seeing you; just let me know when."

"How's tomorrow look for you?"

"Great, meet you at the hotel for cocktails and dinner? Let me know when you arrive."

The next evening, our meeting went better than expected. Marty opened it by telling me that Hal had officially backed out of the deal.

"You're kidding!" I said. "I can't believe Hal did that without giving me the courtesy of a phone call. Hal's decision and actions just reinforced my decision to go with you."

Marty explained that he'd already signed the papers with the bank and the Department of Insurance, so a few simple formalities remained before Gulf Coast was his. If I still agreed to take the position of Gulf Coast's V.P. and western regional manager, he'd match my salary and benefits, and he'd provide an open expense account. He repeated that I could bring everyone with me to our new office in a location of my choosing, and I'd be provided with a credit card and a car allowance when I was ready to make the change.

He also made one more comment, in the form of a promise; one I engraved in my memory: "Lefty," he said, "I'm also going to give you the stock in Gulf Coast that I promised during our planning stages with Hal, because I want it to be 'our' company. When you produce a volume of business for our company that's equal to the annual business Blue Lakes is now receiving through your western regional division, I'll give you a full one-third interest in Gulf Coast. Hal already gave me copies of your production figures. I presented them to the bank as proof of our ability to cover all our operating expenses as well as payments on their loan."

It was actually going to happen—I was going to get an interest in the company, and all I had to do is work my ass off.

"That's quite a welcome surprise. All I can say is, 'Be prepared Marty; I'm not only going to reach that goal, I'm going to exceed it within the first year.' "

"Great! Brian's death knocked Blue Lakes off balance, but we need to deal a significant blow to their production and cash flow as soon as possible if we're going to eliminate them as a competitor—and Hal will do everything he can to stop us.

"Don't leave anyone behind, even if you're unsatisfied with their performance. You can always make changes after the dust settles. Blue Lakes has no plans to expand the bail business, they just want to sell it off. I believe they'll process whatever West Coast business remains through the home office, rather than wasting resources trying to protect or salvage business or employees they don't want anyway."

I suggested, "Let's try to keep a lid on this until our company, and especially the new West Coast office, is prepared to handle business as usual. I'm sure Hal will terminate me the moment he realizes what's going on, so I need your promise to employ anyone and everyone they terminate. And since Teresa will be working with me on locating adequate office space, securing new business phones, purchasing office furniture, office supplies, and other things even before we start talking to the staff about coming aboard, Hal will terminate her as well."

Marty agreed.

"I'll have her gather copies of every bail form we currently use in all the western states, especially things like the bail bond powers of attorney," I said.

The standard industry practice was to plagiarize as many of these forms as possible; it made writing and processing bonds easier for the bail agents, the court recorders, and the clerks.

"We haven't discussed what Hal might do to try and stop us. I doubt he has the balls to do anything. I think he'll wait until it happens and act surprised."

Marty nodded his approval. He said he'd stay overnight and review all the forms Blue Lakes' bail agents were using to transact business, and which of them they'd need from Gulf Coast before they could start transacting business on their behalf. He needed to ensure that we had at least one of everything so Marty could take them to Louisiana and have his printers plagiarize and print them for Gulf Coast as quickly as possible.

It was getting close to dinner time. Marty suggested that we invite Teresa to dinner with us, since she'd spent the day working on the forms packet and was the only other person who knew what was going on. Plus, I wanted her to spend a little out-of-the-office time with Marty to get her perspective on him and our plans.

During dinner, Marty asked what made me so sure I could pull off taking all of Blue Lakes' bail business with me. I explained that I'd been "talking the talk, and walking the walk," for over ten years. That I'd owned two bail businesses, chased my own skips, and used all the tricks of the trade, some in the shadows, and some straight, to maximize business profits. That I'd seen agents misappropriating collateral, late-reporting bonds to their companies, and bribing clerks to accept previously used bond powers, all to pocket the full premium for themselves or cheat the company out of their portion. "I've even seen them pay off a few judges to exonerate forfeitures, in order to pocket some of the cash collateral they were holding.

"I'm not saying I've done it all, but I've seen enough to recognize bullshit when I hear it, and they all respect that I know this business as well, if not better than they do. They also know I'm here to help them, not to hurt them, and not put them out of business when they get into a tough spot. They'll go where I go, rather than take a chance with guys like Hal and his cronies, guys who know little or nothing about how a real bail bond office works. Brian would have been hard to beat if we were going up against him, but Hal's a push-over in comparison.

"I have all the confidence in what I can do, and that I can do even more over the next twelve months. My only concern is whether you'll be ready to deliver my share of the company by then."

I made that last comment in front of Teresa; I wanted her to know what we could both expect from our decision to take this chance.

Marty knew we were all in and ready to get started.

CHAPTER

#29

During the next few weeks, Marty and I talked daily, even on weekends, in preparation for the mass exodus from Blue Lakes to Gulf Coast. It was our intention to take as much information as possible concerning Blue Lakes and their agents without raising suspicions, and to keep everything we gathered in a secure place, out of the office and out of our homes.

Every night and on weekends, I rummaged through the agent files and made copies of all the pertinent information we'd need to prepare new contracts for each of the agencies, as well as to make Department of Insurance appointments for their owners and agents. I put everything back as I found it so none of the staff would know what I was doing. That way, if any of them decided not to move to the new company, they wouldn't be able to accuse me, or any other staff member who moved to Gulf Coast, of conspiring to steal information or properties belonging to Blue Lakes. (Additionally, I wasn't sure if Hal had offered one of them an incentive to spy on me.)

Teresa didn't help me take any confidential materials. I didn't want her implicated or accused of doing something illegal. She was merely leaving the company to take a new job, and her leaving was based solely on the uncertainty surrounding the future because of Brian's untimely death.

By the time Marty was ready to open Gulf Coast, I'd amassed one shit pot of information, not only about the Blue Lakes agents, but also on just about every other licensed bail agent in the western states.

On the last workday of the month, I advised everyone in the office that I was leaving to take a new position with Gulf Coast Insurance and presented each of them with a copy of my resignation letter, which I'd faxed to Hal. I asked those interested in accepting their own, comparable, position with the new company to fax a similar letter of resignation to the Blue Lakes HR department, then pack their personal belongings and meet me at the new Gulf Coast office in Manhattan Beach the next morning.

Everyone except Bob Anderson faxed their resignations. I suspected Bob wasn't being truthful when he thanked me for the job offer, and said he'd have to think about it. So I wasn't surprised when he said he wasn't coming. I think his plan was to slide into my position and save Blue Lakes, which Hal may have suggested as an enticement to stay.

Teresa and I were careful not to do or say anything when Bob was in the office. I had already planned to have everyone's personal tote box checked for any Blue Lakes' stuff as they were leaving; Bob was the best candidate. I needed him to tell Hal he'd personally ensured that no one took anything belonging their former employer.

Within a week after we left, Blue Lakes sent a letter to all their western regional agents, both civil and bail, instructing them to report all future business directly to the home office. Within a week of the letter, they closed the office and fired their one and only western regional employee, Bob Anderson.

I thought Bob had been talking to Hal all along, which would have given Blue Lakes an opportunity to plan to close our office early, hoping to leave all of us without jobs. We beat them to the punch, since I'd kept everyone in the dark about our actual departure date. As it turned out, Bob was the only loser in the transition.

CHAPTER

#30

Everyone showed up at the new office right on time and were all quite impressed. The office was one short block from the ocean in Manhattan Beach, and every desk had a great ocean view. Teresa picked the location, which was a few blocks from both our homes. (She'd also worked with Marty's team to arrange the purchase and delivery of the furniture, typewriters, copy machines, filing cabinets and supplies, while I was made pre-emptive calls to many of the agents I'd become close friends with over the past year. I wanted them to know what we were doing so we could keep in touch, in case Hal decided to fire everyone before we were ready to leave.)

We were ready to kick off the new deal and pick up from where we'd left off that previous Friday. We had a new location, a new company, and a positive future.

Everyone found their new spot and new furniture, settled in, put their personal stuff around to remind them of home, and prepared for our first office meeting.

"Hi, and welcome to Gulf Coast Insurance Company. For those who don't know me, I'm Gulf Coast's new V.P. and western regional manager." Everyone laughed and applauded except Teresa, who rolled her eyes and smiled at me.

Over the weekend, she and I were able to make copies of the comprehensive list of all the bail agents we'd been working with during the past year, as well as those we wanted to contact. Those currently doing business with Blue Lakes were at the top of the list; those working with other surety companies in our region were next. We wanted to make sure everyone knew about our new company.

I passed out the list to everyone.

"I've divided the list into sections, one section for each of us. Today's assignment is for you to start calling everyone; those we know and those we don't. Before the week's over, I want everyone to know who we are, where we are, and that we're offering the best rates, the best underwriting limits, and the best service in the market. We're not the new kids on the block—we're the best!

"Be sure to enter notes next to each name while they're fresh in your mind. And make sure you get their current mailing address. When we're done, we'll exchange lists and start all over again, now with follow-up calls. These second calls, to the Blue Lakes agents, will let them know we've mailed their Gulf Coast agency appointments to the Department of Insurance in each of their respective states, and to make sure we appointed all the agents in their office.

"After we've called everyone at least twice, we'll start sending follow-up letters with a photo of our entire staff. Before we're finished, I want those that haven't done business with us before to feel like they've known us for years. If we play this right, everyone will be calling us as soon as they hear that Blue Lakes has closed its West Coast office in California. When they think about all the changes and sadness surrounding Blue

Lakes, they'll start worrying about losing their bond market, and the first ones they think of will be us!"

Many Blue Lakes agents were the first to switch, not just because we were increasing their underwriting authority, which allowed them to write larger bonds without calling us for approval, but also because they enjoyed doing business with us, people they knew and trusted.

While we were hammering on them to switch companies, Blue Lakes was stepping all over themselves. Closing our office and asking their agents to report their business directly to the home office, then asking them to deal with employees they didn't know and were thousands of miles away, enhanced our opportunity to switch more than half the agents within the first few weeks. After the first six weeks, Blue Lakes was becoming a thing of the past throughout the western region.

Marty was so impressed with our progress that it was easy to persuade him to let my staff begin production and distribution of the first-ever monthly bail publication, which we called "The Bail Reporter." We mailed copies to all the bail agents currently appointed with Gulf Coast, not just those in the western region. Then we expanded distribution to every bail agent throughout the US.

This new marketing plan, using the newsletter—which contained numerous advertisements and articles about Gulf Coast—as a solicitation tool, was working so well, Gulf Coast was almost overwhelmed by new requests for appointments from agents throughout the country. In fact, the entire company, not just the western region, was within reach of the first-year production figures Marty had set during our initial meeting. I felt the reality of receiving my one-third interest in the company was close at hand.

In early February 1978, Marty called to let me know that he was taking the board of directors and the entire senior management staff, myself included, to Mardi Gras in New Orleans for an all-expenses-paid company celebration. He said it would be a great opportunity to meet his dad and get to know the other members of the executive team.

I remember thinking, "This is it. They're going to give me my stock, and maybe put me on the board, I can just feel it." I wanted to bring Teresa along, but I thought it might be the wrong time to let them know we were seriously dating, so I passed on that idea.

When I told her, she agreed. We were concerned they might want her to quit, so we settled on my going it alone while she stayed behind to watch the kids, but I told her I'd make it up to her real soon.

I'd never been to Mardi Gras. In fact, it was my first time in New Orleans. Mardi Gras was the place to be if you were into partying all night. My drinking days were over when I decided to join Blue Lakes, and I carried my abstinence with me into my new job, my new love, and my new family.

I didn't come to see the pageantry, the parades, or drink myself silly. I was here to meet the key players in my new company, and hopefully receive my one-third interest. But Marty insisted that I see the sights and participate in the carnival atmosphere.

"After all, this is in the famous French Quarter, and it is Mardi Gras."

As we stood talking near Bourbon Street, Marty said, "Lefty, you've been working so hard these past few months, and I wanted to show my appreciation by having you come here for a little fun and relaxation. We'll walk around here tonight, have dinner, a few drinks, and take in the sights.

Then tomorrow we'll drive over to my place on the coast in Mississippi, so you can meet my dad, my wife, and the rest of my family."

As we started to walk through the French Quarter, I noted that young people were everywhere, and the bars and restaurants were jammed elbow-to-asshole with people. Women were hanging from every second-story balcony flaunting their naked tits, while the drunks in the streets were cheering them on, yelling, "Take it all off!" Everyone, including the middle-aged groups, was listening to jazz, drinking mint juleps, spilling food all over each other, or dropping it like garbage in the gutters. It was certainly something to watch, but not all night long.

After a few hours of eating, having a couple of light beers, and watching just how crazy grown people could behave, we agreed to meet for breakfast the next morning and parted company. Marty continued to party. I returned to my hotel in the French Quarter and spent at least an hour cleaning street garbage off the only pair of shoes I'd packed for the trip.

Headlines in the morning newspapers listed the total tonnage of trash the city's garbage company cleared off the streets of the French Quarter the previous day. The articles noted that the city fathers measured the success of every annual Mardi Gras by the tonnage of trash scooped off the streets. I thought, based on the amount of shit on my shoes, and the number of people I'd seen roaming the streets, the city fathers could call this one of the most successful, especially if they added an additional ton or two to cover the amount carried home on everyone's shoes.

Marty picked me up around nine the next morning, and we headed to his beach house, just over the border in Mississippi. We arrived in time for lunch with his father, his wife, and their three kids. We spent the afternoon socializing and enjoying the ocean views.

On our way back to New Orleans, Marty started talking business. He said the company had recently passed the eight-month mark, asked how I felt about the company's potential for future growth, and if I had any new ideas up my sleeve to promote the company and pump-up production.

He said not one word about the West Coast office. Nor did he give me credit for the unexpected interest in the company due to our newsletter. Watching his demeanor, I got the impression that we'd not yet hit the production totals needed to secure my one-third interest in the company.

Rather than talking about the totals, I decided to let him in on my latest idea of using the Bail Reporter publication to announce the formation of the first national bail agent's association—the American Association of Professional Bail Agents, or the AAPBA—and having that association host the first-ever national bail agents convention in Las Vegas in May 1978.

The idea was to launch the AAPBA as a neutral entity, so bail agents, general agents, and insurance executives representing the different surety insurance companies from throughout the US would feel comfortable attending, and not discourage their agents from coming as well.

I explained how Vance Parker, the former western regional V.P. for Blue Lakes and now the executive V.P. from Cal Western Insurance, had agreed to proportionately share in the convention's promotional costs, as long as I could get Marty, and our company to agree to cover the rest.

I explained how Vance and I were becoming friendly competitors as a result of the new negative bail legislation pending before the California legislature. And that he wasn't really much of a competitor, because his heart wasn't in the bail business like mine was. And although his company wrote bail bonds and civil bonds, they were licensed to do business only in California.

I wasn't sure how Marty would react to learning that Vance and I were friends, so we staged our first meeting with him as a bid for his approval for the joint distribution of materials opposing the pending legislation. This also gave us a chance to broach the subject of forming the national bail association and hosting its first-ever convention.

Marty said, "I recognize the value of our joining forces, especially since Vance's company is licensed to do business only in California, and it's the only company able to capitalize on all the prospective agents from many of the other states. But I'm skeptical about our chances of pulling off the convention as part of an AAPBA function, without our competitors getting wise that it's tied to Gulf Coast, Cal Western, or both."

I cut him off. "The California legislature is reviewing a proposal to fund a pre-trial release program, and if passed, bail agents from across the country would feel the negative financial impact because 'As California goes, so goes the nation.' This is going to be our 'call to arms' for the convention.

"Plus, I have a friend; actually, a friend of my brother's, named Harlan Fuller. Fuller's agreed to front the entire program as the founder and interim president of the AAPBA . . . for a fee, of course. He's a well-respected independent financial advisor from San Diego, with no traceable affiliation to any bail bond agents, agencies, or surety insurance companies in the business. In fact, outside of me, he's never met another bail agent, or needed their services for himself, his friends, or his family.

"Hell, getting you and Vance to fund the event and the pre-event promotions was the only part of my plan I've been worried about. I've already made contact with one of my old friends in Las Vegas, a mafia capo by named Tommy Costanoto. Tommy sent me a lot of referral business when I was writing bail for Mickey in Vegas. At the time, he was acting only as an observer, sent out West by his boss to protect and ensure the mob's interests. Now he's the casino manager for the MGM. He's agreed to comp the conference room as well as four hotel suites—one for Harlan, one for Vance, one for you, Marty, and one for me. And the MGM Hotel is one of the newest and largest casinos on the Vegas strip."

I continued, "Tommy's take on this national bail convention thing is as strong as mine. In fact, he's setting aside a block of three hundred rooms to accommodate *his* expectations on the turnout. He also plans to post a notice of the event on the hotel's largest Events and Entertainment reader board, located right on the strip. He says that over the years, the MGM Hotel Casino acquired a lot of heavy repeat play from many bail agents throughout the country and he expects they'll come running when they realize that this time, their trip qualifies as a tax write-off."

Marty bought it all. So did Vance.

By now, I thought for sure Marty realized the quality of my work and the potential for success that my marketing ideas were bringing to his new company. Now, sometime between the Mardi Gras and the convention, I felt the time was right to secure my ownership interest in Gulf Coast.

CHAPTER

#31

As a result of all the positive pre-convention publicity, and despite the negative propaganda being sold by our old-time surety competitors, the AAPBA phone, which was set up in my Manhattan Beach office, was ringing off the hook. We got calls from individual agents as well as general agents from across America. Many of them, especially the G.A.s, wanted an opportunity to speak at the convention and participate in some of the committees being set up to discuss the current problems affecting their business. In addition to some of the smaller western states, they came from Florida, Pennsylvania, Tennessee, Iowa, Texas, New York, New Jersey, Washington, Nevada, California and many other parts of the country.

They all made reservations at the MGM. Harlan, our interim president, made sure he scheduled a spot for everyone wanting to speak in order to fill the entire the three-day program. He scheduled agents, general agents, and company representatives regardless of company affiliation; after all, this was an "industry event," not one limited to Gulf Coast.

There were so many people planning to attend that Tommy had to expand the block of rooms to accommodate everyone.

I was the AAPBA's self-appointed convention coordinator, as well as the editor of the monthly newsletter. Everyone wanted an opportunity to meet with me to discuss their local problems and find out more about Gulf Coast—so many, in fact, that I scheduled one-on-one meetings with some of the G.A.s from around the country prior to the convention. I knew that controlling the convention and being able to meet with as many prospects as possible would easily provide enough new business to meet Marty's one-year production goal for the western regional office. It was time to make my call.

"Hey, Marty. I'm sure you've seen the latest projections, as well as the number of new agents we anticipate signing out West, so I'm wondering if we could have a little sit down here in California before the convention. I'm sure the entire staff would appreciate hearing about the good job they're doing, and I'd like to discuss the deal we made almost a year ago. Why not combine a one-day side trip to California on your way to Las Vegas?"

Marty said, "That's a great idea. I have a few things we should get out of the way before we get involved in the Vegas thing, anyway. I'll be there the day after tomorrow. Is that okay with you?"

"You bet. See you then."

I told Teresa that Marty was coming, that he was aware that our first year was just about up, and that this time, we were going to talk about the original deal. I'd started to think about our future, not just with the company, but with each other.

I was hoping Marty would live up to his part of our deal and present me with something proving my one third ownership in Gulf Coast. The next two days were the slowest in my life; at least it seemed that way at the time.

Marty arrived in L.A. in time for lunch, so after congratulating the staff on a job well done, he insisted on taking us all to lunch at the Mexican restaurant across the street from the office.

With everyone in attendance, I felt it was inappropriate to discuss my up-and-coming ownership in the company. He talked about everything else, including the convention in Las Vegas, but failed to say anything about me personally, or my interest in the company.

When everyone settled back to work at the office after lunch, Marty said, "Lefty, why don't we go for a walk around the block to help our digestion."

As soon as we walked onto the large entry deck overlooking the ocean, I asked the only question on my mind, one I'm sure he knew was coming.

"Marty, you know why I wanted you to come here; you know what I want to hear. Now that I met my part of our deal, I need to know if you're ready to meet yours."

He paused to look out over the ocean for what seemed like a lifetime before he looked at me and said, "I know what I said, and at the time I really meant it, but I just can't do it. I can't give up any part of my company. It just means too much to me and to my family. I also know how hard you've worked to keep your end of our deal, so I want to do whatever I can to show my appreciation.

"I've ordered a new Mercedes sedan for you. It will be yours for as long as you're with the company. In addition, I'm raising your salary by 30 percent, and providing a new bonus plan based on the profits from the West Coast production. Hopefully, these tokens of my appreciation with make up for my inability to meet the original terms of our deal."

Now it was my turn to pause. I needed time to calm down. At that moment, I was ready to throw his ass over the guard rail, or strangle him on the spot.

Instead, I was able to get control of my emotions. This provided an opportunity to flash back to something Mickey told me when I started writing bail.

He'd said, "Kid, lots of things can and will happen to you in this business, some good, some not so good. Remember, always keep your cool, and always keep your word. Think before you give it; always be prepared to live with the consequences, good, bad, or indifferent. And if a client, friend, or business associate gives you his word, make sure they live up to it as well, or make sure they pay the consequences. But never get mad. Just get even. Because getting mad will always cost you in the long run. But getting even will cost them for a lifetime."

I turned around, looked Marty in the eye and said, "Thanks for being honest with me. Although I'm disappointed, I understand where you're coming from. Thanks for the car and the raise; I'm sure they'll help put a smile back on my face. In the meantime, any chance we can give the staff a raise as well?"

He agreed and suggested that I put together a list of what I thought each person deserved, based on their contributions to our success.

As we headed back into the office, it took every bit of restraint I could muster to shake his hand rather than punch him in the face.

Marty thanked everyone again for their hard work and told them he was looking forward to spending more time with each of them at the convention. He said his goodbyes, and I took him back to the airport in time to catch his plane for Vegas.

I went back to the office and pulled Teresa aside. "When we talked earlier this week, did you have a premonition about Marty? Because the little prick just backed out on our deal." I told her about the car, the raise, the bonus, and his reneging on his promise. "I guess he thinks I'm stupid enough to accept his cheap-ass gestures while cheating me out of the partial owner-ship of what was supposed to be our company. BULLSHIT!" I ranted about how the company would have fallen on its face if it weren't for our efforts. "I helped build this damn company into one that has the potential of being worth millions, and he gives me a token raise, lets me use some piece-of-shit car, then provides me with another worthless promise. Mickey always told me not to get mad, just get even. Well, I'm mad, and I'm going to get even too! He has no idea what I can do to him and his little company. You can bet your ass that he'll be sorry when I'm finished. I was instrumental in building it, I can be just as instrumental in destroying it and putting it all on his back as the owner."

Although Teresa shared my anger, she was far more ratio-nal. She reminded me to stay calm and get even.

During the two days I'd waited for Marty to arrive and discuss our deal, Vance and I had had an opportunity to discuss a new twist; one that included the possibility of him acquiring an exclusive national managing general agency contract for license and permit bonds with Gulf Coast. Vance felt that Cal Western Insurance wanted out of the bail bond business because some of the newer, inex-perienced bail agents he'd signed were encountering early, extraordinary losses. This caused their board of directors to question management's decision to go into bail bonds in the first place. Vance also said he'd rather focus on solicit-ing license and permit business through his own national managing general agency, rather than continue working as an employee for Cal Western.

I said I'd mention his situation to Marty when he arrived in California. In reality, I'd been thinking how this arrangement could be icing on the cake for closing my ownership deal with Marty. If I was able to pull it off, it would double Gulf Coast's bail business in California, and open up a new, national license and permit division. Gulf Coast would provide all the Cal Western bail agents with new Gulf Coast contracts that would give them an opportunity to continue writing new bonds while liquidating their open liability with Cal Western. This would almost immediately double Gulf Coast's California bail business. In exchange, Cal Western would make sure all their agents agreed to the transition on an exclusive basis with Gulf Coast.

What's more, Vance would receive an exclusive license and permit contract with Gulf Coast, which would put Gulf Coast in the L&P business. This would be in addition to everything Gulf Coast would receive due to the Las Vegas convention exposure.

But now, since I'd gotten screwed out of owning any part of Gulf Coast, my conversation with Marty was going to head in a totally different direction.

I had a great exit strategy for Vance, one that would get him the managing G.A. contact he was looking for, while providing Gulf Coast with a shit-pot full of new business in exchange. First, I'd have to convince Marty to recontract all Cal Western's bail agents with Gulf Coast at their same Cal Western bond cost rate; then agree to help the agents liquidate all their open Cal Western bail bonds while allowing them to use their Cal Western reserve accounts, without placing liens or encumbrances on the existing contract collateral Cal Western was holding.

Vance would then have to convince Cal Western to ensure that all their agents transferred to Gulf Coast and post all their future business through Gulf Coast, instead of through another competitive surety company. He'd need to ensure a complete exodus from Cal Western and entry with Gulf Coast.

This was a great exit strategy for Cal Western, whose senior management were concerned about potential losses in a business they neither liked nor understood. And it was a great way for Gulf Coast to significantly grow their California bail business overnight.

But after getting fucked by Marty, it was time for me to get something more out of this deal.

That night I called Vance and told him "I've decided against talking to Marty about our plan until we have another opportunity to discuss some financial changes we need to make."

"I want to proceed with our plan; I just want to make a few positive financial alterations to directly benefit the two of us. We're not giving Marty Cal Western's bail business for free, nor are we signing any of the new California agents from the Vegas convention with Gulf Coast. We're going to sign them up with Cal Western first. That cheap little bastard is not only going to pay us a percentage on Cal Western's current agents, he's going to pay us for every one of the new guys we sign up with you as well."

Vance chuckled. "Shit, who put a bug up your ass?

"That cheap bastard just backed out of the deal we made when I joined him. He cheated me out of the one third interest in Gulf Coast after I met my part of our deal." I told him about the raise, the car and the bonus, in return for working my ass into the ground. "Big fucking deal! Vance, we know the quality of the Cal Western's bail agents is poor at best, and the company's going face heavy losses the near future and will probably use you as their scapegoat and fire your ass. Then, they'll cancel their bail program. Transferring all Cal Western's agents to Gulf Coast will give the agents an opportunity to keep writing while using their Cal Western loss reserves to clean up some of their early losses. This will give you and me three-plus years to build our new national agency while pocketing kickbacks from Marty. We know this deal will eventually turn to shit, and when it does, it'll be my ass that gets fired for coming up with it.

"There are three types of bail agents: Those that do everything by the book and write bonds with the right intentions, playing it straight, and guaranteeing their clients' appearance in court. There are those that write their business on the edge, willing to work in the shadows whenever they need to return their skips and recover their losses one way or another. These are the guys I've been cultivating over the years for Blue Lakes, and now Gulf Coast. Most of them are long-term players. Then there's the guys you've been signing up—the ones that take drugs or stolen merchandise for collateral from drug dealers, users, or thieves. Stuff they can't sell or will get them killed trying. They also take full cash collateral and could give a shit about justice, or whether their clients show up for court."

Vance stayed quiet as I continued my tirade.

"I want to stick them all with Marty to pay him back for failing to keep his word. I want to milk this deal, and our relationship with Marty, for all we can get over the next few years. While your group of loss agents pile their losses on Gulf Coast, which will hopefully be enough to sink his ship and leave him with 100 percent of nothing, we'll fill our pockets with cash.

"Here's how I see it working. First, we'll sign all the new applicants from the convention with both Cal Western and

Gulf Coast and provide appointments with the Department of Insurance from both companies; Cal Western's appointments first, and then Gulf Coast's. Marty won't know the difference, because I'm the only one taking the calls from new agents, and you're the one providing him with the current list of Cal Western's agents. Nothing in the deal with Cal Western will indicate how long each of the agencies have been with them, or what portion of the overall business each represents.

"Then, after Cal Western and Marty sign off on the deal, we'll begin the transfer process, which will include all the new California ones from the convention." I took a breath.

"Now for the good part. I'll tell Marty that you're getting cold feet, because if this deal goes through, you'll be out of a job. So you need to start your own managing general agency to ensure that you have enough income to sustain your family. Then, I will convince him to pay you 15 percent of the gross income he'll receive from all the agents you and I transfer to Gulf Coast. This compensation is, of course, your payment, under the table, for helping convince Cal Western to transfer all their future bail business to Gulf Coast.

"Of course, you agree to pay me 15 percent of your 15 percent, under the table, plus 49 percent ownership in your new national managing general agency. And you agree to give me a job when Marty cans my ass, which he will when he realizes how bad this deal really was for his company.

"In the meantime, I'll still get paid from Gulf Coast, and I'll receive money from your deal with Marty, which will be enough to make me feel a little better about losing my one third interest in Gulf Coast. Plus, I'll receive a bonus from Marty on all the civil bond business you generate, at least, or until, he decides to screw me again.

"We should have three years, two at the least, before Gulf Coast begins to incur losses that will hopefully cost Marty's company at least a third of its value, which should even the scorecard for not keeping his word."

I said Vance should think about it overnight and let me know, because I wanted to call Marty and explain the new deal to him first thing in the morning. But since Vance would receive 85 percent of the money paid by Marty under this deal, he bought into my scam before I hung up the phone.

The next morning, after Marty agreed to the arrangement, we started to put things in motion. However, I had a nagging thought that one of them would somehow back out. But I had no choice, I had to trust them both, because I wasn't about to sign anything, or put anything in writing that could tie me to a criminal insider deal like this one.

And since Marty had already reneged on his promise to me, I wasn't sure how long it would take before he recognized how bad this deal was and put me out of a job. Hopefully, if it did happen, it would be after Vance's new deal was able to support us both.

Anyway, it was interesting to watch these two young lawyers dance around their ethics while implementing a corrupt insider deal where one of them, Vance, would be tricking his employer, Cal Western, into believing that their surety bail bond business was worthless, then convincing them to transfer their entire book of business to Gulf Coast, Marty's company, rather than putting it on the auction block and selling it to the highest bidder among other surety insurance companies.

All this, while Marty would be paying Vance, Cal Western's vice president in charge of their bail and surety bond division, 15 percent of the gross revenues Gulf Coast would receive from all the Cal Western bail agents, if, and when, he convinced the agents to move to Marty's company.

There's more. During the same negotiating period, Marty also promised to give Vance an exclusive national managing general agent's contract for civil bonds with Gulf Coast, knowing full well that Vance would be operating his new agency in direct competition with his previous employer, Cal Western. And he'd be using the 15 percent kickback from the bail deal with Marty to promote his new civil bond business.

Aha! White-collar crime at its best; even though I'd designed and implemented it, I was innocent of wrongdoing. Thinking about or talking about a potential crime is different from committing it.

In this case, it was Vance and Marty, the two brain trusts with law degrees, who collaborated and initiated the plan to steal the bail bond business from Cal Western and to set Vance up with a contract that enabled him to compete against them in the civil bond business, making them the only two that appeared to benefit from the transaction.

CHAPTER

#32

On May 1, 1978, the first convention in the history of the American bail system took place at the MGM Grand Hotel in Las Vegas and went off without a hitch. Over 350 bail agents and their wives, husbands, girlfriends, boyfriends and guests from across the US filled the MGM's convention halls, gaming tables, hotels rooms and restaurants. Tommy Costanoto and I were elated, while Marty, Vance, and the old guard could hardly believe it.

I went from being broke, bankrupt, and almost out of the bail bond business, to not only hosting the first national convention, but being honored by my fellow agents and competitors from around the country for pulling it off. I needed someone to pinch me, and I knew the person that would do it. Teresa brought me back down to earth by telling me when people start swimming in praise from others, they begin to drown in their own glory.

When I told Tommy I wanted to host a welcome and celebration party for a handful of special guests in my suite the first night of the convention, he said, "Not to worry. I'll send up four bottles of Dom Perignon, and an array of hors d'oeuvres, on the house. You deserve it. What a great turnout!"

In addition to Vance, his wife Sally, Teresa of course, and me, we invited Timmy Walters, his wife Sharon, and my best buddy, Roy Carver, who came down from Reno. I intentionally excluded Marty and his wife from our little party because I was still pissed about his reneging on our deal.

Timmy and his wife operated their own retail bail agency in Rohnert Park, California, and he also managed his parents' bail general agency while his father was ill. All the agents in their general agency did business with Blue Lakes, through Mickey, and then moved with him to Gulf Coast.

We were in the same age group, and fairly good friends, so Timmy and Sharon felt comfortable bringing a little surprise to the party . . . a lid of their home-grown marijuana, together with a six-person water pipe. This was perfect, because Roy never liked to smoke, especially marijuana.

As I remember, the pipe was made in India. It enhanced the effects of grass, and any other smokable substance known to mankind at the time. The seven of us drank champagne, smoked grass through Timmy's pipe (a first for most of us), and laughed our asses off; it was one hell of a great evening.

The next morning, I kicked off the convention with introductions, followed by a long list of speakers including Vance, Marty, and about six of the foremost general agents from across the country.

When Marty spoke, I wanted to stand up and punch him in the face. He started by tooting his own horn and talking about "his company this, and his company that," which was bad enough, since we'd advertised the event as nonpartisan. We'd told Harlan Fuller to schedule other company representatives to speak, but make sure each used their time to talk about the industry and our problems, and not to sell their company.

So when Marty started alluding that the idea of a national organization and the convention was his, I wanted to haul his ass out to the parking lot, throw him in the trunk of a car, and take him for a one-way ride into the desert. Instead, Harlan interrupted him with a polite "time's up," and moved on to the next speaker on the program.

During the first break, Teresa came up to me. "I hope I was the only one that noticed your reaction to Marty's comments; your facial expressions said it all. I'm sure glad you stayed cool and didn't do something stupid! Remember, you're going to get even, not mad."

The next few days saw several workshops and seminars, including skip-chasing techniques presented by Ralph "Papa" Thorsen. As I mentioned earlier, Papa was one of the best bounty hunters in the business. In fact, he authored a book called *The Hunter*, outlining his experiences, which was later made into a movie starring Steve McQueen. Over the next few years, I got to know him pretty well, and used him when some of our agents needed help on some of their bigger skips.

Then it was Vance's turn. He outlined some of the adverse legislation pending throughout several states, including California. He then welcomed Archie Graham, a bail agent from California. Archie was arrested in Oregon for kidnapping when he and one of his buddies apprehended a bail skip from California who had fled north. They were arrested in California on a fugitive kidnaping warrant from Oregon after returning their fugitive to the appropriate California court. They were extradited back, and tried in an Oregon state court, where they were found guilty.

Although the US Supreme Court had previously ruled that bail agents have a legal right to apprehend and return their clients from anywhere in the US, and to cross state lines without the need for a warrant in order to surrender him or her to the proper jurisdiction, it was still necessary for them to appeal their case to the Ninth Circuit Court.

The case was eventually overturned on appeal.

During the remaining two days of the convention, participants broke into smaller workshops and discussion groups to meet and exchange ideas. This resulted in the formation of four national committees: Ethics, Public Information, Industry Liaison, and Education.

On the last day, during my closing speech, there was a motion from the floor suggesting that we host a second convention in Washington D.C. This was overwhelmingly seconded by a roar from the audience, and a date was set for June 1979.

That night, we hosted a formal cocktail party and dinner in the Metro Club on the 26th floor of the MGM. It included a special keynote speaker, District Attorney Jerry Brown Jr. D.A. Brown applauded those that sponsored the convention, as well as the bail professionals in attendance. He said, "Bail agents are an essential part of the criminal justice system." This was met with cheers from the crowd.

At the end of the evening, when Teresa and I headed back to our suite, we were swimming in the glory of our success. Tomorrow we would be saying our goodbyes to everyone, old and new, because it was time to go back to work . . . and to start getting even.

CHAPTER

#33

I'd worked hard for a long time to ensure that Marty and his company were successful. And the success of the convention, together with the number of new agencies Marty signed up because of it, confirmed for me that he'd reneged on our agreement.

Now it was time to implement my plan to bury his company while ensuring the success of my new venture with Vance and his, or should I say, "our" new national managing general agency.

With the blessing, help, and thanks from Cal Western's senior management, we were able to transfer all their bail agencies to Gulf Coast within six weeks of our return from the convention. This transition included the new California agencies Vance and I picked up as a result of their participation in the convention.

Now that Vance was guaranteed a substantial monthly income based on his shady Cal Western transfer deal with Marty and his new national MGA contract for civil bonds with Gulf Coast, it was time to set up his new office. Vance regularly reassured me that we were partners, and emphatically expressed his plan to keep his word. He kept insisting

I start calling it "our" office; and I kept insisting, "Thanks, but not while I'm still working for Gulf Coast."

He selected an office site in Carlsbad, just north of San Diego, and hired two of the female underwriters who had worked in licensing and permitting for Blue Lakes before Brian's death.

Thanks to Cal Western bail agents, along with its new License and Permit Division, Gulf Coast was writing more bail and surety bonds in California than any other company. And with my 30 percent raise, the 15 percent kick-back from Vance on the deal with Marty, and the commission bonuses I was promised on all western regional business, I was starting to make a lot of money. Unfortunately, it was based on Gulf Coast staying in business.

Vance and I knew that the quality of underwriting being used by the Cal Western bail agents, and the collateral they were taking from big-time drug dealers, gang members, and other high-risk clients would get them arrested, or worse yet, killed.

I was certain that many of these guys would end up dead, out of business, or in prison within the next three years. If I was correct, Gulf Coast and Marty Dupree would be left holding millions of dollars in unpaid bail losses throughout California and ten other western states, with zero collateral. Then, if Marty was lucky enough to fend off bankruptcy, or stop the state insurance regulators from shutting down Gulf Coast, he'd come after me with a vengeance. And Vance would lose his bail override and civil bond contract.

We knew from the beginning we needed to secure a new G.A. contract, one that would allow us to continue writing licenses and permit bonds and move a significant number of our friends and good, reliable bail agents, away from Gulf Coast before the shit hit Marty's fan. The race was on.

CHAPTER

#34

While Vance was on the road looking for new national insurance carriers and expanding our civil bond business, I was struck with a more pressing personal problem. In early 1978, the Los Angeles County School Board developed a plan to desegregate the county's public schools by busing African American and Mexican American kids from the inner-city to the beach community schools, while busing all the beach communities' Caucasian kids to the inner-city schools. The state intended to initiate the busing program at the beginning of the upcoming school year, in September.

Two lawsuits were filed to stop them from implementing the program, which would later be combined into one complaint titled "Bus Stop vs. LA Board of Education." Our decision to move out of L.A. had nothing to do with prejudice and everything to do with safety. The idea of having Bonnie and Ella bused sixteen miles each way, from the beach communities to Watts every day on some of the busiest freeways in the world, was enough to unnerve any parent, and it scared the shit out of Teresa and me.

Our decision to move sounded pretty good until we started listing the hurdles involved. Where do we move? What about our jobs? What kind of new housing cost will we be looking at? What about Vance, and our new joint venture? All these questions needed quick answers if we were to be settled someplace new in time for the kids to start school.

After days and nights of discussion after discussion, we realized we needed to come up with an ideal place to move, one that was uncongested, beautiful, and offered some of the best schools. And if I was going to continue managing the bail operations throughout the western states for Marty or Vance, our new home base had to be in an area large enough to provide easy access to interstate highways, and within a one-hour drive of a major airport.

Finding the perfect place turned out to be easier than expected, thanks to Teresa.

While attending the University of Oregon in Eugene, she'd fallen in love with everything about the state—except the rain. But she remembered a visit during a semester break to a high school girlfriend who had moved from Las Vegas to San Rafael, California. Teresa had flown from Eugene to San Francisco, where her girlfriend Diane picked her up and drove them the short distance to San Rafael. During the ride, Teresa was in awe of the beauty of the region, and how much it reminded her of Oregon. The area had more sunny days and less annual rainfall than Oregon, which prompted a comment to Diane that "Someday, I'd really like to live here."

It had been a few years since then, so Teresa called Diane and scheduled another visit. Meanwhile, I called our bail agent friends from Sonoma County, Timmy and Sharon Walters, those with the water pipe in Vegas. They lived in Novato, a short drive from San Rafael, and had both their bail office and their real estate office in a small business complex they owned just north on the 101.

During Teresa's visit, she researched the grade schools for our girls. They were now going on six and seven and about to start school. She also checked out a few office locations, including some vacant space in Timmy's complex, and talked to him about the local housing market.

At the time, we hadn't the faintest idea what, if anything, Marty would say, or agree to, so it was premature to secure something. But Timmy drove her through the neighborhoods and surrounding school districts anyway.

She came back to L.A. convinced that Novato was the perfect place for us to move. She also found a great school, and two modest tract homes for sale on the same block, within easy walking distance from the school she thought was the best.

She decided that two homes would be better because moving to a new city would be hard enough on the girls without trying to explain that we would be living together full time in the same house. Plus, it would be easier to convince Marty that Teresa was moving because of the opportunity rather than because we were an item, which he didn't yet know.

Timmy talked to the owners of the houses and got them both to accept tentative offers, with nothing down, and a two-week grace period to back out if our moving plans failed to materialize.

As well as the overwhelming amount of information Teresa brought home, she surprised us with two new boxer puppies; one for Ella and one for Bonnie. Diane's show dog had delivered a new litter six weeks earlier. So, of course, Teresa had to bring one for each of the kids.

Although I was elated about the idea of moving, I wasn't quite as excited about the puppies. However, once the kids saw them, there was no sending them back. The puppies gave the kids something else to focus on while Teresa and I began orchestrating the big move.

Now that we knew where we wanted to live, we had to convince Marty that Gulf Coast needed to open a new western regional branch office in Northern California, have him pay the moving expenses for every member of the staff willing to relocate to the new office, hire the necessary replacements for those moving north, and any additional employees needed for the new office.

Using Teresa as my sounding board, I spent the next few days thinking and planning something I thought would work. When Marty and I connected, I explained that the state of California was too big to supervise from one location, especially with the new agents coming on board as a result of his deal with Cal Western, which I emphasized was "his deal." Plus, we were taking on a significant number of new agents from the other ten western states. I said things were bordering on "overwhelming;" and I didn't want to impact profits from a lack of supervision.

Then I explained my plan to divide the Western Region into two parts: a Northern Division, to be located in Novato, California, and the Southern Division, which would remain in Manhattan Beach. The northern office would supervise Washington, Oregon, Idaho, Wyoming, Montana, northern California and northern Nevada, while the southern office would service southern California, southern Nevada, Arizona, Utah and New Mexico.

I said I would personally oversee both offices from Novato, while promoting Beth, my senior assistant in L.A., to the southern division manager, and I'd be moving to Novato with certain members of our existing staff, to open the new northern branch office just as soon as he approved the plan.

Marty was so elated with the results of the convention and the Cal Western deal that he bought right into the idea. He expressed concern over the company's ability to properly service all the business, and he said this idea fit right into the plan he had been working on as well.

In fact, I convinced him to advance money from my future bonuses to purchase a home rather than having to rent, and to provide the mortgage company with a written estimate from our CFO on my future earnings, which included both my salary and my anticipated bonuses. I said I'd need these same references for Teresa, and anyone else interested in moving with us. Of course, the advance I asked for was enough to cover the down payments both houses.

With Marty's approval, I asked Timmy to prepare the paperwork on both houses, and, while he was at it, to prepare a lease for the vacant office space in his complex. Gulf Coast would take it all.

During our next conference call, I explained how we had three people moving to Novato, two staff members and me. We would need to hire two replacements in the L.A. office, and three new members, besides the three of us that were moving.

Since school started in September, and it was already mid-June, we had to move fast. I called Vance to fill him in. He not only agreed, but suggested we include room in our new office for a civil bond clerk so we could list a branch office in all his new promotional pieces. I recommended that Teresa obtain her insurance license so she could be the civil bond underwriter for all the Northern California agents through Parker Surety Bonding, and through our new western regional branch as well. I didn't bother to tell either Marty or Vance that Teresa would be doing two jobs in the same office, working the same schedule, while earning commissions from Vance, and a salary from Marty. What they didn't know wouldn't hurt them.

Everything worked without a hitch, thanks to Timmy and Teresa. We got the kids in school, closed escrow on the two houses, re-staffed the southern office, and hired a few new people for Northern California.

Work itself was a different story. I had problems up the ass trying to keep Vance's old bail agents in line. Every day I was being asked to approve $20,000 bonds on bikers who had no collateral except a signature from a couple of club members, or some $30,000 bonds on drug smugglers, traffickers, or dealers with worthless deeds of trust on over-mortgaged property. What's more, those agents who had higher underwriting authorities and didn't need my approval to write bonds up to $50,000, were merely taking clients' drugs, or nothing at all as collateral.

I always had to choose between Vance getting his kickback percentage, and the company taking a loss due to poor underwriting. Most of the time it was an easy choice, since, thanks to Marty, I didn't own a piece of the company. Big premiums with under-collateralized bonds usually won; unless it was so blatant it would appear as though I was purposely negligent.

One day, shortly after a client was released from custody on one of those questionable drug bonds, the bail agent who wrote it was shot and killed in his office. The killer ransacked the office, retrieved the drugs given to the agent as collateral, and ripped off everything of value he could get his hands on, including collateral from earlier bonds written the same day. The police believed the person who delivered the drugs for collateral must have returned to retrieve them once their boss was released.

Shit like this usually happened when agents got greedy. Then I was left with a dead agent on my hands, and a ton of outstanding bonds on some really bad dudes who obviously don't mind killing people. I had to hire some of the best bounty hunters in the business, guys like Papa Thorson and Joel Castro, a California based Bounty Hunter with strong ties in Mexico, to find, arrest, and surrender as many of these asshole drug dealers as they could. And since the bail agent was dead, and the cops confiscated everything that slightly resembled evidence, including files and receipt books, I was left explaining the whole mess to Marty.

Every time one of these problems reared its ugly face, I called Vance and said, "You better find that new company soon, because this stuff from Cal Western and their agents is trash. It's shoddier than I thought, and it's getting worse by the day. We've been lucky to catch a few of these guys, but I'm not sure how long our luck will hold out. I'm not sure Marty will keep paying you an override, or even keep me on the payroll if or when this gets worse."

Around six months after establishing the new Northern California branch office, Vance received a call out of the blue from a general agent in Miami Beach named Randy Fallon. Vance and I had met Randy in Las Vegas during the bail convention, and we'd promised to do some business together if the opportunity presented itself.

Randy and his partner, Butch Hogan, were originally from New York. Their "Bada Bing Bada Boom" vibe reminded me of the New York mob guys I'd met while writing bail in Vegas.

Randy told Vance he was having trouble getting his company to increase his bail underwriting limits so he could write larger bonds on some of his preferred customers. We assumed these "preferred customers" were connected guys from New York or Chicago running scams out of Atlantic City or Las Vegas who were snatched up by the cops in Miami on warrants.

Randy said he was looking for a new company. Could we help him out? Vance explained that I was still working with Gulf Coast, they weren't yet licensed in Florida, and he was able to take on only a few smaller California-based surety companies, limited to doing license and permit business, and wanted nothing to do with bail.

Vance said he and I were working together in hopes of finding a national fifty-state carrier willing to take on the entire line of surety business, which included bail, and do it by providing an exclusive underwriting contract through an experienced national managing general agency like his, which included me, of course.

Randy replied that he recently met with the president of a well-established full-line insurance company based in Miami called United Colonial Insurance. Although it was approved to write surety bonds in all fifty states, it had yet to enter the surety market.

When he'd met with the president of the company, he was intrigued with the idea of going into in the bail bond business but felt he wouldn't get his board of directors to approve the upfront costs needed to establish a new surety processing division for a single bail bond agency, even if that agency was based in Miami. Randy remembered that Vance was a lawyer with significant experience in surety insurance on a company level. He also knew Vance also had numerous contacts in the bail bond and surety bond industries in all fifty states. He suggested that Vance put together a presentation while Randy worked on setting up another meeting with United Colonial.

Vance immediately agreed.

My part was to provide Vance with a list of the regional bail general agents throughout the country I'd met during the convention and devise a plan for bringing them all together within the framework of Parker Surety Bonding, so he could show United Colonial how we could provide them with nation-wide surety business, in bail, as well as license and permit.

Although Vance wanted me to accompany him to Miami and present the bail program, I declined. I said we could lose Gulf Coast if word got out that we were working together to find a national market. I added that I needed to stay in the shadows and protect our relationship with Marty, or whatever was left of it. Plus, it was too early to tell if we could reel in this new one. Any contract that might emerge from his meeting would ultimately be with Parker Surety Bonding, and we were partners.

He agreed.

Randy set up the meeting and Vance scheduled his trip.

I couldn't believe it. We were looking at the possibility of actually securing a fifty-state contract for surety with a company that had materialized through a contact we made during the convention. That simple idea, hosting a national convention, was about to provide another life-changing opportunity for Vance and me.

CHAPTER

#35

Vance's meeting went exceptionally well. United Colonial was excited about the program as he presented it. They were 100 percent in. But because Vance was unable to provide any bail revenue on our financial statement, and we had less than a year of revenues from the license and permit business Vance had been developing through his contract with Gulf Coast, our financial statement was weak.

The president told Vance his board would approve the contract with us if we came up with a $100,000 security deposit. They would hold this deposit in a premium trust account to ensure that we paid them their portion of the premiums we collected each month on the civil bonds written by independent insurance agents through Parker Surety Bonding, and the bail bonds posted by our independent bail agents and general agents across the US.

They would hold this deposit until we satisfied their auditors that our corporate premium trust account held at least $100,000 in excess capital over and above the premiums we owed them during any single audit period, at which time, our deposit would be returned to us.

They also wanted to see at least an additional $150,000 in operating capital to ensure that we were able to promote our managing general agency throughout the country.

All we had to do to secure this new dream was to come up with $250,000 in ready cash. They agreed to a six-month moratorium, during which time they would not discuss or enter into any meetings or negotiations with any other parties, individuals, or companies regarding their entry into the surety business.

When Vance's returned from Miami, he contacted a banker friend to see about an unsecured personal loan that would not appear on our corporate financial statement. The banker said we were asking the impossible, since the corporation was not conducting enough business, and our personal financial statements would not support that size loan. He suggested that we obtain a startup loan through a private investor.

Vance asked if I knew anyone with that kind of money. He suggested finding someone willing to invest in exchange for a one third interest in our company. As long as he and I controlled two-thirds interest, he said, we'd always be in control.

After we talked, I put on my thinking cap. I thought about Mickey, but figured he had his money tied up in his new venture. Then I thought about Joey Glover, one of the bail agents I'd met in Northern California who was writing millions of dollars in business annually and making a ton of money. He was one of a small group of good-quality guys I'd brought along from my Blue Lakes days.

Even though the business he was writing owed a lot to the Satan's Raiders motorcycle gang and their drug business, he was not one of the bums we got from Cal Western. He had the experience and the money to protect us against losses and had proven himself time and again by writing a hefty number of large bonds over the past couple of years. Many of them were $100,000 or larger and always required my approval. Many were federal bonds on members of the Raiders. In fact, Joey wrote so many individual bonds in one case that the federal judge requested a qualified representative from the insurance company appear in his court to testify, under oath, as to the type of collateral our agent was taking on each of these bonds, and the amount of the premium charged.

I testified that based upon the past performance of our bail agent and his history of ensuring that the members of the Raiders always made their appearances (and if not, they were returned to the agent's custody by other members of the club) I gave the agent complete authority to underwrite, and execute these bonds as he saw fit, but only after we discussed them.

Consequently, the company was satisfied with a single promissory note for the full amount of each premium, as well as the full amount of each bond, on every defendant, which was signed by each elected officer of their club.

The judge was irate. "You mean to tell me that your company is satisfied holding millions of dollars in worthless notes as collateral on these thugs?"

My response didn't make him any happier.

"Your Honor, in our business we've learned that everyone is innocent until proven guilty, and everyone must be treated equally. In this case, being a member of a motorcycle club doesn't make them thugs or guilty of any crimes. Many of these individuals have proven their trustworthiness by assisting us in returning any every member that has ever failed to appear on one of our bonds."

I got the impression that neither the judge nor the prosecutor was pleased with my testimony. Within a few weeks, my suspicions were reinforced by some surprising encounters.

Teresa and I were now settled in Novato, in two homes down the street from each other. After a year of having dinners and sleepovers with the kids almost every night, first at her place, then at mine, and working together every day, we decided to ask the kids how they felt about us getting married and all of us living together. They couldn't have been happier.

We decided I should sell my house and use the money to remodel hers. We wanted to expand the master bedroom and bath, convert the guest room into a media room, and cut out the wall out between the two small bedrooms, replacing it with pocket doors, so the kids could open them when they wanted to play together, and close them if they wanted privacy. We also decided to expand the patio and add an inground plastic-lined swimming pool in the backyard.

After Teresa and I agreed on the changes, with the goal of completing them before our marriage, I put my house up for sale. Then I hired a carpenter friend, and the two of us got to work.

Shortly after my testimony in federal court, the carpenter and I began framing the addition to the master bedroom at Teresa's house. We completed the walls and were working on the roof when, from my bird's eye view on the roof, I noticed a strange car and driver parked down the street. At first, I thought nothing of it, but after about a week or so of seeing it every day, I got suspicious. One day I climbed down, went into the house, out the back door, climbed over the neighbor's back fence, stepped into the street and came up behind the driver. His window was down. I said, "Hello!" This nearly scared the shit out of him.

I said I'd noticed him watching our house for over a week, and was wondering what he was doing? He gave me some bullshit answer about wanting to remodel his house and checking out construction sites like ours to learn more about how home remodeling is done.

"Well, then," I said. "You're welcome to come on over and take a closer look, unless you're still on duty."

He looked surprised, apologized, said he was sorry he bothered us, started his car and pulled away from the curb. I copied down the license plate number and called Timmy to have one of his cop friends run it. Turns out the car came from the federal motor pool; probably the F.B.I. I'm sure they thought I was getting my money from the Satan's Raiders as a payoff for my testimony, because a few days later I noticed another suspicious car parked at different times and locations around our office. They must have wanted photos of some of the Raiders coming and going from my house or the office, to connect me to their drug operation.

No luck there: I did all my business with Joey. We had a deal. I always approved his large bonds, especially on the Raiders, and he always slipped me a few grand in cash every time he needed to post one. My cut came from all the large bail bonds Joey wrote, not just from those on the Raiders.

As a result of our little arrangement, Joey and I were pretty good friends long before I was called to testify in federal court. Since I knew he was making a pot full of money through his bail business, I figured he might be interested in buying an interest in our new national general agency for $250,000. When I asked him, he wanted to know if we had a financial prospectus available to show investors.

I explained that we were concerned about a prospectus falling into the wrong hands and possibly causing us big problems with Gulf Coast and our other insurance companies. "But maybe I could get Vance to put something together for your eyes only."

"I'll give you a $50,000 deposit, as a good faith gesture," he said, "and a promise not to discuss our arrangement with anyone else except my financial advisor. But I just can't put up a quarter mil without more information."

I told Vance, and after a lengthy discussion we decided that our options were few, and time was of the essence if we were to close the deal with United Colonial. We accepted his deal. Vance provided a copy of our business plan together with a copy of a hastily developed prospectus. I delivered it and collected the $50,000 deposit, all in cash, in a small green duffel bag.

There were no security check points at the airports in those days, so I caught the next plane to San Diego and delivered the cash to Vance.

Within twenty-four hours, Joey called. "My financial advisor said the deal looks good, so I'm all in. You can pick up the rest of the money whenever you get back."

I stayed over that night to celebrate, and Vance joined me the next day on my return flight. He wanted to meet Joey, thank him for the investment, and get the rest of the money.

I didn't care whether he came along or not; I had just one question for him.

"What if he gives us all cash?"

Vance said, "I really don't care. I just want our deal with United Colonial, and getting the money is worth a third interest, no matter who gives it to us, as long as we still control the company."

CHAPTER

#36

Joey came up with the money we needed, all $250,000—In cash, as I'd expected. Many bail agents had numerous ways of skimming cash from their businesses. As an example, they would collect cash collateral from a client, knowing in advance that he or she had no intention of showing up for trial. The agent would sit back and wait for the court to forfeiture their client's bond. Then, instead of using the cash to pay the loss, they would write a check from their business account for the full amount and post the transaction as a total loss on their taxes, leaving them free to pocket the cash.

I had no way of knowing exactly where Joey got this kind of money, but at the time, I didn't care. All I knew was that we'd need a bigger duffel bag.

Vance and I didn't count it in front of him. We didn't want our new relationship starting off on the wrong foot with him thinking we didn't trust him. Vance did ask, "Is it all right to take all this to the bank?" We all laughed, but I'm sure for different reasons.

Joey said, "You might scare the hell out of your banker if you take it all to him at the same time; unless you know him well enough, of course."

At the time we were putting this transaction together, the Feds hadn't enacted their regulations restricting banks from accepting cash deposits of $10,000 or more without reporting the transaction to the IRS. If they had, we'd all have been arrested, including the banker.

Fortunately, Vance knew one of the officers at a small local bank. The guy had helped him manage his campaign contributions when he was running for state assembly; he'd also helped Vance set up the original Parker Surety Bonding bank accounts.

His banker friend told him to deposit $12,500 in cash every few business days, together with his regular business deposit . . . maybe $11,000 plus some checks today, then $13,000 tomorrow, etc. That way, by the end of each week, they could transfer the cash portion of Vance's daily deposits from the Parker Surety operating account into a special interest-bearing savings account, while leaving the business portion of the deposits in his operating account. Then, when we needed the $100,000 security deposit for United Colonial, Vance could simply authorize a wire transfer from his account to theirs.

The plan worked perfectly. With the banker's help and Joey's $250,000, Parker Surety Bonding Group was able to notify United Colonial that we had the funds necessary to move our relationship to the next level.

Within days, Parker Surety Bonding would become the national managing general agency for United Colonial Insurance Company, which meant we'd be able to write surety bail bonds, as well as license and permit bonds, through licensed surety insurance agents and bail bondsmen throughout the US.

When it was official, the first thing we did was let Joey know that we'd successfully secured our national contract and were appointing him and his office as our first United Colonial bail agency. Vance also signed up Randy Fallon, since he was the guy from Miami who'd introduced us to United Colonial.

We still needed the kickback money Marty Dupree was paying Vance for their Cal Western scam to maintain his level of personal income, which meant I had to continue working with Gulf Coast. This also meant Vance would have to continue promoting both the civil and bail business for a while longer and start signing some of the larger general agents we met during the convention with United Colonial without my help.

Our charade went on for about ninety days before Dupree got wind of what Vance was doing. He must have heard about it from one of our disgruntled competitors. Fortunately, it didn't take much to appease Dupree's concerns—for another month. I told him Vance was having to do civil bonds with other companies in certain areas because Gulf Coast was not yet qualified to do so.

I also said Vance wanted to start promoting his MGA as a national market, and Gulf Coast wasn't expanding their filings or receiving additional state approvals fast enough to suit him.

What I purposely failed to mention was the two bail appointments Vance already made, and that he was bragging about our new company having bail agents from coast to coast. Nor did I say anything about him signing many of the general agencies we'd met at the bail convention.

About this same time, I learned that Marty was still riding high, believing everything was going well. And since the company's future looked favorable, he decided to buy himself a few bonus gifts with the profits his company was making as a result of my efforts and my earlier marketing strategies.

He bought a custom 1980 Clenet Series One Roadster for somewhere around $90,000. He remodeled his beach house on the Gulf Coast and bought a new, larger home for his family. When I heard all this, I laughed. I knew it was short-lived, and that he was too busy playing the part of a rich kid to keep a close eye on his business. As the cliché goes, "The bigger they are, the harder they fall." I was almost certain he was going to fall, and fall hard.

At the same time, I also heard that he'd been visiting Southern California more frequently. I was puzzled that he never notified me or ask me to join him there. He never came to my office in Northern California, either. But he did continue to call and check in with me almost daily.

He also never visited Vance, even though Vance's Carlsbad office was less than an hour's drive from his Manhattan Beach office.

When my curiosity got the best of me, I asked a few of my bail buddies with offices down South to snoop around and see if they could learn what he was up to. Their reports almost knocked me out of my chair. Marty's trips were of a personal nature. Rumor had it he was having an affair with Beth Williams, the woman I had appointed to supervise Gulf Coast's Southern California office when I moved north. I assumed she would be reporting everything directly to me in Northern California, including Marty's visits.

I knew she wanted my job, but I hadn't realized how far she was willing to go to get it. I wasn't sure if she started by cheating on her husband, then turned against me to justify her actions. Or it was the other way around? Either way, I could no longer trust her. My agent friends also learned she was telling Marty that I was letting a group of our more questionable agents write high-risk bonds with limited or no collateral, regardless of their size, as long as they reported the bonds within a week of executing them.

Since Beth was never privy to what Vance and I were doing, she couldn't have told Marty much, because we held our discussions over the phone, long distance.

Her efforts to undermine me allowed me to learn what she and Marty were doing. Plenty of our agents were more than willing to spy on her as a means of protecting their working relationship with me. They knew I was the one protecting their contracts, and approving their large bonds, not her.

One of the most noteworthy things my Southern California friends discovered occurred about fifteen months after Vance started looking for our national carrier: Marty was going to attend the second annual bail convention held in Washington D.C., and he was going to take Beth, not me.

However, the second national convention never materialized because Marty made the mistake of withdrawing all his financial support and downplaying Gulf Coast's involvement in the national association altogether. This left the door wide open for his other competitors, the old-time insurance executives, to provide funding, take over the organization, and appoint their cronies to the board of directors, which they did.

Their justification in changing everything, at least in their own minds, was to ensure that I didn't receive any credit or recognition from the second convention.

Their first order of business at the convention was to change the organization's name from the AAPBA (American Association of Professional Bail Agents) to PBUS (Professional Bail Agents of the United States.)

Their convention was not anywhere near as successful as the first one we put on in Las Vegas. I can't say whether it was the result of choosing Washington D.C. as opposed to Vegas, or because Vance and I signed up a significant number of new agents and general agents who, knowing we weren't going to be there, elected not to attend.

However, Marty and Beth were there, and so were a few agents who called to let me know they would be providing pictures of them together. At the time, I felt the scenes depicted in the photos would trump any accusations from them concerning my alleged inadequate supervision of the company's bail agents. So I decided to tuck the pictures away for a rainy day, or for use in any future court proceedings against me, if it ever became necessary. I still have them, after all these years.

CHAPTER

#37

While I was busy protecting our override income from Marty, Vance continued to contact the general agents who expressed interest in doing business with us. I had him stay away from some of the southern states and California to ensure that we didn't accidently contact someone friendly to Marty or Beth. Vance successfully began signing some from Texas, Iowa, Pennsylvania, Idaho, Washington, North Carolina, New Mexico and Tennessee. When we coupled these new guys with Randy in Miami, we were able to project millions of dollars in annual bail premiums.

When Marty heard that these new agents were reporting their bail business through Vance, he stopped paying Vance the Western States override. In addition, he sent him a letter cancelling his exclusive MGA contract for civil bonds with Gulf Coast.

Then, unbeknownst to Vance or me, Marty also cancelled Joey's bail contract when he found out about his affiliation with Vance.

On a stand-alone basis, Marty's letter to Joey didn't mean much, since we wanted him to start placing his business through

Vance anyway. But one day, Joey called me in a panic. "Lefty, if Marty really has cancelled me, I'll have to start placing all my new Satan's Raiders business with Vance and Parker Financial."

"So what?"

"Well, the Feds just brought indictments against a significant number of the Satan's Raiders for murder, drug trafficking, money laundering and racketeering, among numerous other charges; they're cracking down on Satan's drug business. They're going to have trouble coming up with all the bail premiums needed to get their gang members out of jail."

I asked again, "What's that got to do with us?"

"You guys might have to wait for your share of the premiums. You know, float their bonds indefinitely, until their cases are either dismissed or we bail them out so they can get back to making money."

"Joey" I said, "unfortunately, your appointment with United Colonial, not to mention our relationship with them, is too new. If we were caught floating bonds by reporting them late, or not at all, *especially* those on members of a notorious motorcycle gang, they'd probably cancel our national contract immediately, especially if they received an earful of complaints from the federal judge who's already unhappy about some of these gang members getting out earlier on similar charges through Gulf Coast.

"Look, I'll have to think this shit through before we can move forward. Give me an hour; I'll call you back."

If that news wasn't bad enough, Vance called minutes after I hung up with Joey.

"Goddammit Lefty, the Satan's Raiders just sent three of their enforcers to our Carlsbad office. According to Sandy, our office manager, three of the biggest, ugliest bikers you can imagine roared up on their choppers and parked in front of the office door. They strutted into the reception area like they owned the place. One stood guard inside the front door while one of the other two walked over to Sandy's desk, sat down, leaned back in the chair, and put his dirty motorcycle boots on her desk. Then he insisted that she get me.

"She was frightened and on the verge of tears. But she managed to say I was out of town and wouldn't be back until tomorrow. She asked if there was anything she could help him with."

"He said, 'You can tell your asshole boss we came to pick up our first dividend payment. The one he owes the club for the investment we made in his little business here. And, as his new partners, we figure $10,000 a month should cover it.'

"Sandy said, 'I'm not sure I understand the message.'

"He yelled, 'You don't have to, Bitch! Just tell him what I said when he calls, and, let him know we'll be back tomorrow to collect. Either we get the ten grand, or we cut his nuts off and present them to the club in a glass jar when we get back home. We really don't give a rat's ass which one we take back, his nuts in the jar, or the cash.'

"Apparently his sidekick chimed in with, 'Yeah, and we don't accept no checks.' The leader stood up, kicked his chair across the room, and they all walked together. They started their choppers, which rattled the windows, and roared off.

"Poor Sandy. She was in tears when she called my house. Thank God she didn't tell them I was home. It took her a few minutes to calm down and explain what happened. I told her to close the office immediately and go home. I didn't want them coming back. So here we are."

Vance sighed. "How about telling me what the hell is going on? What have you gotten us into? How are these gang members our partners, and why are they demanding ten grand a month?

You'd better ask Joey what the hell they're talking about, and get this shit fixed before they come back. You know as well as I do we can't afford to start paying that kind of money . . . not now, not ever! For Christ sakes, fix this!"

"Look, Vance," I said. "This is the first I've heard of it. I don't know what they're talking about either; I'll find out and get back to you after I talk to Joey."

After a couple of hours of calling around for him, Joey finally called me back.

"Lefty, I told you the Raiders are in big trouble; many of them have been arrested, and the ones still on the loose are hiding out from the Feds. I'm afraid I may be next."

When I asked, "What the hell are you talking about, Joey?" he proceeded to drop a bombshell, one I never expected.

"I've been investing the Raiders' drug profits for years, buying small pieces of a few local businesses; that's why they've been coming to me whenever their club members needed bail. The money I invested with you actually came from them, not me.

"When I talked to them about investing in your business, they laughed and said it was like buying an irrevocable 'Get out of Jail Free' card."

Joey told me the Feds had raided their clubhouse, confiscated all their cash, and were hunting them down, especially their officers, drug handlers, and enforcers. He added that some of their "no bail" arrest warrants were for murder, kidnapping, and violations of the Federal Racketeering Act, not just sales and possession of drugs.

"This is some heavy shit, Lefty! I'm sure, with their drug operation shut down, they're badly in need of cash to cover their attorney's fees in hopes of having him get reasonable bail set on everyone or begin making deals to reduce the charges.

Your operation is not the only one being squeezed. They want dividends from every business they invested in, and they want it yesterday!"

Then he dropped a second bombshell.

"The Feds not only confiscated all their cash, they seized every business record they could find in the clubhouse. Most of them listed, or at least mentioned, something about every investment I made for them. I'm not sure if they scooped up the copy of your business plan as well, but you may want to prepare for the worst."

My heart was about to fall out of my ass. My response was mixed, to say the least. "There's no way we can afford to pay them now! We're just about to get our heads above water, so we need every penny we've got to keep promoting the business."

I paused and collected my thoughts. Then I asked the question I didn't want the answer to: "What do you mean you're pretty sure they got our business plan?"

"I don't know for sure, because the Raiders were still talking to their attorney about securing our deal the last time I talked to them, so their attorney may still have it."

"Joey" I said, "this is bullshit. I can't believe you thought we'd be stupid enough or desperate enough to get in bed with these guys. We had no idea you were investing their money in our business.

"And since you put your relationship with them first, above ours, there's no way I'm going to let you post another bond for any of them. I'm temporarily suspending your United Colonial appointment. I strongly suggest you start surrendering any club member who has an open Gulf Coast bond pending on their previous arrests. Especially those the Feds have scooped up on these new charges.

"I'm going to call Vance as soon as we hang up, and you better hope he and I can come up with a solution for getting our ass out of this mess. In the meantime, I suggest you get in touch with your attorney and start explaining just how you duped us."

CHAPTER

#38

I called Vance.

"It's worse than we thought. Apparently, we're not the first business he's duped into believing it was his money being invested. He's been investing the club's drug profits in other businesses for quite a while."

I explained about the FBI raids and confiscation of records, which might have included our business plan, the one Joey was supposed to return to us.

"Joey believes that outside of that one copy, there are no other documents relating to us or indicating that we concluded a deal with them, or received any money."

About this time, Teresa came into my office. "Joey's on the other line," she said. "He needs to talk to you right away."

"Hang on, Vance, Joey's calling, and says its important."

"What's up Joey?"

"The Feds just hooked Rocky Bowman, the club's treasurer, which is really bad news for the club, and for me. But it may be good for you and Vance, if you guys can get in touch with his attorney."

"What good would that do?"

"Their attorney just told me they never finalized the paper-work needed to complete the purchase of the one-third interest in your company. You might be able to arrange for Vance to return their money to them, through their attorney, as though you never closed the deal, or that it never took place."

"Sounds like it might work," I said, "except no one's stupid enough to trust lawyers with that kind of cash; especially those willing to deal with biker gangs. And we'd have to get Rocky to agree never to try and squeeze us again. Listen, I've got Vance on hold; I'll get back to you."

I told Vance what Joey had suggested and my concerns about trusting their attorney to let Rocky know we'd changed our minds and would give their $250,000 in cash to their attorney. In other words, we refused their offer.

We also had to consider where we'd get a quarter of a million dollars on short notice.

Vance came up with the perfect solution for both concerns. But pulling it off would potentially create a whole new set of problems.

"I'll go to the jail facility with their attorney, provide the jailer with my bar association card, have their attorney confirm that I'm there as part of Rocky's legal team, and we need to speak with him right away. I'll outline the deal like this: They get every penny of their money back, short of any interest or dividends we may have been forced to pay their goons in the meantime. When we have the money, I'll deliver it directly to their attorney, which we know is exactly what needs to happen. Then the attorney and I will make a second trip to the jail and let Rocky know the attorney has it. In exchange, Rocky gives me his word, on behalf of the club, that neither he nor they, will ever come after us for anything, especially a future extortion."

Vance continued, "I'll go to my banker who helped me process my campaign contributions and ask for his help. I'm sure he'll work with us because he's the one that orchestrated all the cash deposits from Joey's original $250,000.

"I'll ask him for the money, secured by our property—your home and mine. We'll split the total stock in the company, including the third interest we offered Joey. That means we'll own the company. I'll take 51 percent, and you'll get the remaining 49 percent."

At first blush, this sounded plausible. But after I hung up, I thought about how I'd lost my first home and everything else I owned because of a stupid deal gone bad. I couldn't get involved in something that could cause me to lose everything again.

I called Vance back and refused the deal. There was no guarantee that this would work, and I had too much to lose. He and I had had many conversations about our pasts; he knew I'd lost my home, my businesses, and my family once before.

I said, "It's one of those 'been there, done that' kind of things you never forget. I can't take the chance it might happen again . . .

"But if you can pull this off without using my property, and you're successful in getting the loan, you can take 80 percent of the company, and I'll take the remaining 20 percent. You can give the bank your home, and all the stock in our company, including my shares, as collateral."

Vance said he understood my position but added that he didn't want to proceed without knowing for sure that I'd be satisfied with a smaller percentage of our company. Unlike Marty Dupree, Vance knew the value of being partners, and of keeping his word. We both agreed to the new deal.

After a few days of negotiations with the bank, he was able to secure a commitment for the loan and arranged to meet

Rocky and his attorney in the conference room reserved for attorneys, which we knew was designed specifically to protect attorney/client confidentiality.

When they met, Rocky told Vance that everyone involved in all the other deals with the club kept their money and turned on them in order to save their asses; some went as far as to make deals with the Feds to testify against them. As a result, the club had little chance of securing good legal representation without receiving the money we were returning to them. At the time, they had zero access to any other money because of the Fed crackdown.

So, when Vance made his offer to call off a deal that we never knew existed and give them back the money we never knew was theirs, Rocky was shocked. In fact, he thought the offer was so good that it must be a setup.

But after his attorney assured him that everything we were discussing in the privacy of the jail conference room was not only confidential, but protected by attorney/client privilege, Rocky got excited, gave them both a handshake, a hug, and a promise.

"Vance, if you deliver the money in a way that satisfies our attorney here, and we're able to secure his representation for our club members, you'll never hear from us again. I'll let the members know that you're a standup guy, the only one who gave us back our money when we really needed it, and that we owe you a favor, if you ever need one that is, after we get out of this mess."

The attorney told Rocky, "Don't mention any of this to anyone, especially Joey; we're not sure whose side he's on anymore. He's been acting as the club's bail agent, so he can visit any of your members in jail or out under the pretense of discussing previous bail bonds, or cases that are still active.

He could be passing on information to the Feds to make a deal for himself."

He turned to Vance. "Get in touch with whoever's been working with Joey and see what he's up to. See if he's been asking any questions, has any news, or is acting suspicious."

When the meeting ended, Vance called me and relayed the good news and all the particulars about the attorney's cautions to Rocky and to us. "We can't tell Joey about any of this," Vance said. "We don't know whose side he's on. The attorney wants you to see what he's up to as soon as possible."

At first blush, my task seemed simple. I'd show up at Joey's office and ask him. If the Feds were watching, I had good reason for being there; good reason for asking him to what extent he was involved; and if he had any idea what was coming down, since I worked for the insurance company that was underwriting all his bail business.

When I got to his office about an hour after my conversation with Vance, Joey wasn't there, but his assistant was. She said, "I haven't seen or heard from Joey in over a week, and I'm worried sick because he's never gone more than 24 hours without checking in to see how business is going.

"I've been calling his home two or three times a day for almost a week, and neither he nor his wife answered. I even had one of our bounty hunters stop by to see if anyone was home. Lefty, I'm not sure what else I should be doing."

Since she was his office manager, and pretty much ran his business anyway, I said, "Have his employees continue to post bonds and be sure to keep the office open as usual. Also, have your bounty hunter continue to look for Joey and call me as soon as you hear anything."

I also instructed her to call me for any large bond approvals, especially those that exceeded the normal underwriting authority that Joey gave her, and on any large bonds, for that matter. "For the time being, don't bail any of the Satan's Raiders. Leave those for Joey and me to discuss when he returns to work."

I emphasized the importance of continuing to do business as usual until we found out what was going on, and why Joey was out of touch.

"You should also make all your regular premium deposits, prepare all the weekly business reports, write checks as needed to pay everything, including the insurance company, the agents, bounty hunters, and yourself. Operate Joey's business as though nothing was wrong. In the meantime, I'll see what I can find out. Remember, if you hear anything, or talk to Joey, call me immediately, day or night."

I left the office and looked for the nearest phone booth to call Vance. I relayed everything Joey's office manager had told me. I added, "Joey must be gone because he helped launder money for the Raiders. Knowing it's a matter of time before he's arrested, maybe he and his wife took off. Or maybe the Feds made him a deal he couldn't refuse, so he agreed to testify in exchange for them moving him and his wife into witness protection. Of course, most likely, the Satan's Raiders scared them off . . ."

". . . Or they're both dead!" Vance put in.

"I've been thinking. If we do this right, it won't matter where Joey is, or what deal he makes with anyone, including the Feds. Once we get the loan from the bank and give the money to Rocky's attorney, we'll be able to prove that we changed our minds on making a deal with Joey, and we decided to borrow the money from the bank instead.

"The attorney will be happy to go along with this scenario because he can claim he was working on the deal between

Parker Financial Corporation and Joey, which had nothing to do with the Satan's Raiders. And as far as he knows, the money actually belongs to Joey.

"Keep in mind, we can also show where Joey gave us cash, a few thousand bucks at a time. You have matching weekly bank deposit receipts to prove it. The reason we didn't think anything of it was because he was writing enough bail business to justify paying us weekly in cash.

"By giving the attorney a cashier's check from your bank, we're all in the clear, because Joey never received documents proving that our deal with him, or anyone else, was ever concluded.

"You, me, and Joey are the only ones who know he gave us all the money at one time, and that we decided to deposit it weekly. So in addition to numerous deposit slips to back up our story, it will always be two against one, his word against ours, should it come to that."

Vance simply listened, so I continued.

"Their attorney can also present a scenario where he was representing Joey, that it was Joey's money, not the Raiders', and he'll be holding it in his trust account awaiting Joey's return to claim it. Joey can use the money to pay the attorney whatever the Raiders owe him for defending them to ensure that they made their appearances in court on all the open cases where Joey had posted their bail.

"If Joey doesn't show up within a reasonable length of time, the attorney can use Joey's money to pay himself under that same 'scenario.'"

Vance agreed with me and called the attorney to set up a meeting. He wasn't sure if his phones were tapped, so he waited until they met in person to lay out my proposal. As far as we knew, it worked. We didn't hear anything to the contrary from the attorney, Joey, or the Feds.

And since this was a deal that Vance and Joey's attorney made, I could have Joey's office manager revoke all the open Gulf Coast bail bonds on the Satan's Raiders, one by one, as they were rearrested on the new, federal charges.

Surrendering them put a smile on the faces of the prosecutor and the judge. After all, they were ones who'd subpoenaed me earlier that year to learn why I'd approved an unbelievable number of large bonds on these bad guys with nothing more than a promise to appear from their leader as collateral.

Surrendering them also turned out to be my parting gift to Gulf Coast, since it saved Marty Dupree millions of dollars in potential forfeitures or, at the very least, some significant bounty hunting and investigative fees. As it turned out, most of the defendants were apprehended by the Feds under the new federal warrants. This allowed Joey's staff to surrender them before they were scheduled to appear in state court on their previous cases.

About two months later, I got a call from Vance. "Lefty, I just heard from the Raiders' attorney. He thought we might be interested to know that the Feds came to his office today. They informed him that they were unable to locate Joey, and therefore, were unable to substantiate the information they found during their raid concerning the alleged business deal Joey was working on between us and the gang. They also wanted him to know that in the future, they'd be keeping a close eye on you, me, and Joey."

I concluded from their conversation that the federal government was more interested in stopping the flow of illegal drugs and drug trafficking than in money laundering; and that they knew all along where Joey was, but never needed his testimony.

"Vance, it appears that either Joey was dead, or he played dumb when it came to giving them any information on you or me. We can all breathe a little easier."

The FBI concluded they would open a file and keep a close eye on us, so I relaxed, knowing that all they needed to do was update the file they already had on me from when I was working with Mickey in Reno and Vegas.

My hunch was that Joey was buried in the California desert somewhere, or would be, once the Raiders found out his new identity and address.

Vance and I, on the other hand, stopped worrying about the other proverbial shoe dropping regarding our deal with Joey. Although we'd closed out one of the ugliest chapters in what was about to become a long and financially successful business relationship, there would be plenty more to deal with.

CHAPTER

#39

With the Satan's Raiders issue behind us, our new agency started to grow by leaps and bounds. Vance was promoting the hell out of the civil bond business, and I was still working behind the scenes on the bail side for Martin Dupree and Gulf Coast.

My predictions about losses were beginning to come true. Some of the initial Cal Western bail agents were having to scramble to find their skips, and when the bounty hunters found one, the agents struggled to pay them for their help. This, in turn, made it almost impossible to get their help on future cases.

Gulf Coast also had to assist agents in paying off the full amount of the bonds when the agents were unable to locate and return the fugitives to custody in the timeframe allotted by law. If the agents failed to pay these losses, the courts would refuse to accept any more Gulf Coast bonds and turn them over to the Department of Insurance, at which point, all the Gulf Coast agents throughout the state would be suspended from posting future bonds, not just those owing the court money.

Marty's honeymoon period in the bail bond business was just about over, at least in California, and he knew it.

He also started to recognize the obvious. He'd really fucked up when he failed to keep his word with me. Although he couldn't prove it, he knew that I started setting him up for failure the minute he reneged on his promise.

Although only a few of the Satan's Raiders' bail bonds were forfeited, there were enough other losses from the rest of the Cal Western agents to bury Marty's company. And it was all the result of his greed.

I could tell from our phone conversations that Marty wasn't happy, which meant my days with Gulf Coast were numbered.

Soon after, Marty showed up in our Northern California office with no warning. The first thing he did was cancel Timmy's bail contract—not because his general agency was one of those creating loss problems, but because Timmy was the landlord for the Northern California office, which Marty closed, effective that day.

In addition to giving Timmy his notice, he fired me, and all the Gulf Coast personnel in my office. He gave each of us our final paychecks. He didn't give me my bonus or any of us a single penny in severance. He merely handed everyone their check and left one of his cronies behind to supervise gathering Gulf Coast's records, files, and furniture. He did, however, ask me for the keys to the Mercedes he'd given me to "use." He got in it and drove away.

His henchmen stayed back to help remove everything that belonged to Gulf Coast, which Marty later found out was only the actual Gulf Coast agent files. Everything else, including the filing cabinets, desks, chairs, and other furniture, belonged to Timmy, who was now our landlord.

I'm sure Marty's intention was to shock and scare everyone, but the only one shocked or scared was him—because the moment Marty's team was gone, I got Vance on the phone, and Parker Surety Services immediately hired everyone. The transition was as easy as changing hats, since everyone still had their same desk, chair, and everything else.

Teresa was the exception. She'd kept all the Parker Surety paperwork, civil bond files, and other related materials in a separate file room on Tim's side of the building. This way, Marty couldn't accuse any employee in our section of the office of working for Vance, nor could he threaten or intimidate us with an employee/employer breach. After the movers left, we moved all of Vance's files and supplies into our side of the office building,

When they were settled, the staff was able to use Timmy's office phones to begin notifying the bail agents, while Teresa and I used Vance's phone, which was in her office.

Within a few days, we arranged for new phone services and started to notify everyone that we were now working for Vance's new company. I began to openly solicit the last of the largest bail producers and general agents in the country, those who hadn't already taken a contract with Vance.

As a result of our reputation (through forming the first national bail association and the convention in Vegas), guys signed with us without hesitation. Vance's national managing general agency now had two offices, one in Southern and one in Northern California. I ran the soliciting, contracting, and underwriting of bail agents across the country from my office in northern California. Vance handled the internal processing and reporting of all their business to the insurance company in addition to all the civil bonds.

Within a few months, the money started pouring in. Just as quickly, Vance and his wife started to spend it. They bought a new home in one of the more prominent areas of Southern California and rented out their old one.

To this day, I'm not sure who started providing them with illegal drugs, but their new lifestyle and their newfound wealth was the right formula for getting them hooked on cocaine and alcohol in a big way.

Vance became the neighborhood big shot and began hosting neighborhood parties for his wealthy friends and neighbors. Sally provided everyone with food, alcohol, and entertainment, while Vance provided them with marijuana and cocaine . . . all free, of course. Fortunately, neither Vance nor Sally were stupid enough to take any money for drugs. Taking money for anything would have tarnished not only Vance's image, it would likely have gotten them arrested. So everything was always at Vance's expense.

Some of these parties ended up being wild, partner-swapping gatherings. At the beginning of our business relationship, I stayed at Vance's house during my regular monthly business trip to our Southern California office, and he would inevitably host a party. Although I drank more than I should have most of the time, I never had sex with anyone, and I never smoked or snorted drugs. I found my fun watching the ladies take off all their clothes and jump into the pool while the old farts embarrassed themselves trying to make it with some other guy's younger wife or girlfriend. But I always went to bed alone, and long before all the real fun started.

One night, just after the swimming party began, I said my goodnights to everyone and went to the guest room, where I passed out on the bed with my clothes on. To this day, I believe Vance, or most likely Sally, spiked my drink, because when I woke up a few hours later, I was naked and handcuffed to the headboard.

I made a futile effort to free myself about the time Vance and Sally walked into the room. She was nude; he had on a long robe. She came over and began fondling me. Vance sat down in the recliner across the room and watched.

I began yelling, "Goddammit, uncuff me and get the hell out of my room." My screams startled her. She stopped touching me and went to stand next to Vance.

"Take these handcuffs off . . . NOW! And get the hell out of here! If you keep this up, you'll regret it before the fun's over, I promise you!"

Obviously, I'd made my point. Vance unlocked the handcuffs while Sally muttered, "Gee, we really thought you'd enjoy this." I got dressed and left the house as fast as I could. Although our friendship stayed intact after that incident, my future trips to Southern California included hotel reservations.

The business started to suffer from Vance's mismanagement. In addition to all the parties and drugs, he started spending money like he really had it. He leased both a new Ferrari for himself and new Rolls Royce in the company's name, with the intention of starting a limousine service. He also hired a couple of drivers and provided them with the traditional chauffeur's suitcoats and caps.

His rationale was, "We'll use the Rolls and the drivers to pick up visiting bail agents at the airport and provide them with expert transportation during their visit. This will give our national managing general agency the look and feel of financially stability."

The concept sounded great, but unfortunately, Sally began using the limo for shopping trips, luncheons with girlfriends, and nightly restaurant trips for her, Vance, and some of their neighbors. This meant we always needed a staff member to pick up the visiting agents, dignitaries, and of course, me, in one of their personal cars. This wasn't quite as classy as Vance described it when he made his sales pitch for justifying the Rolls, but he owned 80 percent of the company and did whatever he wanted.

A few months later, Vance met the owner of an Italian restaurant located on a lagoon near San Clemente. He was so impressed with the guy and the quality of his food that he offered to partner with him in a new, larger place, but only if he agreed to move the restaurant to a more prominent location nearby, with an ocean view—at our company's expense. When it opened for business, it became Vance's hangout—days, nights, and weekends, at another significant cost to the company.

The cost of Vance and Sally's drug habits, which were already out of control, plus their colorful parties, flamboyant behavior, extravagant wardrobes, and flashy investments increased the amount of cash he took out of the company.

Over the course of our first three years, our chief financial officer, Paul Edwards, cornered me numerous times during my visits to the home office to fill me in on the company's true financial situation.

One time, his concerns were somewhat unusual. He said, "Lefty, since you're the company's only other stockholder, I feel you should know that we're on the verge of being out of trust—we're spending more than our share of the premiums we collect from the agents, both bail and civil.

"Until now, I've been able to shake a few trees to keep us in trust, but Vance is asking me to stop processing some of the incoming monthly business from the bail agents while continuing to deposit their premium checks. He said to do whatever I need to, to cover our shortages and continue paying the bills. That the new agents we're putting on will eventually provide enough new revenue to pay our bills, especially those relating to his lifestyle, which, we know, includes his drug habit. I'm afraid holding back business while depositing the agents' checks will create a huge backlog of unreported bonds.

"He's asking me to skim money off the top to increase the company's cash flow. I'm not concerned for myself, because I'm following the directions of the majority stockholder. But I am concerned that if the Department of Insurance discovers this, everyone—Vance, you, and the company—could all lose your licenses, and possibly go to jail, and the rest of us will be looking for work. Since you're the only other stockholder, I felt it was important for you to know."

Although I knew he was covering his ass by telling me, I thanked him for being forthcoming. I realized I'd let my guard down. I'd forgotten my own rule about limiting the number of people involved in any illegal activity. There were now three of us: Paul, Vance, and me. That was one too many, especially since Paul wasn't receiving any piece of the forbidden fruit.

I decided to confront Vance's potential problem head on, so I set up a meeting with him. That's when I remembered something Mickey always said: "Kid, always try to be part of the solution rather than a part of the problem, no matter how big the problem is, or who owns it." So before I met with Vance, I went back to my office to think about what Paul had dumped on me.

After spending a few hours of pacing, I decided to have lunch with Vance. I wanted our meeting to be someplace other than the office or his favorite Italian hangout; I wanted to ensure that we weren't overheard or constantly interrupted by our staff, his friendly neighbors, or his restaurant owner.

CHAPTER

#40

Although the solution came easily, it was meant to be temporary, because Vance's spending was the real problem, and we needed to get it under control as quickly as possible.

My idea was simple. We had already secured contracts with more than five hundred bail agencies across the country, all of which were posting their bonds with United Colonial, either through one of our regional managing general agencies or on a direct basis through our home office. All we needed to do was tap into a new revenue source that many of our smaller direct agents and managing general agents were missing.

Over time, I'd noticed that most of these smaller agencies were passing up larger bail bonds because they felt they weren't financially strong enough to satisfy a loss in the event that one of these larger bonds went into forfeiture.

My idea was to offer these agents a new program; one where our agency, together with the posting agency, would split the bond liability, with each of us taking some part of the potential risk in exchange for a proportional part of the premium.

These agents could take whatever part of the risk they were comfortable with, and our agency would take the rest. This new program would offer them an opportunity to better service their clients, while getting a percentage of these bonds, rather than giving them up entirely, which could also mean losing their client to a competitor.

As an example, let's say someone needed a $100,000 bail bond and they had the $10,000 premium, but the agent felt his client did not have enough collateral to insure the loss in the event he failed to appear. Before turning this bond down, the agent could call me, offer to retain whatever portion of the risk he was comfortable with, and our agency would take on the balance.

If he were comfortable taking $25,000 of the risk, and keeping $2,500 of the premium, we would take $75,000 of the risk and take $7,500 of the premium.

The agent would then report the entire $100,000 bond, but only include his check for the bond cost on his $25,000 portion and hold our $7,500 share of the premium, in cash, for me; I would provide him with a separate "hold harmless agreement" for the $75K upon receipt of the $7,500.

Depending on how large our portion of these bonds were, and how many we secured during any given time period, I would have the agents send our portion, together with their weekly reports. But if our percentage of the premium was ten grand or more, I wanted our share of the cash right away. I'd take the next flight out, review the collateral, drop off the "hold harmless" agreement for our share of the bond, pick up their special bond report, and pocket our share of the premium.

I arranged this program directly with Vance so we could keep it outside the company. It was my job to underwrite these risks to ensure that we didn't end up with a loss we couldn't cover if the defendant failed to appear. I made it a point to collect our portion of the premium in cash and I provided a cashier's check to our general agency for the balance of the bond cost due the insurance company on our portion of each of these bonds. I always made sure our agency got the bond cost before I split the remainder with Vance, on our normal 80/20 basis.

This arrangement generated thousands of dollars a month for both of us, and because I oversaw it, I was assured of receiving my split. Based on the revenues Vance was receiving from this new program, Paul, our CFO, was not only able to stop holding back bail agent reports, he was able to clear the backlog of unreported bonds he'd been holding. At the time, it appeared as though we were able to avoid another potential financial disaster, but only for a short while.

In fact, this program worked so well I had to hire a friend of Timmy Walters, Sandy (Bones) Carmella, to travel around the country and pick up cash and paperwork on our bond splits. Meanwhile, I stayed in the office, processed the paperwork, and kept tabs on Vance. In addition to being my personal gofer, Bones was one of my lead bounty hunters. I never asked where (or why) he got his nickname, because he was six three, weighed 260 pounds, and could easily intimidate anyone he encountered, including me. I figured his nickname came from breaking a few bones while working skips for Timmy, which was none of my business.

Bones lived in Northern California and hung around our office, so he was also available when one of my agents needed help skip chasing. I usually brought him along when I traveled, even to the home office, because I felt comfortable with him watching my back. Whenever I had time, I'd also go along on one of his skip-chasing cases, just for the fun of it. But mostly

I used him to pick up our splits, especially if our share of the premium was large and in cash. I considered him a friend as well as an employee, so when we weren't busy, we played a little golf, had lunch with agents, or stopped off after work for a few drinks.

Unfortunately, while the business was going well thanks to the bond splits, Vance and Sally's drug use and spending habits got worse. They began traveling to New York and Hawaii on a regular basis We had just signed two new general agents in these locations. Since Vance was looking for ways to run all his expenses through the company, he would write off these trips as a business expense and not have to take a personal draw.

They also started traveling to Vegas, which inevitably meant Vance would join in on high roller gambling. This happened so often that the new cash flow from our bond splitting program wasn't enough to sustain their bad habits.

Vance not only started to push the envelope on putting the company's trust account in jeopardy again, he started having some of the agents, those who were splitting bonds with us on a regular basis, report them directly to him in an effort to cut me out of my 20 percent split. Most of the agents knew what he was doing, and they kept me in the loop, especially since Vance never provided them with our hold-harmless agreements. They always called me concerning his paperwork, so I was able to collect my 20 percent one way or another. I'm sure he thought he was cheating me out of it, but I was able to take a larger portion from those I worked on to offset his greed.

The only time I traveled to Vegas with Vance was when the new agent's association held one of their conventions there. As I've mentioned, some of our competitors, the long-time surety companies that hated us, had grouped together and taken control of the AAPBA, which we'd founded, and even changed its name. But no matter how hard they tried, they were never able to obtain our level of success, or our level of attendance, regardless of where they held it: Washington, D.C., Texas, or anywhere else.

In this latest attempt they returned to Las Vegas in hopes of improving membership participation, which provided us with a good excuse to see what our competitors were up to.

Although we had no intention of participating in any of the events, we invited a bunch of our agents and their wives to meet us there. The plan was to socialize with some new prospects while keeping an eye on what our own agents were doing.

Just before leaving for Vegas, I finished a large bond split with one of our agents. Our share was $10,000 after bond cost, so I invited the agent to meet us in Vegas at our expense. I told him we'd have a little fun and he could pick up his hold harmless. I, on the other hand, wanted to get my $2,000 plus the company's share first, then make sure Vance got his $8,000 so he didn't hit the company's Trust Account for gambling money.

Soon after our arrival, I met with Vance in his suite, and gave him his $8K. He looked at it, laid it on the coffee table, and said thanks. Then I left.

Later that night, Teresa and I went to the party Vance was hosting for our agents. Shortly after we arrived Teresa said she had seen enough of Sally drinking, smoking, and snorting. She excused herself for the evening and retired to our room.

I, on the other hand, stayed at the party for a while longer, and I'm glad I did. Because soon after Teresa left, Sally started ragging on Vance about their private lives in front of everybody in the room. Before anyone knew what was happening, Sally stood up, grabbed the envelope with the $8K in cash Vance had left on the table earlier, and started screaming, "This is all you really care about . . . You asshole! Money! Money! Money! Watch this!" She ran into one of the bathrooms and started flushing handfuls of cash down the toilet. By the time we were able to stop her, she had flushed more than $6K down the drain.

Vance was too wasted to realize what she'd done; he shrugged his shoulders and continued talking to his guests. About ten minutes after running into their bedroom and locking the door, Sally came out stark-ass naked! She ran out the door, down the hall, and into the glass-enclosed elevator before anyone could stop her. On the way down, she stood against the glass, facing the casino for all to see, including hotel security.

As the elevator door opened on the ground floor, a security guard strongly suggested that she put on the suitcoat he'd conveniently borrowed from one of the pit bosses. He gave her two options: "Ma'am, either you put on this coat and let us escort you back to your suite or we will escort you outside to a waiting police car. The choice is yours."

She put on the coat, stepped back into the elevator with the guards, and returned to her room.

I'd had enough excitement for one night, so I stopped by our room, told Teresa what Sally had done, and let her know that I was taking a cab downtown to check out my old stomping grounds. I wanted to see how many new bail offices there were around the jails and the courthouse and if I knew any of the agents on duty.

As I went from office to office, saying hello to the agents, and shooting the shit with a few of the ones I knew, I came across a new agency that was owned and operated by a woman. Although it wasn't that unusual to see a woman in a bail office, it was unusual to see one wearing a fashionable dress, high heels, and costume jewelry, rather than a conservative pantsuit and flats.

After introducing myself and explaining who I was and that I used to write bail in Las Vegas a few years earlier, I asked if I could give her some friendly advice.

"You're welcome to share any advice about the business, and I'm more than willing to listen. Just as long as you understand I'm not necessarily going to agree or accept it."

I nodded and said, "I think you're dressed quite handsomely for a legal office, or for a court employee, but it's not necessarily suitable for a bail office, especially the jewelry. And assuredly not one in a transient area like Vegas. I believe you might be inviting trouble, especially if you were to bail out the wrong person."

She asked, "I don't understand. What are you trying to say?"

"Well," I said, "After thirty-plus years in the business, I know that we meet all kinds in our business, and a significant number of them aren't very nice, to say the least. If any of us were doing business in Vegas, as you are, and we bailed some guy from out-of-state who was staying at a local hotel, we might have to take him to his room to collect our premium or some type of collateral. At that point, he, or they, might attempt to assault the agent or worse, if the agent was a woman. And, in your attire, they might get the impression that you're weak or fragile."

She laughed and said, "Thanks for the advice but I'm capable of taking care of myself. You think I'm another weak, stupid female, who should be home nursing a dozen kids rather than dealing with bad guys."

I realized she wasn't interested in discussing my concerns any further. I apologized for any misunderstanding and told her I was only making an observation from years of experience in the business. I told her it was a pleasure meeting her, handed her my card and said, "Please feel free to call me if you ever need a new insurance carrier to back your action." I said good night, hailed a cab, and returned to my hotel.

Shortly after that trip, several unfortunate things happened.

I got a call from one of my agent friends in Vegas. He called to let me know that the female agent I'd met during my trip had been physically and sexually assaulted. She was handcuffed to a bed in one of the hotels on the Strip, so she must have taken a man back to his hotel to collect her bond premium, and/or some collateral. The police figured that her client, or possibly an accomplice who may have been waiting in the room, smashed her in the face, knocked her out, ripped off her clothes, cuffed her to the bed frame and sexually assaulted her for hours. Then, after ransacking her handbag and briefcase for valuables, he (or they) took her wallet.

The maids found her at checkout time, still nude and handcuffed to the bed. Security called the police and the paramedics. The investigators found out that the information her assailant had given to the hotel clerk, and later to the jailers during his initial arrest, was false. And, since his fingerprints didn't show up on the national crime identification database (NCIC) or with the FBI, they had no way of knowing who he was, or where he was from. After flashing his mugshot at the airport, the bus depot, and the train station, they came up empty, and figured the suspect or suspects must have been traveling by car.

After filling me in on the assault, the bail agent shared that when the woman got out of the hospital, she closed her bail office and planned to leave Las Vegas. When we hung up, I felt as though I must have had a premonition, because I'd never given that kind of advice or warning to anyone else. I do remember having a strong feeling of concern for her safety when I saw her through her office window. I really didn't know what might happen, or that it would be violent; especially when she was so confident about being able to take care of herself. But I did know that being dressed as she was, and looking like she did while working in a bail office, was asking for trouble. This was one time I wished I was wrong.

If that wasn't enough to spoil my week, Vance called a few days after we returned from Vegas. He and Sally had a major falling out; they were officially separated, and she was filing for divorce. He also said he'd moved out of their house and planned to purchase a $1.5 million beachfront home.

Under normal circumstances I wouldn't have given the divorce a second thought, because breaking up was inevitable given their problems with drinking and drugs. But with the company suffering from the financial strain of their wild lifestyle, this was not the ideal time for Vance to become physically troubled and emotionally bankrupt, which I knew would happen.

It was time for someone to have a serious talk with him. Unfortunately, I was the only one he'd listen to. If things went south, Teresa and I had the most to lose, so I asked for her help as well.

We both agreed that the time had come to tell him, face-to-face, what he already knew. The drinking and the drugs were killing him, his wife, and their marriage. If he continued along this path, he would also kill our financial golden goose . . . the bail and bonding business.

This was the first, but not the last, time Teresa and I would convince him to check into a substance abuse rehab center in Northern California. The place we agreed upon was within an hour's drive from our home, which would give me an opportunity to meet with him at least weekly. The rehab center agreed to my regular visits as long as we restricted our conversations to business-related updates and financial issues only. No personal problems.

CHAPTER

#41

The first time Vance was released from rehab he was as good as new, and back on his game.

While in rehab, he had an opportunity to talk with a lot of the local staff, some of whom were illegal immigrants from South American countries. Many had been arrested by the U.S. Border Patrol or the Immigration and Naturalization Service while attempting to cross into the United States near San Diego. At the time (1985), they were all required to post a $2,500 immigration bond, and those who couldn't were deported back to their home country.

This was the first time Vance had heard about immigration bonds. He decided to research them. On his release from the center, we flew to Los Angeles and had his limo pick us up and take us to the federal immigration office.

I'll never forget driving through the gates of the immigration facility in our stretch. You could see and feel all the gawking eyes on us. There was at least one person in every office window of the three-story building. From the looks of it, they were all wondering who was arriving in such style. Little did they know, it was only two bail bondsmen.

We spent the better part of the afternoon learning the qualifications for posting immigration bonds, what type of charges illegals were being held on, the size of bonds required, and what kind of volume passed through the Southern California points of entry.

It turned out that most of the bond amounts were small, mostly $2,500, but the number of bonds being posted daily was in the hundreds. And the qualifications for posting them were simple. All we needed was a federally qualified surety insurance company to underwrite the bonds, and a licensed California surety insurance agent to negotiate and post them.

After leaving the federal building and knowing that United Colonial was already qualified, we went looking for a suitable office site; within a month, Vance opened our first and only immigration office. In the process, he hired a friend who not only held a valid insurance license, but also spoke Spanish, and happened to need a job. We were off and running, and it seemed Vance had settled into his normal business routine.

I wasn't home a week before I got a call from Paul, our CFO. He said Vance had decided to separate the immigration bond office from the main company, and that he'd be reporting the immigration bonds as bail bonds but wanted us to catalog them as civil bonds. The difference is that the civil bond premium for any $2,500 civil bond was far less than the premium on bail bonds, which meant the insurance company would receive a significantly smaller amount, while still being financially liable for all the losses.

So they were written as bail bonds and cataloged and reported to the company as civil bonds, which meant Vance was able to retain the lion's share of each $250 premium with no financial responsibility for the losses. And since the bail agents are held financially liable to the company, as well as the courts, for any loss, they are authorized to hold all the collateral, including all cash deposits.

Vance not only required that every defendant have a co-signer, someone who would sign to guarantee the immigrant's appearance before the Immigration and Naturalization Service, but they were also required to deposit a minimum of $50 per week, or more, as bond collateral until the entire $2,500 amount was reached. At that time, the cosigner would be released from any future financial responsibility for the immigrant's appearance.

He also required that all bond files be held in his downtown bond office, not in our home office. In addition, he kept all the cash collateral as well as the receipt books in his safe at home.

This would have been acceptable underwriting policy, except for the fact that Vance began pocketing all the collateral money.

As he painstakingly outlined it to Paul, he wanted to be the only one with access to all premium files, bond records, and collateral receipt books. He felt that we should try and keep all the information pertaining to this new program away from United Colonial Insurance, the California Department of Insurance, and anyone else who might snoop around, until he was satisfied with its success. In other words, he wanted to make sure he could skim off the collateral for his personal use.

In the event any auditors showed up at the immigration bond office, they would be limited to noting that most immigration bonds are small in nature and required only a co-signer as security in almost every instance; and none of the files would reflect cash collateral ever being taken.

The new office almost instantly began writing hundreds of immigration bonds weekly. This meant that Vance now had access to a new and almost unlimited amount of premium money and cash collateral, which he could siphon off for his own personal use without anyone being the wiser.

The company's involvement in this office and in the immigration bond program was limited, and that's the way I liked it. Every person that gave this new office money got a receipt, regardless of whether it was for premium or collateral. So if any of these people produced their receipts and complained, the whole program would backfire and land on Vance, and him alone.

The only question that would fall on our managing general agency would be whether we were reporting these immigration bonds properly to United Colonial. To be on the safe side, I told Vance he should hire some of the best insurance lawyers in California to protect him from the meddling eyes of the Department of Insurance.

One of our general agents, a guy named Hal Taylor, who reinsured a few retail bail offices in cities located near the Mexican-American border, got wind that Vance was writing immigration bonds, and wanted in on the action.

When Vance said no, a couple of other general agents joined Hal in an attempt to take their bail business directly to United Colonial and circumvent our managing general agency in hopes of gaining access to writing immigration bonds. They thought they could break our exclusive arrangement by informing United Colonial's president about Vance's cocaine addiction, his wild parties, his flamboyant spending habits, and last, but not least, his need to acquire a new residence, due to his marital problems.

At first, I didn't think Vance created the immigration program outside of our managing general agency in an effort to cheat me out of my 20 percent. Instead, I believed he did it as an opportunity to control the amount of money he'd been siphoning from our company. He needed a new source of revenue to help settle his inevitable divorce without having to open the company's financial records to anyone.

CHAPTER

#42

To make sure Hal Taylor and his general agent buddies didn't get a direct contract with United Colonial, Vance worked out a deal with Randy Fallon, our general agent friend from Miami. We knew that Randy was in tight with the president of United, as he'd originally introduced Vance back when we were looking for our first national market.

The idea was to have Vance find a new company, one we could move all our business to while we helped Randy obtain a new, exclusive MGA contract with United Colonial for bail only, with our blessing.

Randy's contract would include taking all the independent bail agents as well as all the general agents in the eastern states, including Hal Taylor's group, as well those represented by his general agent buddies.

We had lost all trust in Hal but didn't want him gaining direct access to United Colonial or obtaining authority to start writing immigration business. We were willing to give up a percentage of our bail business in an effort to stop Hal. We figured the cost for the long-distance supervision of the business we were giving to Randy amounted to almost 50 percent of their revenue. So this new deal made good sense.

Randy would pay us 50 percent of all the gross income from his new G.A., which would go into effect as soon as we signed our new exclusive MGA contract with the new company Vance had found, American Sentinel Insurance. American Sentinel's national contract included civil, bail, and immigration bonds. So if the deal went south with Randy, we could still contract with bail agents on the east coast.

Our deal had to be built on trust, because there was no way we could check with United Colonial to find out if Randy was paying us everything he had agreed to. And since some of my past ventures taught me to "trust, but check," I convinced Vance to hire my best buddy from Reno, Roy Carver, and send him to Miami as insurance that we regularly got our percentage of the business.

We sweetened the pot for Roy's inevitable move to Miami by insisting that Randy hire him as the liaison between our office and his. This meant Roy would get two paychecks, one from each side of this deal. He packed his bags and arrived in Miami within a week.

With Roy in place, Vance secured our new national contract with American Sentinel Insurance. They were chomping at the bit to take on our business, so our staff started moving all the direct agents while he worked out a suitable exit strategy with United Colonial and Randy Fallon.

While this business transition was happening, Vance was having a hard time accepting his pending divorce. He was calling me daily, telling me how much he loved Sally and wanted them to get back together.

Unfortunately, Sally had flipped out after years of cocaine and alcohol use. She began to drive Vance crazy with her financial demands surrounding their divorce. She insisted that he continue supplying her with cocaine, which meant he was once again being exposed to drugs. It was a bad situation.

Much of the money Vance was using to sustain their ongoing lifestyle was still being misappropriated from numerous sources within the business, and he couldn't afford to have the company's finances scrutinized by a team of his wife's divorce lawyers or by the Department of Insurance. His only solution was to stoop to her demands and purchase her half of their 80 percent interest in the company for an agreed upon price of $7.5 million, payable at a rate of $1.5 million per year for five years.

He also agreed to pay her attorney fees and transfer full ownership of the two homes they owned together; their original home in Rancho Bernardo, which was now a rental, and their existing residence in San Clemente. In exchange for all this, he retained all stock and voting rights in our company.

When it was all over, he ended up owning 80 percent of the company (which was almost worthless based on our trust position, among other things) and the new beach house he'd recently acquired (which, at that point, had little to no equity).

The CFO and I had a good laugh about Vance's wife getting more from him than Johnny Carson gave his wife for their divorce, which happened around the same time as Vance's. The difference being, Carson could afford to pay his wife. Vance, on the other hand, couldn't.

The worst part of their divorce was Vance getting hooked on drugs again. The stress of losing Sally, together with the avalanche of debt he was facing from the divorce, could easily break anyone, especially a recovering addict.

To top it off, I got a call from Butch Hogan, one of our bail agents in Houston. He'd recently written a $500,000 bond with American Sentinel on some rancher's son. The kid was a single, twenty-five-year-old cowboy arrested for manslaughter. He allegedly shot and killed a poacher on his old man's ranch.

We split the bond 50/50 with Butch. We took our half, $25,000, and the old man's ranch for collateral. A few weeks later, the kid failed to appear for his arraignment. The judge forfeited our half-million-dollar bond and gave Butch forty-five days to bring him in or pay the full $500,000 to the court.

This wasn't the first $500,000 bond we wrote, but it was the first, and only one, on American Sentinel Insurance at the time.

The last thing we needed was ask our new insurance carrier for help in paying off a bond this size; especially since we'd just started writing bail through them and they were holding less than $100,000 in our loss reserve. I was afraid if we asked, they would panic and cancel our entire contract.

The next day, Butch called and said, "The kid's dad just got a collect call from him. He's in Miami and heading for the Bahamas. The kid told the old man he was sorry, but he couldn't face life in prison. I guess he was hoping his father understood and wouldn't lose his ranch over this whole mess.

"Lefty, what should I do? You guys got half this bond. You've got to help me out on this, I don't want to lose my bail business."

The only thing I could think to do was take Bones, together with one of his regular backup bounty hunters, and go find this little asshole.

I told Butch, "I'm going to charter a private jet and bring a few guys with me. We need you to pick up a copy of the kid's latest mug shot, the one taken just before you bailed him. And meet us at your airport. Pack light, because we're all going to Miami."

Then I called my old high school buddy Roy and told him what was up. I let him know when we'd arrive in Miami and asked him to pick us up. I told him to rent a van because there would be five of us, and if we found the fugitive, we'd jam him in the luggage compartment or tie him to the roof.

I charted a private jet large enough to hold five passengers. I packed my brass knuckles, drove to the Oakland airport, boarded the plane with Bones and his buddies, and was in the air ninety minutes later. We flew to Texas, picked up Butch, and headed to Miami.

Roy met us at the private terminal in a seven-passenger van and we took off.

After introductions all around, Roy said, "The best place to start looking for a young, single, twenty-five-year-old punk with a messed-up life is inside one of those strip bars along Miami Beach where the girls dance nude on tabletops. Some of them also allow private parties in private rooms for customers willing to pay. If this kid is looking at prison, or hiding out in the Bahamas, he's probably looking for a little soft and comfy companionship before he takes off."

We agreed and headed for Miami Beach. We hit places like Tootsie's Cabaret, Scarlett's, Miami Velvet and Booby Trap, and ended up at the Pink Pussy.

I was beginning to think I'd made a mistake spending $10K on a private jet based on information we got from a phone call. But as luck would have it, our last stop was the charm. It looked like he'd just arrived, because he was sitting alone at the bar.

During our van ride, we'd passed around his mugshot, so we all knew what he looked like. Roy and I teamed up and cased the joint looking for the back door, the restrooms, and any other entries or exits in relation to the bar, and where he was sitting.

Now that we were certain he was there, I went up to one of the security bouncers, a guy who looked like he might be in charge, or at least be the last one standing in a bar fight. I handed him $1,500, which instantly got his attention. Then I told him who I was, what we were doing there, and what he needed to do to keep the money.

My plan was simple. All he needed to do was have one of the working girls, one he trusted, walk over and sit in the empty chair next to our boy. Then she would cozy up and convince him to go with her to one of the private rooms in the back, the one closest to the rear exit. I slipped him another $500 for her.

"You let us into that private room shortly before she arrives with our boy. Let him enter the room first; we'll take it from there. After we've secured him, you need to escort us to the exit, with the exception of the girl of course, so we can load him into our van."

I assured him that our boy wouldn't be in any condition to make a scene when we left the room, but not to worry, he would still be breathing.

I sent Roy and Butch to the van and had them move it around back. Then the bouncer led us to the empty room in the back so we could get ready.

After a few minutes, the girl convinced our cowboy to come with her. She nodded to the bouncer, and he escorted them to the room. He negotiated a fee with the kid so he wouldn't get wise to what was about to come down, collected his money, and let him enter first.

As the kid walked through the door, Bones and his buddy each grabbed an arm, and I hit him square in the face with my brass knuckles. He dropped like a log. We handcuffed him, shackled his ankles, and carried him to the van. On our way out, the bouncer and the dancer thanked us for making their evening fun, exciting, and profitable.

Halfway to the airport, the cowboy woke up, looked around, and said, "Jesus, who are you guys, and where the hell are you taking me?"

I said, "Don't you remember this guy?" and pointed to Butch. "He's your bail bondsman, and the rest of us are your worst nightmare. We're taking you on a little airplane ride back to see your daddy, and then to jail."

He started screaming. "You can't put me on a plane. I'm afraid to fly."

"Aw, gee," I said, "you've been watching too much TV. You're either going to fly quietly while you're still breathing, or when you're not, the choice is yours—because our choice is to bring you back dead or alive, but we are going to bring you back."

The pilot was at the airport when we arrived; he'd filed the flight plan we discussed on the phone after Bones and his buddy spotted the kid. I told him our first stop was Texas, to drop off Butch, the fugitive, and the two bounty hunters; then he and I would fly home to California.

At the airport, Bones and his buddy literally had to carry the kid onto the plane, then I had them tie him into his seat, handcuffs and all.

While saying our thanks and farewells to Roy he took me aside and said he'd had just recently been talking to Abe Ardeen, one of Butch Hogan's general agents in Louisiana, and heard that Martin Dupree's company, Gulf Coast Insurance, went belly-up; in addition, Martin's wife divorced him, and he was killed in a one-car accident. He allegedly lost control of his roadster and crashed.

I was at a loss for words, so as I stepped in the plane, I told Roy I'd send him five grand for his help, and we took off for Houston.

Roy's message was all I could think about on the return trip. I'd hated Marty for what he did to me, and I wanted his company to go broke, but I had mixed emotions about his family, and his death.

When we landed in Houston, I told Butch that my two bounty hunters would stay behind in Texas to make damn sure the kid got into jail, and to buy them both first-class tickets home when they were done. After all, the kid's dad would be paying all our expenses.

Including the bail premium and my padded expense report for finding and returning his son to jail, it cost the old man a little over $100,000. But thanks to us, he kept his ranch, and saved $400,000.

When it was over, we were all happy—except for the cowboy.

By the time I returned from Florida, Vance was doing so much coke and had so many friends, especially girls, coming and going from his place on the beach, he was getting paranoid, and started to fear for his safety. So he hired a bodyguard, Frankie Milo.

Some nights Vance and Frankie would sit out on the deck and watch the sunset while Vance drank wine and snorted coke. Frankie, on the other hand, just looked around, always with his trusty shotgun at the ready. What a mess! I tried to talk sense into two of them, suggesting they keep a lower profile and asking them to tone down their outer appearance. In other words, I said, no drugs, alcohol, or guns in sight. It was starting to look like an armed fortress, or worse yet, a serious drug house. The last thing we needed was to have Vance arrested or involved in a shootout trying to protect his stash of drugs. All my concerns fell on deaf ears.

With financial issues hanging over his head, Vance started looking for some new revenue sources. One day he decided that if he owned his own insurance company, he could keep the entire premium on every bond we were writing, be it civil or bail. This would immediately put an additional 12 percent of our gross bail revenues into his pocket without increasing our expenses, not to mention a significant cash flow from civil bonds, since we were already doing all the work while the insurance company sat back and collected some hefty revenues from us.

Vance hired one of his hanger on-type friends, a guy named Richard Sanders. Rick, as he liked to be called, was a has-been financial advisor who had some experience with public offerings through the stock market. Rumor had it that he participated and managed to take a couple of them public. But the key issue here was "not lately."

Rick convinced Vance that our managing general agency, with the enormous revenues we were collecting, made us a perfect candidate for supporting a public offering to raise enough cash reserves to either purchase an existing national insurance company or qualify for a new California charter. And he was the perfect person to help us.

After almost a year of messing around and getting paid $800,000, in the process, Rick accomplished nothing other than pushing Vance further into debt. He needed to come up with a plausible reason why things were standing still.

One day, Rick cornered Vance in his office and explained that the biggest problem he was having in getting Vance's new insurance company off the ground was me, and the fact that I owned 20 percent of the agency.

He convinced Vance that the Department of Insurance would never let him own his own company if I was involved as an employee, and most especially a part owner. During their conversation, Rick implied that he was on a first-name basis with the D.O.I. investigator who had previously caused problems for Vance. This female investigator allegedly suggested that getting rid of me would solve all their future problems with the department.

Based on the financial settlement Vance had made with Sally and the fact that I knew the actual net worth of the company after factoring out the millions of dollars he'd siphoned, we arrived at a value for the company at $10 million, which placed the value on my 20 percent at $2 million.

They agreed to pay me $750,000 up front, and the balance of $1.25 million on notes payable monthly, with an 8 percent annual interest on any unpaid balance. In addition, the purchase had to be from Vance personally, rather than through the company, because they didn't want to show this debt on any future financials.

The buyout deal sounded great. However, knowing the company's true financial picture and Vance's personal finances I was concerned about ever getting the rest of my money. However, considering Vance's drug relapse and Rick's attempt to use me as his scapegoat for all his delays, $750,000 up front was hard to turn down. As the expression goes, "A bird in the hand . . ."

CHAPTER

#43

As an early tenth wedding anniversary present to ourselves, Teresa and I used some of the money Vance paid us to buy a small condo in Palm Desert. With the girls both living away at college, we intended to spend at least six summer months each year in Northern California and the winter months in the desert. As it turned out, my hiatus from the company lasted just short of a year.

In late November 1989, Vance called and asked me to come back to work and help him dig himself out of the hole Rick Sanders had put him in. I agreed to return, but only as a consultant, and only on two conditions. First, I'd have carte blanche in running the company; second, he'd let Teresa and me check him into the Napa Rehab center again. He agreed.

During my first week back in the office, I found out that after making millions of dollars in bond revenues over the past few years, not counting the money from Vance's personal bail and immigration offices, the company was now almost $3 million out of trust; $800,000 of which went to pay Rick Sanders, and another $750,000 went toward purchasing my 20 percent of the company. The rest went to pay Sally's alimony.

Additionally, Vance had spent well over a million dollars in immigration collateral paying off his wife's attorney fees, making monthly payments on his beach house, and supporting his drug addiction and parties.

Although the immigration collateral problem was his, and his alone, the premium trust shortage belonged to the company, and if I ever wanted to see the remainder of the money Vance owed me for my interest in the company, I had to help fix this mess as fast as I could.

Just prior to my return, Vance fired Rick and replaced him with another loser, Boyd Thatcher. Boyd was as worthless as tits on a bull, and just about as stupid, especially when it came to managing a company in financial trouble, or with an owner like Vance.

So when Vance announced my return, and that I would be running the company in his absence, my first decision was to relegate Boyd to an office in the rear of our executive wing and give him a deck of cards to keep him busy. I did, however, leave him at full pay in the hope that he wouldn't cause problems.

After everything settled down, I devised a plan to redirect some of the company's incoming revenues through a falsified reporting program. My plan called for having certain agents report to a parallel company I set up in Nevada. That way, we could avoid problems with insurance regulators and investigators, especially those from the California Department of Insurance, because the new portion of our operation was in Nevada, out of their jurisdiction and out of sight to everyone except Mom and me.

We used Mom's address as my home office and hired her as my only employee. She went to her bank, which was within walking distance of her home, to open a couple of new accounts in the name of Parker Surety Bonding. She was able to obtain two blank signature cards from a female bank executive by using their long-term friendship and her little old lady charm to convince her friend that Vance was in the hospital, and unable to come into the bank, but not to worry, she had witnessed him signing all the necessary bank forms right in front of her.

In 1989, small businesses were just barely entering the computer age, with computer typewriters and punch-card-style data-entry systems. Both the independent agents and our main office staff were still manually preparing and processing weekly bail bond production reports and sending copies to the insurance company as required by our contract.

These reports contained all the pertinent information on each defendant released on bond, such as his or her name, the charges against them, the amount of their bail, and a court date and time for their initial appearance.

We were reporting thousands of bail bonds at a time, from over five hundred agencies across the country, and the insurance company required that we use a batch system. If each agency wrote just four bonds a day, and reported twenty-eight bonds a week, we would process over fourteen thousand bonds each week.

Each batch we sent to the company required a cover sheet that included the total number of individual bonds in the batch, the total liability written to the courts, the total premiums charged, and a corresponding check and check number for the amount of bond cost owed and paid to the company.

As an example, one report might reflect a total of fifteen hundred bonds totaling $1.5 million in liability to the court, with $150,000 in premium collected by the agent. We'd attach our check #123 in the amount of $12,000, which represented

.08 percent of the premium charged by the agents. In reality, we were actually reporting over ten times that much weekly. Many of the bail bonds were written on weekends and closed out and exonerated by the courts the following Monday when the defendants appeared in court. In quite a few of these cases, the charges would be dropped by the prosecutor for lack of evidence, while other cases were closed because the defendants pled guilty, and either paid a fine or were sentenced to a number of community service hours. The bail bonds on all these types of cases were always exonerated when the cases were closed.

Because they were written and closed within the same batch, and there was never a chance that the company would ever receive a notice from the court questioning or suggesting a defendant's failure to appear, or requiring a payment of a forfeiture on them, we were able to mark these bonds as void rather than pay the company their portion of the premium.

When we included them in our weekly batch reports, it wasn't necessary to include the liability, or pay the company bond cost for them, because they were void. Consequently, the batch totals, those that we reported and paid for, always balanced.

The company employees entered these bonds into their records, noted the batch number used to report them and the fact that they were either exonerated or voided, and were closed out within the same batch. No one ever suspected that these were never paid. They assumed that because they were listed and voided on the same report, the agent must not have written them. And since the entry clerks were processing thousands of these weekly, errors were not uncommon. The accounting department saw to it that the premiums due for written bonds always matched with the amount of the check we were providing to the company and that all the bonds, including the voided ones, ended up with a batch number.

The batch system we were using to report and track thousands of these transactions was not only archaic, it was based on the honor system. Potential policy liabilities resulting from bail bond transactions never impacted the insurance company's capital or surplus, because unlike every other line of insurance, bail bonds were indemnified by cosigners, secured by collateral, and guaranteed by bail agent contracts.

The insurance regulators required every insurance company to enter their surety and bail business differently than every other line of insurance, because none of the other lines secured the company against loss by taking personal indemnity or collateral.

Without computers, the sheer volume of bonds written through our company made it almost impossible to find or track reporting errors on closed bonds. The companies only verified that a bond had been written when they received a notice of forfeiture or a demand for payment from a court. Neither of these would ever happen on these voided bonds, because they were all posted by individual agents and closed by the courts prior to their being reported. As a result, there was no chance the company would receive a request or demand regarding them.

Beginning in 1989, I devised every trick in the book to reduce the amount of premiums we needed to pay the insurance company while still depositing all the premiums we were collecting from hundreds of agents on many of these types of short-term bonds.

By April 1994, this falsified reporting program had been running like a Swiss clock for just over three years. In addition, I had managed to stop Vance from drawing excessive amounts of money from the company by convincing him that it was safer for him to use the immigration collateral for his special needs while we worked on balancing the managing general agency books and paying our bills, which included the payment on my note from selling my stock back to the company.

We were now more than halfway home; somewhere around $1.6 million dollars out of trust, with that figure dropping every month. And only two people, not counting me, knew what, or how we were doing it.

Meanwhile, Vance had been in and out of rehab in Napa two more times, but this third time he was doing much better. He was long past his divorce; he sold his beach house to a couple of rich guys from Japan and retired his bodyguards. This helped bring his finances more in line with his income. His self-confidence was coming back, and he was ready to return to work.

Once again, timing and lighting were everything. Boyd Thatcher, who was being paid an executive salary while playing solitaire in the back office, couldn't stand that I was turning the company around, or that Vance was turning his life around. He ran to American Sentinel Insurance and spilled his guts. Fortunately for us, he knew only what had gone on before I came back to work, and nothing about what we were doing now . . . or the actual amount the company was out of trust.

Boyd told them he thought the trust deficit was "somewhere around two million dollars or more," but he couldn't give them an accurate number because he'd been shut out of the financial loop for quite a while.

American Sentinel Insurance took Boyd's written statement to a federal judge and got him to sign a cease-and-desist order against Vance and the company. We got wind of this, so the next day, Vance flew to Hartford, Connecticut, to meet with Truman Whiting, the president and CEO of Mid-Atlantic

Insurance Group. In the past, Whiting had shown some serious interest in Vance's surety business, as well as his bail operation.

During their meeting, Vance told Truman everything, including his battle with drugs, his divorce, and the amount the company was out of trust. He didn't divulge any information about his retail bail operations or the immigration bond program, because they weren't part of the company.

Truman struck a deal with Vance to purchase the civil bond division of Vance's company for $2 million. Truman instructed his CFO to issue two checks, one for $1.8 million, made payable to American Sentinel Insurance, and the other to Parker Surety for $200,000. Upon his return, Vance and his attorney met Sentinel's group as they were entering Vance's office and handed them the $1.8 million cashier's check, which happened to be more than the amount they were showing as being out of trust. He also showed them a deposit slip to our trust account for an additional $200,000 which, combined with the $1,800,000 cashier's check, was more than the amount shown in the judge's order.

Instead of closing Vance down, they went home with their tails between their legs, because they had been misled by Boyd Thatcher. They were also about to lose all of Vance's business. Truman provided the financial assistance Vance needed, and gave him a national contract with one of his companies for his surety bail bond operation. Vance's attorney advised Sentinel that we would be moving the entire bond operation to the new company, and that if they tried to interfere in any way with the transition, Vance and the new owner of his civil bond division would sue them for business interference based on the false accusations they'd misrepresented to the federal judge.

CHAPTER

#44

Vance and Truman hit it off. While Vance worked with Truman to move all the license and permit business to Truman's insurance company, I worked with the bail general agents and the smaller retail bail independents to ensure a smooth transition to the Mid-Atlantic Insurance Group.

Parker Surety, which housed the wholesale bail business, still belonged to Vance, so my involvement was strictly with Vance, and I had little interaction with anyone from the new company.

Mark's Bail Bonds in El Cajon and the immigration office in downtown Chula Vista were both still owned by Vance. He was still processing immigration as bail, rather than surety, and they remained independent entities directly under Vance's control. As a result, Vance was responsible for everything his agents and employees did there.

We were successful in moving all our independents and general agents to Mid-Atlantic, and Truman's company began to realize significant profits from his deal with Vance. So much so, he wanted to see if he could improve his return by working a new deal with Vance for bail. He didn't want anything to do with our normal wholesale operation, but he was interested in opening Mid-Atlantic's own retail bail offices and acquiring some of the more profitable independent ones. He wanted his company and his employees to deal directly with clients and post their bonds with the jails and courts, similar to those owned by Vance, and those owned by me back in Reno and Vegas twenty-plus years earlier.

Truman knew about Vance's ownership of two retail bail offices in Chula Vista and El Cajon, and how Vance was captivated by the thought of gaining a "bad guy" persona as the owner. Playing on that, he made Vance an offer he couldn't refuse. Truman suggested that the two of them form a new retail bail-bond operation and acquire as many successful independent retail bail agencies throughout California as they could handle. Truman would provide the acquisition money, while Vance would manage their retail operation and research all future possibilities for acquisitions.

They would not only acquire the actual business; they would offer the existing agent/owner a job managing his or her old agency. When they started offering agents a million dollars for their business, together with a job doing exactly what they'd been doing for years, living in their own hometown, and managing their old offices, why wouldn't they sell? After all, it provided them with the opportunity to liquidate all their open bonds and receive hundreds of thousands of dollars from their loss-reserve monies held by their old insurance company while collecting an additional million dollars for their business.

The deal between Truman and Vance provided each of them with equal shares in the new venture. And their partnership agreement provided each with a substantial life-insurance policy, with all proceeds going to their individual estates. In addition, their contract included a survival clause that automatically transferred their portion of the entire business to the surviving partner.

Truman told Vance that owning retail bail agencies and controlling the entire bail bond premium instead of the ten or fifteen percent provided through his general agency contract was the only way to make any big money.

Truman also believed that having quality in-house investigators, or bounty hunters, on salary, rather than hiring freelance bikers or ex-cops who charged more than the original premium to return a fugitive to jail, was a better way to control the agency's underwriting, and provided the agents and employees with a better opportunity to write more bonds with less security.

They began using Truman's millions to buy up agencies while paying his insurance company the same bond rate as all the other agents reporting through Vance's general agency; the difference being, Truman and Vance were pocketing the majority of the premiums through their own retail agencies, just as Vance and all the other retail bail agents were doing.

When the number of their acquisitions grew to the point of feasibility, they began grouping them under one trade name, Swift Freedom Bail Bonds, and began purchasing radio and TV advertising to promote them. In addition, they were able to offer credit to those who qualified through their own loan company.

The phones began ringing off the hook, and they were able to bail at least 90 percent of all those who called.

Truman's influence with the California Department of Insurance kept their investigators at bay, which allowed me to continue working as a consultant, managing Parker Surety while they built their Swift Freedom agencies.

The best part of having Truman involved was that he kept Vance away from drugs and provided him with enough honest revenue to sustain his lifestyle, without having to work in the shadows. Things were going so well, in fact, that Vance decided to start dating again. Over time, he met a lovely woman named Kristin, and they ended up getting married.

Unfortunately, just short of a year after the wedding, Truman died from a massive heart attack, leaving the entire retail bail operation to Vance, as per their partnership agreement.

I say "unfortunately" because shortly thereafter, some of the Vance's retail bail competitors began filing complaints with local jail commanders as well as the Department of Insurance, alleging that this newly formed chain of retail bail agencies was having their agents solicit clients in and around the jails and courthouses, or they were paying jailers and arresting officers to suggest that they call Swift Freedom instead of the competition.

Even though there was no proof to support these accusations regarding the Swift Freedom Bail Bonds offices, Vance knew the wolves were at his door, looking for blood.

We knew that without Truman around to fend them off, it was only a matter of time before the Department of Insurance would initiate an investigation—because they didn't like either of us and they'd always felt we were doing something illegal, but couldn't find any solid evidence to hang their hats on.

Until now.

CHAPTER

#45

While Vance and I were busy dotting our i's and crossing our t's with regard to Parker Surety and Swift Freedom Bail Bonds, we forgot about the two California retail bail agencies and the immigration bond office Vance owned and operated outside the scope of supervision provided by our home office. Unbeknownst to us, these were the cornerstone of the case the state was building against us.

My arrest happened on one of those bright and sunny October days, like so many others I'd enjoyed over the past twenty years in Southern California. Teresa and I spent the six coldest months of each year in our Palm Desert home, and the other six months living in the northern California wine country. Our friends, those who lived full time in one place or the other, would always tell us how lucky we were to have the best of both worlds, with sunshine and good weather year-round.

I always believed it, too. I loved the sunshine, as well as the fact that we could afford two homes and two country club memberships. We could play golf year-round; almost every day if we wanted. But it wasn't always like that. When I was growing up, Mom had worked hard for every penny we had.

My arrest happened on a day when we were in our Palm Desert home. I had spent the better part of the morning commuting to Parker Surety Bonding Corporation's Southern California office, which was located just north of San Diego in Carlsbad.

It was almost always one of those really nice days, the ones on which I would rather have stayed home, lying by the pool after finishing 18 holes of golf. Instead, I'd be dealing with business issues and new problems over dinner at Vance's place. But work had always come first, ever since I was fifteen years old.

Shortly after I arrived at our company headquarters and said all my hellos to the staff, I went to my private office and started reviewing the current list of pending issues that Vance's secretary had placed on my desk earlier. I always tried to arrive about an hour or so before our scheduled meetings to ensure that I was up to speed on all the pending issues. I never liked surprises.

Within twenty minutes of my arrival, dozens of state regulators and law enforcement officers converged on our office. I later learned that they also hit our Northern California branch office, as well as the two retail bail offices and the one immigration office Vance owned in Southern California. They hit them all at the same time. I guess timing and lighting is everything with law enforcement, especially when they're after some real bad guys.

When I heard all the noise coming from the lobby, just down the hall from the executive suites, I thought, *God damn it*! *What the hell is going on out there*? As I stormed down the hall to find out, I ran into a wall of blue uniforms. The obvious hit me like a ton of shit. State and local law enforcement agencies were raiding our office. But why would they? Why would all these cops come charging into our office wanting a piece of our ass? My next thought was, *What in the hell has Vance gotten us into now?*

That's when I saw two detectives I knew from Palm Desert. These were two guys I knew pretty well, and I thought were friends. However, I remembered one of the first things Mickey Colter told me when he was teaching me the bail bond business.

"Kid," he'd said, "don't think for one minute that police officers, or law enforcement officers of any kind, will ever love your skinny little ass, or want to be real friends, as long as you're in the bail bond business. It's not just you; that goes for every other bail agent in this business. You just need to ask yourself one simple question: Why would they? Why should they, when we make tens of thousands of dollars helping the bad guys get out of jail, while they get paid a pittance for risking their lives arresting them. The cops, the ones you may think are your closest buddies, even those on the take, are the ones that will jump at any chance to slap the cuffs on and arrest you."

I started asking myself if I could have done something or said something that caused these two detectives to think Vance and I were guilty of a crime. Was this raid on our offices my fault?

Rather than pointing a finger at Vance, maybe he was the one who should be asking, *What the hell did you do, Lefty; why are we being arrested?*

I was surprised when this loosely organized mixture of deputies and regulators from various law enforcement agencies came charging into our office, but I also found it a bit comical. All these cops in one place at one time reminded me of an old-time western posse, the kind you'd see in the movies. Everyone was wearing different clothes, carrying different weapons, and moving in different directions waving warrants like some kind of "Wanted Dead or Alive" posters, and telling everyone to "stay in their seats and place their hands flat on their desks" and threatening people with evidence tampering "should they touch anything."

Then, someone in a position of authority said, "This is an authorized police raid. We have seizure warrants authorizing us to confiscate everything in these offices, including your files, personal notes, accounting records, memory typewriters, and computers. When you are permitted to leave, do not try to take anything with you."

I expected somebody to say something like "Cut! That's a wrap." Unfortunately, this wasn't a movie set. It was real life. And these were real cops.

Then I saw the lead officer, one of my so-called friends, Larry Hastings, explaining to the lead receptionist, "We will also need to serve three arrest warrants; one on Robert Wayne, one on Edward Vance Parker, and one on Andrew Sanders." As he looked down the hall and saw me coming, he said, "I see Mr. Wayne is here; to your knowledge are the other two, Mr. Parker and Mr. Sanders, in the office as well? If so, would you please ask them to come to the lobby."

She pointed down the hall and said, "Mr. Parker is in his office across the hall. And Mr. Sanders doesn't work in this office. He should be available in the Riverside office if you're looking for him."

Hastings handed me a copy of my arrest warrant and had me sit down, while his number two man, my other so-called buddy, Mike Adams, was heading toward Vance's office. Meanwhile, a few of their uniformed officers were systematically confiscating everything in sight, while some of the other suits started to interview each member of our staff.

Within minutes after Detective Adams brought Vance out of his office, we were moved to the lobby and handcuffed in front of the staff. While we sat together on display, the suits interviewing our staff began sending them home, except for our accountant, our office manager, and the receptionist. Those three were asked to stay for additional questioning, and to witness the ongoing events as they were unfolding. After a couple of hours, I wanted to be on my way, but I knew that wouldn't be happening for a while; probably a long while.

That's when I asked Hastings and Adams, in a more serious executive voice of course, "Is this really necessary? The handcuffs, I mean. Do you guys really think we look like guys that would attempt to escape from a room full of cops? I'm sure that any one of the fifty cops you brought with you could tackle two fat, middle-aged guys like us before we reached the office door!"

About that time, an investigator from the Department of Insurance started reading the contents of a DOI Cease and Desist Order aloud. When he was finished reading, he proudly served it on Vance. This immediately shut down our operation—both our civil and our bond divisions. This meant the office was closed, and we were effectively out of business, on a temporary basis. The D.O.I. Cease and Desist Order is the equivalent of a normal judicial restraining order. It limited the shutdown until the court held a mandatory hearing to determine if there was enough evidence to make the order permanent. I was sure the company's attorney would have us back in business within a few days. Of course, I had my fingers crossed.

At the time of our arrest, none of the cops "Mirandized" us. In other words, they never read us our rights, but then, they never asked us any questions until after we were booked into the San Diego County Jail. I was sure that their failure to read us our rights wouldn't be enough to vacate our arrests. To top it off, they never let us read any of the arrest warrants or the list of charges against us. They just stuffed the papers into our suitcoat pockets, knowing full well that with our hands cuffed behind us, we'd never be able to reach them. Then, after we were booked, the booking officers took them back, placed them in our property bags, and locked them away for safekeeping. So much for knowing why we were in jail or how much our bail was. At least for awhile.

Having enough experience in dealing with warrants, arrests, and bail procedures surrounding release options for the accused, which is what we were now, Vance and I knew bail had most assuredly been set by the grand jury, or the presiding judge at the time he or she authorized the raid.

That was standard procedure at the time. But these guys didn't want us to know the charges, the bail, or anything else. They just wanted us to squirm for awhile.

In retrospect, I doubt if many people, short of suspected drug dealers or gangsters, have ever experienced fifty or more cops from numerous law enforcement agencies converging on their place of business. It was certainly a first for me.

From the beginning, you could tell the suits were in charge, and that my so-called buddies from the desert were the ones in charge of all the uniformed cops. The detectives were the ones waving the search and seizure warrants, and doing all the talking, while the uniforms (the grunts) were the ones tagging and confiscating file cabinets, computers, accounting records, notes, letters, and unopened mail and loading it all into waiting police vans.

While this was going on, Adams placed Vance and me in the backseat of a police car. He left us sitting there for almost an hour, without a clue as to what in the hell was happening.

There we were, on display in the middle of a crowd. People from the surrounding office buildings in our complex were gathering and gawking, trying to see what was going on—what had caused so many police cars and cops to show up in their parking lot, and of course, who had they come to arrest.

I felt like yelling, "Break it up; it's only Vance and me, getting our sorry asses arrested for no good reason." That's when one of the arresting officers came by the car and said, "Gee! I don't think I've ever had this much fun arresting someone in the twenty years I've been on the force. It's about time we're hauling your fat asses off to jail."

You could tell from his tone, this detective assumed we were responsible for many of the criminals being released from jails throughout the country; after all, we represented more than five hundred bail agencies across the United States. Like most police officers, he didn't appreciate the obvious and unmistakable success we'd achieved in helping criminals obtain their release from jail.

He also mistakenly believed I was still one of the principals in Vance's current operation, because he kept saying "you guys" and "your business." True, I was running the bail division again, but only as a consultant and board member, not an owner. And I was only back as a consultant because Vance had asked me to come in and help save his company. There I was, on my way to jail, wondering which one of us caused this mess.

I sat in silence reviewing every encounter, friendly or otherwise, I'd ever had with Hastings or Adams. Why now? Why ransack the offices? Why bring fifty cops? What did they expect to find?

That's when I started to panic. Did they raid my house? Did they arrest Teresa? *Why would they? She hadn't worked for, or had anything to do with the company in years. Are all of our neighbors and friends watching her being handcuffed and placed into a cop car like I am? Oh my God! I need to talk to Hastings.*

I leaned out the window and asked the wise-ass cop, the one who was gloating earlier, "Hey, I hate to interrupt your fun, but could you ask Detective Hastings to come down and talk to me for a minute? I have something important he might be interested in discussing."

As I sat back into the seat, I wondered if they'd reached the conclusion that we were idiots, stupid enough to leave a paper trail in our offices? Did they stop to think for one minute that we might keep all the incriminating evidence (if there was any) somewhere besides our offices? Surely they would give us that much credit. They must have thought it would be somewhere away from the prying eyes of staff members. But where? Did they think we took it home? Had Hastings or Adams seen something at my house? Something that would lead them to believe they could tear the house apart and find some real juicy evidence? If they found something, anything, would they arrest Teresa as an accomplice? I began to think the worst, since I had no idea why we were being arrested or what kind of incriminating evidence they were looking for.

My head was spinning, trying to figure out what Vance had gotten us into, and if Teresa was being arrested. After what seemed like hours in the backseat of that car next to my ex-partner, it dawned on me that being placed in the police car with him was no mistake. It was a setup in hopes that we would be intimidated or scared enough to start talking to each other . . . spilling our guts, while the officer in the front seat would simply take notes, or better yet, record self-incriminating conversations. Did they really think we were stupid enough to say something like, "Oh Shit! Do you think they'll find the millions in laundered money we've got hidden behind the fake wall in your office, or better yet, in my house?" What a joke!

Actually, this was no joke. But it wasn't my first rodeo, either. Law enforcement officers have tried to intimidate me in the past in hopes of getting me to spill my guts, so this show didn't really scare me. But until I could talk to Hastings about Teresa, there was nothing I could do, except worry some more. I took a deep breath and convinced myself to focus on what I could do here and now, which meant I needed to focus my attention on Vance. He was more than a bit nervous; in fact, he was shaking. This verified, at least in my mind, that he knew more about what was going on than I did.

I leaned over to him. "Hey, relax, we can both use a little vacation away from the office for a few days."

"Very funny," he said, with a small smile.

I said, "Don't ask anyone questions or say anything about what's going on until we have a chance to call our lawyers."

The only thing I really wanted to say was, "You stupid fuck! "WHAT THE HELL IS GOING ON, AND WHY THE HELL ARE THEY ARRESTING ME?" But if I did, and he *was* responsible for all this, he might break down and start spilling his guts in front of the cops, which is what they were hoping would happen.

Instead of asking Hastings to come and talk to me like I'd asked, the detective, who must have given up hope that we'd incriminate ourselves, told the officer behind the wheel to take us to the station for processing. That's when I lost my cool for a minute. "Thanks for the courtesy of informing Hastings I wanted to talk to him, you fat little fucker!" I complained. I could have expanded my thanks by threatening him with bodily harm, but that would have added another criminal charge for threatening a police officer, so I elected to stick with calling him the nastiest name I could think of at the time.

When we arrived in booking, the jailers completed the paperwork and fingerprinted us. Then, without dressing us in their famous orange coveralls, they locked us in separate, cozy little maximum-security cells; the kind that hold a single inmate. Each one was about six feet wide and ten feet deep—just large enough to accommodate a stainless-steel toilet/sink combo and a single bed. These solitary cells are used to house inmates on suicide watch, or to separate aggressive inmates who are causing problems with other prisoners. We were neither of those, so I wasn't sure why we were so lucky.

Each cell had a steel bar door with an opening in the middle about waist high that the guards used to pass food trays, or other essentials like toilet paper or legal papers to be read or signed by the inmate. There was a single light overhead, encased in wire, and a small metal shelf mounted just above the back of the sink, which could hold a toothbrush or extra toilet paper. Trust me when I tell you, the toilet paper they provide is not the soft and cozy grade. It's more like sandpaper. There was no bedding, just an old, stained mattress, and a pillow with no case. I guess they didn't want anyone using county linen to hang themselves from the light fixture.

Having been in and out of jails across the country conducting interviews with prisoners and posting bonds, I knew what to expect. Earlier, when I said we were lucky, it was because I knew we could have been locked in a cell built and furnished to hold ten inmates. And because of jail overcrowding issues throughout the country, these larger cells were regularly packed with twice that number. The furniture consisted of five-year-old, rusted double bunk-beds with filthy mattresses, a few spotted pillows without pillowcases, and no sheets. A few extra mattresses were spread around on the floor. These were used more for sitting than sleeping. Plus, they all smelled from piss or vomit.

Although these larger cells usually held inmates charged with less serious crimes, those who were often released within a few hours of their arrest or first thing in the morning after arraignment in court, I always wondered why anyone in their right mind would want to commit a second or third crime that would put them back into a situation like that.

Detainees being held on lesser charges were offered unlimited access to telephones and given an opportunity to call as many bail bond agencies or family members as needed to accomplish their speedy release. On the other hand, the more serious offenders, guys like me and Vance, were restricted to one call every so often, whenever the jailers were not too busy, or not too lazy to bring them out to the wall phones, which were in the booking area.

The real advantages to being held in one of these smaller cells were things like receiving unlimited visits from your attorney and not having your thoughts interrupted by fellow inmates bitching, moaning, and complaining every five minutes about how they were falsely arrested, or victims of police brutality.

Although being held in a solitary cell provided more privacy, it let me know that the charges against me were of a more serious nature, and my release would require a much larger bond; large enough for me, and the deputies, to realize I wouldn't be leaving any time soon.

The thought of having to stay in this shithole did not appeal to me, but then, like I said before, spending tens or hundreds of thousands of dollars on a bail bond appealed even less.

Worrying about my wife, speculating about the charges against me, or venturing a guess about the size of my bail were all I could think about while held incommunicado in this shoebox-size private cell rather than in the general population.

None of this made sense, especially since I knew I was innocent. And so far, nothing had given me any hope of learning what the hell was going on. The only person I knew who had the answers was Vance, and he was nowhere within sight or sound. All I could do was wait and see what would happen next, and try to focus on what, if anything, a small, completely isolated private jail cell had to offer.

Around that time, the sound of my cell door being electronically unlocked interrupted my thoughts. Detective Hastings stood before me. I'd gotten to know him pretty well, because he was regularly assigned to protect some of the golf pros and celebrities that played in many of the Pro Am celebrity golf tournaments, like the Bob Hope Classic and the Dinah Shore Women's Open, which were held at the Mission Hills Country Club in Palm Springs. Our house was located on the sixteenth fairway of the Dinah Shore course; one of three courses within the complex. Teresa and I regularly invited Hastings and Adams to over for lunch, cocktails, or dinner during one of the major events.

"Hey, Lefty! Is it still okay to call you Lefty? Listen, you've known me and that I'm a detective with the Riverside Sheriff's Office for quite awhile, so our visit to your office this morning shouldn't have come as a great surprise. I've come to read you your rights, and make sure you understand them. I will inform you of all the charges listed in the indictment, as well as the amount of your bail. I assume, since you're familiar with the judicial system, that you know your bail was set by the presiding judge, Michael Smith, at the time he issued the warrant for your arrest. So, where would you like me to begin?

I said, "I guess the best place to start is by thanking you for giving me a heads-up prior to raiding our office and arresting me. Oh wait, I'm sorry, you didn't, did you? Before we begin this charade, I do have one question. Did you guys raid my house, or arrest Teresa?"

Hastings instantly replied, "Geez, Lefty, cut me some slack; I'm a cop first, and a friend second. I couldn't give you a heads-up, and you know it. But I was able to stop them from raiding your home and upsetting Teresa. And I made it clear to everyone from day one that she was never a target for arrest.

"Well," I said, "Thanks for watching out for her.

That's when Hastings said, "Your bail is $2.5 million dollars."

That's when I felt my heart skip a beat or two.

Hastings started to read the list of charges, all 250 of them. After he'd read about thirty, I interrupted him. "You can stop reading now, this is all bullshit, with a capital B."

I was charged with numerous counts of bribing law enforcement officers, including jailers, beat cops, and jail trustees (prisoners convicted of a crime punishable by a year or less in county jail). Hastings shared that Vance and Andrew Sanders, Vance's lead retail agent in his personal bail operations, were included in the same indictment and charged with the same crimes.

With that last little tidbit, I was willing to bet my life that it was Sanders, or a member of his retail bail staff, who had caused our current problems. Sanders must have been paying certain jailers, beat cops, or trustees a percentage of the bail premium commissions in exchange for recommending that defendants call their offices for bail. And since Vance owned 100 percent of both the wholesale bail operation and these retail agencies, he and I were branded as alleged accomplices to their crimes.

It became crystal clear that some of the agencies involved in the raid were looking for evidence to prove we had prior knowledge that certain defendants would not show up in court, and that we accepted payments from them in cash, not only for their bail, but to hire attorneys and pay bribes to ensure that their case files were either lost, destroyed, dismissed or reduced to a misdemeanor.

In addition to looking for evidence of collusion on our part, they were also looking for names, and evidence on the lawyers, clerks, or judges that helped us corrupt the entire criminal justice system for their own personal financial gain, as well as ours.

That's when I grasped how stupid they thought we were. To think that "if" we'd been smart enough to pull off these crimes, we'd be stupid enough to keep records of payoffs and/or bribes to provide fugitives with receipts that would not only justify any expenditures on their behalf but also prove our complicity in a crime. Oh yeah! These were the kind of corrupt business transactions where everybody was expecting or demanding detailed receipts for fixing cases. Or better yet, for tax purposes, since we were conducting criminal activities for profit and wouldn't want to get snagged like Al Capone for evading taxes. It was comical.

I knew that under normal conditions, many of these lesser charges would be dismissed during early court proceedings as part of plea bargaining—that is, if and when we ever got into a courtroom. But these were not normal circumstances, and I was not a normal defendant.

"Listen, Hastings," I said, "It's important that everyone understands what I'm about to say. I would never turn on

Vance and provide the State with evidence, even if I could; nor would I ever enter a plea of guilty in exchange for a more lenient sentence. You can all kiss my ass. If anyone ever asks you about how I responded to your questions, let them know they can shove this whole thing up where the sun never shines. It's all bullshit, at least as far as my involvement is concerned."

My thoughts flashed on the number of charges against us, and the fact that our bail was set in the millions. I realized we would be staying longer than the usual arrestees. This was a high-profile case, with high-profile defendants like local judges, clerks, and lawyers. The media would want the whole story, including as many names as possible. I was sure the detectives weren't ready to provide these names, because they hadn't finished going through the materials confiscated from our offices that day. I was also sure they'd instructed the jailers to keep us out of sight for as long as they could.

Hastings interrupted my thoughts again. "Do you want me to continue reading?"

"No thanks, and no deal. I'll waive my right to hear the rest, and let my attorney fill me in. But I do want my copy of the arrest warrant. The jailers put it in my property bag when I was booked. Listen, Detective, I hate to be rude, but I'd like to make my phone call now, and since I'll be talking to my wife, I'd appreciate some privacy."

On his way out, Hastings made it a point to say, "Look, Lefty, unlike many of the others involved in this case, I have no axe to grind with you. I'll make sure you get your call as soon as possible and that you can use the attorney conference room to ensure complete privacy. I'll also stop by on my way home tonight to make sure Teresa is doing okay, and if she needs anything."

Since I felt I could no longer trust him, I took his offer to assist Teresa as the beginning of their normal "good cop/bad cop" routine, the one every cop is taught at the police academy, and the one they try out on every arrest they ever make from then on. I wondered how long it would be before Detective Adams would show up and debut his "bad cop" routine.

I decided to make my one call to Teresa, rather than to my attorney, because I was almost certain the raid and our arrests would soon be blasted all over the news. After all these years, I found myself sitting in jail, about to call my wife and use some of the lamest excuses ever used by my clients to try and explain what was happening. It was the part about being innocent that made this almost laughable. She would imagine the chances of that were between slim to none.

When she answered the phone, I could tell she had already heard, and was frantic.

"Honey, relax. I'm not totally sure what's going on, but the one thing I am sure of is I'm not involved in this one. This is all Vance, and some of the clowns he has working for him in his retail offices."

She started to cry and asked if she should call one of our many close bail bond friends, or Dennis, our family attorney.

"Honey, listen. I've spent years convincing clients, the suckers who got swept up and arrested, that they should pay 10 percent of their bail and have me post their bond rather than waiting it out in jail. I knew full well they could save their money if the charges were dropped the next day, or if they pled guilty and used the 10 percent to pay their fine. But once you've paid the bail bondsman, too bad! It's gone forever."

I knew from the first day in the business that the law is clear: A bail bondsman earns his or her premium the minute their client is released from jail on a bond, regardless of whether they're found guilty or innocent, or if they're out for ten minutes, ten days, or ten months. I'm just as sure there isn't a bail agent in America who would refund my quarter-of-a-million-dollar premium.

"Sweetheart, the answer is, absolutely not! Don't call a bail agent. Just call Dennis. For that kind of money, I'm content staying here as long as it takes, because I'm innocent. I'm going to wait it out in my cell for a while and see what happens next. Plus, it will give me time to think. I love you, sweetie, more than anything. Please don't worry about me; remember, you have access to everything we own. Stay calm and try to go about life as normal as possible; or at least as normal as you can without me being around to help.

"Oh! One more thing: If the kids hear about this from college, let them know it's a big mistake, and I'll be home in a few days."

I hung up, not knowing if I was going to get out at all, let alone in a few days.

CHAPTER

#46

I heard the clamor of metal against metal, and the slamming of jail doors for the second time. The jailers and trustees were delivering meals. They'd taken my watch and other valuables during the booking process, and this cell had no window, so I'd lost track of time. I wasn't sure if the guard was about to serve lunch or dinner. Either way, I was about to enjoy my first sample of fine prison cuisine.

As the trustee began to pass my food tray through the slot in the jail door, I took one look and figured it had to be lunch. It contained some lunch meat I'd never before seen, pressed between two pieces of white bread and surrounded by unrecognizable fruit in a cup. I passed on the sandwich because it smelled as bad as it looked and ate the best parts of the fruit.

I hoped my next meal would be a little better, but decided it wouldn't, because slop is slop, no matter what time of day they serve it. Jail cuisine would never match the cuisine I'd grown accustomed to . . . but then again, neither would my current surroundings match the comfort and beauty of my home.

On the brighter side, if I stayed in this shithole long enough, I would surely lose the twenty extra pounds my doctor always complained about during my annual physicals.

On day two, the only thing I had left from my normal life was my $2,800 double-breasted, custom-tailored Armani suit, my dress shirt, my socks, and my underwear. They took my belt and my tie. I guess they thought I'd be yelling "Uncle" by now and want to post my $2.5 million bail or try to hang myself at the thought having to pay someone else to get out.

I decided to hunker down. Mealtimes became my clock, because they were served three times a day, every day, at the same time. I started putting a small mark on the wall every time a meal showed up. Three marks equaled one day. When I finished any meal, at least as much as I could stand, it was time for another mark on the wall.

Although sleeping left a lot to be desired, much of the time spent in a county jail is routine. There are three types of inmates: those just arrested and waiting to be released on bail; those unable or unwilling to post bail who are awaiting trial or court hearings; and trustees, those convicted of a crime punishable by a year or less in the county jail. Trustees are assigned odd jobs like cleaning the heads, working in the kitchen, and delivering meals.

Because I was one of the inmates awaiting a court hearing and refusing to post bail, they told me I could take a shower every day unless they got too busy. But according to one of the trustees that delivered my meals, the showers were as dumpy as the rest of this place. The shower room was broken into individual stalls, without curtains.

The trustee in charge of the showers said I'd eventually get a clean pair of orange coveralls every other day and would be allowed to walk around the outside exercise area every morning for thirty minutes. Then it would be back to my cell for the rest of the day.

On the second day however, things were a little different, for two reasons. First, I exchanged my Armani suit for my first pair of orange coveralls, and second, I met with my attorney, Dennis, as opposed to seeing just jailers and law enforcement people. Dennis had been my attorney since I opened my bail bond offices in Reno, and fortunately, he was qualified to practice law in California, as well as in federal court. I was glad Teresa called him. But I was sure she thought I was acting like some tough guy, trying to stick it out in this shithole, and that played a part in her calling him, too.

I told her more than once that there's a time to be a tough guy and a time to be practical. Now, I was being practical. I couldn't see parting with $250,000 dollars for bail when I wasn't guilty of anything other than being Vance's friend.

It appeared that being friends with Dennis for over forty years had its benefits. The jailer said, "Your attorney told your wife he was taking the first available flight from Reno. He instructed her to call the jail and advise us that she has retained him as your attorney, and he'd arrive before lunch. We figured you might want to spiff up a bit."

"Thanks for the info. Any chance I could get my suit back in time for the meeting? Or did you guys have something else in mind for spiffing up?"

"Sorry, you'll get your fancy suit back when you go before a jury, not a judge. For now, the judge only likes seeing inmates dressed in orange."

I hoped Dennis would sit down with Teresa and tell her he agreed with me. He'd remind her how stubborn I am when it comes to spending money—and paying a quarter of a million to get out of jail was beyond wasteful. He needed to let her know that he would do everything possible to bring me home without bankrupting us in the process.

CHAPTER

#47

My first meeting with Dennis went well, considering that I was still in jail. I can see now that having all the charges dropped and being released without a single court appearance was expecting a bit much.

"I met with the prosecutor before coming here to see you," Dennis said. "I wanted to tell him we'd be waiving the need for your timely arraignment, and that I was preparing to file a bail-reduction motion. I also wanted to see how he felt about separating you from the other two defendants in this case, because one is an owner and the other is an employee of the company, while you're just a consultant. That's correct, isn't it?"

I nodded and said nothing.

"These two motions are longshots, but it will give me time to review all the charges, the probable cause for your arrest, and any possibilities for a complete dismissal. I'm hoping they might have overlooked something in their haste to arrest you.

"By the way, I agree: Paying a quarter million for bail is a waste. I'm going to meet with Teresa when we're done here and I'll let her know. It means you'll have to stay here a little longer, but I'm sure you can handle it. By the way, did anyone ever tell you that orange is really your color?"

When he was finished laughing at his little joke, he called for the guard, and left.

I admit, seeing Dennis leave made me wish I were going with him. Just the thought of going home, hugging Teresa, sitting out on the patio discussing my case with her and Dennis over a glass of wine while waiting for one of her home-cooked meals was almost enough to make me give in. But I knew paying $250,000 to do it would be crazy, especially with Dennis working to make that happen without having to pay a dime.

The jailer took me back to my cell. Rather than continue to focus on my current situation, I tried to reflect on what I might do first, after I get out.

CHAPTER

#48

Thanks to a joint request from Dennis and from Vance's attorney, the judge approved a video arraignment from jail. Vance's attorney was also able to pull a few strings and arrange for the use of a private attorney/client conference room in the jail the day of our arraignment.

It was the first time I'd seen Vance since our arrest, about ten days earlier, as we rode to jail together in the police car. We were now waiting in a private room with our attorneys present, the first opportunity we'd had to speak openly about our situation.

Vance started. "I'm sorry about all this. I know you had nothing to do with it. Andy Sanders is the guilty one, and the little prick is nowhere to be found, which is probably better, because I'd kill him and never get out of here."

I said, "Who the hell is Andy Sanders?" Vance said, "You know, he's the son of Rick Sanders, that asshole investment banker who was going to take the company public and damn near bankrupt me and the company in the process."

His attorney said, "Vance already explained that you had no part in any of this, and I explained all of that to your attorney while we were waiting for the jailers to bring you two down.

"Best-case scenario, we're hoping to either get all the charges dropped against you, or, at the very least, get you released on your own recognizance during the preliminary hearing. If things go right, the hearing should be in about ten days, or maybe less, depending on the judge's calendar. As for Vance, I'll let him explain."

Vance said, "Because I own the retail agency Andy was managing in Riverside, and the prosecutor believes I knew, or should have known, what was going on in my own business. The best I can hope for is having my bail reduced to somewhere around two million.

"That being the case, Lefty, I need to know that you're willing to help me, because you're the only guy I know that can pull off getting one of our agents to post a bond for two million bucks without costing me $200,000."

I interrupted him. "We've been friends and business associates for over twenty years. We've not only helped each other through some real shit, we've also pulled off a lot of deals that made us both a lot of money. I'm not about to give up on you now.

"I'm not sure what the hell Sanders did," I continued, "or how much you knew about it, but if you and the attorneys are able to get me out of this crap without having to pay, I'll do everything I can to pull off one of my fucking large-bond miracles for you.

"But let's be honest. You either knew what was going on, or you let your guard down somewhere along the way, which allowed Sanders to fuck you over pretty good. It doesn't matter either way; we're still friends, and you can count on my help, if I ever get out of here.

"Let's wait and see what evidence the prosecutor has against you, and whether he buys into my innocence before you get nervous and spill your guts in hopes for a better deal. We both know you're better off dealing from outside this shithole, rather than inside.

"They can't have much on me because I'm just a consultant, and everyone in the system knows that. Andy Sanders is the guilty one, so this case has to be based on activities surrounding your retail bail agencies, and not your corporate managing general agency.

"Outside of entering a not guilty plea to all charges, there's not much to say until we get to the preliminary hearing. Let's let the attorneys do their jobs so we can both get out of here, one way or another."

Shortly after our conversation, our video arraignment started, and we entered pleas of not guilty. The judge said he'd take our motions for bail reductions under advisement and put our preliminary hearing on the fast track, so we should be hearing something soon.

Dennis then called for the guard; we all commented about next time, referring to the preliminary hearing. I shook Vance's hand, hugged him, and whispered in his ear, "I'm all in, we're friends to the end, and I'll get you out of here on bond if I have to commit forgery to do it."

When I got back to my cell, I started to think about all the things Vance and I did over the past twenty years that could have gone wrong, and all the reasons why they didn't.

CHAPTER

#49

*T*he *Preliminary Hearing*

During our preliminary hearing, the judge listened while the prosecutor laid out his case. It turned out that Andrew Sanders, the third person indicted in this bullshit case, was not only the principal suspect, he was the only person the prosecution was able to produce evidence against. It appeared that the investigators found a pocket-size ledger locked in his desk drawer at his retail bail bond office. It listed the names and amounts of every bribe or payoff he made while he was the lead bail agent and manager of Vance's retail bail office.

This ledger appeared to support all 250 of the charges against him, Vance, and me, which the prosecutor used not only to have us arrested, but also as the basis for establishing our bail. Two hundred and fifty counts at $1,000 per entry apparently gave the judge justification in setting our bail at $2.5 million.

In addition, the prosecutor alleged that since Vance was the owner and licensed agent for the office in question, as well as Andy's boss, Vance should have known about any criminal activity going on within his office.

It was obvious that this whole case consisted of evidence involving Andy Sanders, and possibly Vance, but nothing was mentioned about me, or how I was somehow involved, until the end of the prosecutor's presentation.

"Your Honor, Mr. Wayne has been a friend and business associate of Mr. Parker for well over twenty years. And as such, I believe he had full knowledge of everything going on in all of Mr. Parker's bail offices. He claims that he's only a consultant, but as such, his years of experience in the bail business, coupled with his knowledge of Mr. Parker, would have been enough for him to know, or at least question, Mr. Parker about what was going on. Although Mr. Parker swears that Mr. Wayne had nothing to do with it, the whole thing smells. It's a clear case of 'Let's blame it all on Andrew Sanders,' the third and only other defendant, and the only one we're unable to locate. For all we know, Vance Parker and Lefty Wayne collaborated in Mr. Sanders's flight, or worse."

Dennis and Vance's attorneys jumped out of their chairs and virtually yelled in harmony, "Objection!" Dennis continued his outburst: "The prosecutor is alleging that both defendants have collaborated in Mr. Sanders' disappearance, or worse. And he's made these serious accusations without presenting one shred of evidence against either of them.

"This is just another example of the prosecution fabricating ideas in order to keep the co-defendants in this case, especially my client, in jail, hoping my client will implicate Mr. Parker in their fabricated scheme in exchange for leniency from the court. The only thing my client is guilty of is being Mr. Parker's friend, and to my knowledge, that's not a crime in this state.

"Therefore, I respectfully move to have all the charges against Mr. Wayne dropped, and that he be released from custody immediately."

The judge strongly reprimanded the prosecutor for his remarks, which he indicated were totally out of line. He went on to say he would take everything under consideration, except the inappropriate outburst from the prosecutor. And he'd render his decisions regarding whether to proceed with the case against us, and if he choose to do so, he would also render a decision on the motions for bail reductions.

"Court adjourned."

I asked Dennis how long he thought it would take the judge to make a decision.

"Only the judge knows that. In the meantime, I'll see if I can arrange for a visitor. I'm thinking about bringing Teresa into the attorney's room as my assistant so you two can have a real visit—you know, holding hands and all that shit, instead of talking through a glass window on the visitor's phone. I'll keep you posted. Just hang in there."

The next day, Dennis was able to bring Teresa with him. We kissed, hugged, and held hands during the entire meeting as Dennis explained what had happened in court the previous day. It was clear from the testimony that Andy Sanders was the agent making all the payoffs to the jailers, the court clerks, and one particular judge, through two different attorneys. All three of these individuals had yet to be named.

It was no coincidence that the numbers in Andy's ledger matched the number of charges in our indictment. This meant the snitch for the prosecutor's office must have copied Andy's ledger and given it to the prosecutor in order to have Vance scooped up, along with me, if, and when, they had enough evidence.

Andy could have been the snitch, but I doubted it. He didn't know enough about my relationship with Vance to provide the prosecutor with enough information for Andy to testify against us. Andy would have had to justify any missing premiums, or collateral, to someone in the home office when he turned in his weekly production reports, because they always included the matching premium and collateral deposits.

That meant there had to be someone else in Vance's office working with the prosecutor, and that someone had to know enough about the two of us and our past dealings to interest the prosecutor in offering him or her a deal in exchange for their testimony. The only logical person in my mind was Vance's chief financial officer, Paul Edwards.

Paul must have gotten wind of the fact that the police or the D.A.'s office were investigating Vance's retail operations, and figured it was a matter of time before they came busting through the office door to arrest everyone in sight. He was the only one who could have implicated me, since we'd had numerous discussions regarding all the past shady financial transactions we carried out to keep the managing general agency open and operating before I sold my interest.

It was Paul who had come to me often over the years to discuss how Vance's spending habits resulted in the company's negative financial condition.

One thing is certain: If the prosecutor asked Paul to name someone who could corroborate his story, other than Vance, he wouldn't hesitate to throw me under the bus.

Talking about me, and the things Vance and I did over the years to keep the company alive, could have been just enough to convince the prosecutor that if he arrested me too, he might be able to squeeze me into substantiating Paul's story about Vance, and make his case.

If that's all they had, I was home free, because we'd passed the statute of limitations on my previous dealings with Vance, and his attorney had told the prosecutor I had nothing to do with the retail bail bond offices operated by Andy and owned by Vance. Small relief, I guess.

CHAPTER

#50

*T*he Judge's Ruling

That's part of why the two of us were still in jail awaiting decisions from the judge. It was our understanding that he was reviewing all the evidence and motions presented during our preliminary hearing in order to make his rulings.

According to a phone call from Dennis, today was the day. He said the judge was prepared to rule on who, if anyone, would be going home, and who would remain in jail awaiting trial. The judge would also rule on the motions regarding bail reductions for anyone left behind.

Dennis also said that because our hearing was on for that afternoon, he arranged to have the jailers return my Armani suit, as well as all the other clothes I'd need for court. He said Teresa would be in court, so he was doing his part to help make me presentable. "I lied before; orange is not your color," he told me as he hung up.

After the better part of three weeks, which I'd calculated by counting the scratches I'd put on the wall of my jail cell, my day in court had finally arrived. I hoped and prayed that this was my last day in jail and that Dennis had convinced the judge to dismiss this whole mess, because I really was innocent.

About an hour or so after his call, a jailer brought my clothes and said, "We'll be taking you and Vance over to the courthouse within the hour, so be ready." Luckily, I had nothing else on my calendar that day.

Putting on my suit made me feel like a new man. I was somebody again—not just an inmate.

Vance and I arrived in court and said hello.

The bailiff called the court to order and announced the entry of the judge.

After we were reseated, the judge said he would first respond to the motions for dismissal that had been filed by each of our attorneys and move on from there.

He asked Dennis and me to stand. He said that in his opinion, the state had not demonstrated to the court's satisfaction that I was involved in any of the transactions cited in the warrants, and therefore he was dismissing the entire action against me and ordered my immediate release from custody.

Wow! I couldn't believe my ears! I was a free man, and without the need for bail. I'd made the right decision to stay in jail and save myself a quarter of a million dollars.

After Dennis and I sat down, he called for Vance and his attorney to stand. He proceeded to tell them the opposite: The state had provided sufficient evidence to bind Vance over for trial, and he set a trial date approximately two months out.

He did, however, provide some good news for Vance. He ruled that Vance's bail was excessive and reduced it to one million.

As soon as Vance heard the ruling, he looked at me. I knew from his expression he was counting on me to have him out on the street before sunset.

While he and I were in jail awaiting our hearing, his attorneys worked to get both the retail bail operations, as well as the wholesale general agency, up and running again. They successfully argued that as a result of reviewing the case with the prosecutor's office, they were able to show where all the instances noted in the indictment were from Vance's personal retail bail offices and had nothing to do with the Parker General Agency, or the Swift Freedom Bail Bond operation. They had a valid California licensee overseeing them, so they should be allowed to reopen.

Fortunately, before Truman died, he'd had Vance's new wife, Kristin, licensed and listed as the principal owner in the event of Vance's untimely death or inability to operate as owner.

Vance's lawyer went on to say that not reopening would do irreparable harm, not only to the business, but to all the employees of these entities as well.

They won the argument regarding the two companies, but not the retail agencies owned directly by Vance; the ones that got him in this mess. However, the judge stipulated that if, or when, Vance was released on bail, he could not have anything to do with these operations until after his trial. And then, only if he was found innocent.

CHAPTER

#51

Upon my release from jail, I called Arnold Goldman, one of my best friends in the bail business. Arnie was one of the bail agents I used to help me place our portion of the large bonds we split, the ones I wrote to offset those where Vance was keeping my 20 percent.

I told Arnie I needed a favor.

"Lefty, I was hoping to hear from you, I know you're in jail. I wanted to see what I could do to help get you out of there."

"Well," I said, "I'm out, but unfortunately Vance is still in, and I need your help to get him out. I need to have you post his million dollar bond without collecting the premium. I'll cover the bond cost to the company, wave your reserve deposit, and guarantee his appearance, but you won't be making a nickel off this one. Vance can't write it on himself, and I'm not licensed in California, so I need you to do it."

Arnie said, "No problem, Lefty. I'll do it, but you'll have to get me a bond power of attorney large enough. My current one on file with the court and the Department of Insurance only covers $500,000."

I said, "Great, Arnie, I knew I could count on you. I'll pick up a bond from the office and meet you by the jail. Not in front; I don't want anyone thinking I have anything to do with his release. The prosecutor may try to stop him from getting out if he thinks I'm involved."

I called Peggy Richards, Vance's office manager, and said I needed a million-dollar bond power for Arnie Goldman. I asked her to meet me at the office as soon as possible.

Once I got the bond power, I called Arnie, we met at a place near the jail, and I gave him the bond. Arnie posted Vance's bond within two hours of my release and waited for him at the jail. When Vance was released, Arnie took him to his office where Vance's wife Kristin and I were waiting.

Getting Vance out of jail was the easy part. Now we had to figure out what to do about his business. Since Vance was the sole owner of the retail bail businesses, including the immigration office, he couldn't have anything to do with them.

More importantly, at least for Teresa and me, was to figure out what to do with Swift Freedom and Parker Surety.

We left Arnie's office and started to drive Vance and Kristin home. He thanked me for getting him out as quickly as I did, and he said he was sure this whole jail and trial thing was going to turn out this way, so he'd been thinking about what he was going to do.

"I'm going to shut down both the retail operations I own separately from Parker Surety and Swift Freedom Bail, including the immigration office.

"Also, my attorney has been working with a group of lawyers. I think you and Teresa met them at one of my 'black tie dinners' a couple years ago. Anyway, they're interested in buying Parker Surety and Swift Freedom Bail Bonds; they're willing to pay somewhere around $15 million over a five-year period. They'll continue to pay your note off as well. They want to take the company nationwide, which is fine with me, because I want out."

He continued, "I'm going to accept a settlement offer my attorney has been working on with the prosecutor. I'm going to enter a guilty plea on 250 misdemeanors, pay a $500,000 fine, and surrender my bail license for life. Pleading guilty to misdemeanors with time served will allow me to retain my law license and open my own practice and see how it goes.

"I'm sure the new boys will phase out the entire wholesale-bail bond operation after they buy up a few more the retail agencies that Truman and I were eyeing before his death. They want to expand into other states. I'm sure they'll be calling you one of these days. I told them there's nobody better . . .

"You're the man, Lefty; I owe it all to you. Let's go out to dinner, get some real food for a change, and celebrate our new start on life!"

After dinner, Teresa and I drove out to our desert home and watched the sunset from our patio. After spending weeks in a jail cell without windows, I can testify that nothing takes the place of freedom.

The next day, while having a nice breakfast on the patio and watching the golfers flub their shots, the phone rang.

"Hello . . . Yes, this is Lefty."

After listening for a few minutes, I said, "Well, I appreciate the compliments, and the offer, but, as you know, I just got out of jail and need time to think about it and to discuss it with my wife. Can I give you my answer tomorrow?"

The gentleman on the other end said, "Sure, say hello to Teresa, and I'll wait for your call."

Teresa asked, "Who was that?"

"The lead lawyer for the group that will be taking over Vance's operations. He said Vance accepted the plea bargain, so he's officially out, and they're in.

"He offered me a job as the director of bail operations for their new company. He wants me to expand Swift Freedom Bail Bonds into a number of other states and offered to relocate us to a state of our choosing to begin the expansion.

"It's a lot to think about on my first full day out of jail, so right now, let's just drink up the fresh air of freedom, and give him our answer later."

Teresa smiled and said, "If you take it, you'd better behave yourself and stay out of trouble, because next time I may just ask Dennis to leave you in jail."

THE END
(For Now)

ABOUT THE AUTHOR

The author grew up in Reno, Nevada, graduated from high school in 1961, and immediately joined the Marines. Upon his return home, he elected to attend the University of Nevada, Reno, in an effort to find his calling. Shortly after classes started, he realized the need to find a part-time job, which led him to becoming a licensed insurance agent specializing in writing surety bail bonds. Rather than finishing school, he chose to direct all his interests into the bail bond business.

After spending a number of years writing bonds as an employee for a local bail bond agency in Reno, and later in Las Vegas, he opened two of his own agencies in Reno. Certain financial roadblocks forced him to sell his agencies and take a job as the western regional manager for a number of different surety insurance companies. From there he established a national managing general agency with a friend and associate. It provided bail contracts to over five hundred different bail agencies and general agencies across the United States.

Although his career spanned over fifty years of writing bail bonds for his own clients, and helping fellow bail agents throughout the country to underwrite their bonds and apprehend their fugitives, he has never been arrested (despite the story you've just read), convicted, or sentenced to jail.

I hope you enjoyed this book.
Would you do me a favor?

Like all authors, I rely on online reviews to encourage future sales. Your opinion is invaluable. Would you take a few moments now to share your assessment of my book at the review site of your choice? Your opinion will help the book marketplace become more transparent and useful to all.

Thank you very much!

www.ingramcontent.com/pod-product-compliance
Lightning Source LLC
Chambersburg PA
CBHW030234030426
42336CB00009B/95